Latino Voices in New England

Latino Voices in New England

Edited by
David Carey Jr.
and
Robert Atkinson

excelsior editions
State University of New York Press
Albany, New York

Published by
State University of New York Press, Albany

Printed in the United States of America

For information, contact State University of New York Press, Albany, NY
www.sunypress.edu

Production by Marilyn P. Semerad
Marketing by Anne M. Valentine

Library of Congress Cataloging in Publication Data

Latino voices in New England / edited by David Carey Jr. and Robert Atkinson.
p. cm.
Includes bibliographical references and index.
ISBN 978-0-7914-9377-9 (hardcover : alk. paper) — ISBN 978-0-7914-9378-6 (pbk. : alk. paper) 1. Hispanic Americans—Maine—Portland—Social conditions. 2. Hispanic Americans—Ethnic identity—Maine—Portland. 3. Hispanic Americans—Maine—Portland—Biography. 4. Oral history—Maine—Portland. 5. Portland (Me.)—Social conditions. 6. Portland (Me.)—Ethnic relations. I. Carey Jr., David, 1967- II. Atkinson, Robert, Ph. D.
F29.P9L37 2009
974.1'9100468073—dc22

2008018973

10 9 8 7 6 5 4 3 2 1

Contents

List of Illustrations vii

Foreword
Elsa Nuñez ix

Acknowledgments xiii

Introduction: Situating Latino Voices in a New England Community
David Carey Jr. 1

1. It's About Dream Building
Blanca Santiago 51

2. I Wanted to Free Myself
Adrian Bravo Chavez 67

3. We're Very United, All the Latinos
Ana Manza and Eliseo Brea 83

4. Swimming in a Different Ocean
Laura Ochoa 97

5. It's About Community Building
John Connors 111

6. Answering the Call
The Reverend Virginia Marie Rincón 129

7. We Left because of the War
Hernán and Marta 137

8. My Life Has Always Included Change
Victoria Chicón 155

9. Roots Are Important
Juan González 169

10. Trying to Move Forward
Lourdes Carpenter 175

11. Everything Has Its Good Sides and Its Bad
Iván Cantor 185

12. You've Got to Practice It
Olga Alicea 195

Conclusion: Toward a Fluid Latino Identity
Robert Atkinson 207

Appendix: English and Spanish Interview Questions 229

Index 231

Illustrations

All photographs by Victor Damian.

Map of Portland Latino Locations, by Rosemary Mosher 3

Martinez Auto Service 5

The Gold Boot Two Shoe Shine & Shoe Repair 7

Sacred Heart Catholic Church 11

The Center for Cultural Exchange 18

Hacienda Pancho Villa Mexican Restaurant and Cantina 19

La Bodega Latina 21

Tu Casa Restaurant 23

Lourdes' International Beauty Salon 24

White Memorial Seventh-day Adventist Church 31

Immanuel Baptist Church 33

Immigrant Legal Advocacy Project 35

Blanca Santiago 50

Adrian Bravo Chavez 66

Ana Manza and Eliseo Brea 82

Laura Ochoa, and her daughter Diana 96

John Connors 110

The Reverend Virginia Marie Rincón 128

Tu Casa Restaurant Salvadoreño 136

Victoria Chicón 154

Juan González 168

Lourdes Carpenter 174

Iván Cantor's mentor Armando Vives 184

Olga Alicea 194

Foreword

The immigration wave that is changing the face of America has reached parts of Maine, bringing large numbers of southeast Asians, Latin Americans, and Africans. The profound demographic changes that are occurring strike at key issues for all of us, whether we are educators, social workers, or business owners. Whether we are grappling with how to teach English to the children of immigrants, bring appropriate health care to their families, or integrate them legally into the work force, we are faced with complex issues that need to be fully understood before solutions can be developed and implemented. In order to welcome them into these communities and better serve them, we need to understand their perspectives so that we are prepared to embrace the changes their presence has brought.

Marty Baron, the editor of the *Boston Globe*, received the Pulitzer Prize for Journalism for his coverage of the Elián González story in Miami, where nine out of ten members of the Cuban community wanted Elián to stay in the United States. Yet, nine out of ten Americans wanted him returned to Cuba. Why was there such a clash in values between these two communities? In a speech Baron gave to the Association for Education in Journalism and Mass Communication, he emphasized the fact that the American people missed an opportunity to really get to know the Cuban American community because of the biased media coverage the story received. He stated, referring to Cubans and the anti-Cuban sentiment that was fostered during that period, that a better understanding of the Cuban community and their perspective was necessary in order to appreciate the nuances of the Elian case: "You have to understand their history. You have to understand their personal experience, their culture, and their religion. You have to listen. You have to listen hard."

The editors of *Latino Voices in New England*, David Carey Jr. and Robert Atkinson, did exactly this. They carefully listened to Latino/as in Portland, Maine and recorded their experiences so that we could better understand their culture, religion, history, and personal perspective. They examined the specific experiences of Latino/as who moved to Maine, and the stories told inform us about the nature of community and how cities and neighborhoods change when new and different groups of people move in and establish a home.

The number of Latino/as living in Maine has been steadily growing for years, and now numbers close to 10,000 people. Central and South Americans, Mexicans and Puerto Ricans all come together to worship, shop, and socialize. In Portland, Latino/as have created a vibrant community, starting restaurants, grocery stores, and Spanish-speaking churches. But the book tells more than that one-dimensional story. It talks about finding community beyond language and culture, giving us a clear picture of what they are thinking and feeling.

Since Maine has not traditionally been a racially diverse state, except for African Americans that settled in Bangor in the early part of the twentieth century, the reality of new ethnic groups and cultures settling here often leads to misconceptions, lack of understanding, and nonacceptance—all issues explored by those interviewed for this book. In substantive ways, Maine's experiences mirror those of the United States.

America is a land of immigrants, and each successive wave has brought its own traditions and culture, which often threatened the communities in which they settled. In many cities, those groups were often regarded with suspicion or even prejudice. The experience of these immigrants shows that proximity to those unlike you does not automatically create community. It is important to examine, and begin to rethink, how we define and view community. These compelling stories help us do that. Is a community simply an accident of geography, people who just happen to live near one another? Or is it something more fluid, more based in shared history, culture, and experiences?

In the case of immigrants, new and old, the struggle came when a community held together by one language and culture moved into a community bound by a different language and culture. In most cases, the two communities do not always become one, sometimes opting for relatively peaceful coexistence through mutual segregation. This is the way communities have worked for decades, but in many cities things are beginning to change.

Both the increasingly mobile workforce and the emergence of new technologies have increased the speed with which communities undergo substantial change. People move much more frequently now than they once did, leading to progressively more diverse cities and towns. In most cities, the old barriers that once separated the "Latino" part of town from that of another ethnic group are fast disappearing. Part of this is undoubtedly due to the homogenizing effect of popular culture, but some of it is also simply an increased acceptance of people who might be different from us.

Another factor is the increasing view of community as people with shared interests. The rise of communications technology has led to the creation of virtual "communities" online, where like-minded people gather to engage in discussion and share information. This communication can take place in a very long list of languages. These communities exist completely apart from geographical, cultural, or racial boundaries and yet thrive all over the Internet. As increased travel, diversity, and technology challenge the traditional concept of community, we are forced to examine it from a new perspective, one that gives us a greater ability to communicate and even interact in ways that were never possible before. The inevitable changes that result as the world comes in closer contact emphasize the complexities of understanding what makes a community.

The editors of this book have given us firsthand accounts of how it feels to be Latino in Portland in an effort to give us an understanding of Latino culture in Maine. It is true that these individuals through their culture add to the vibrancy of this state, but the book poses many issues that Americans need to explore so that we are more open to saying that those who look, speak, and act differently from us are helping us define and build communities in ways that are different from previous generations.

Elsa Nuñez
President, Eastern Connecticut State University
(formerly Vice Chancellor for Academic and
Student Affairs, University of Maine System)

Acknowledgments

We are grateful for the support of many individuals during the preparation of this book. We first want to especially thank all those whose inspiring stories grace these pages; they provided us with the rare and rewarding opportunity to step inside their lives, share their journeys, and pass their challenges and triumphs on to you, the reader. We are indebted to Blanca Santiago for the interviews she carried out, as well as for her continuing feedback, guidance, and insights throughout the project. We want to thank Victor Damian for so skillfully catching the essence of each of the storytellers with his photographs. We thank Rosemary Mosher for working so patiently with us on the many iterations of the map. We also thank Malvina Gregory and Janice Jaffe for their transcriptions and translations of the interviews.

Avi Chomsky, Gina Pérez, Jo Radner, and the anonymous reviewers at SUNY Press all offered valuable critiques and comments on earlier versions of this manuscript and we offer our thanks to them. The Maine Humanities Council, University of Southern Maine Faculty Senate, Provost Joe Wood, Dean Betty Lou Whitford, Dean Devinder Malhotra, and the Office of Sponsored Research all generously supported this project. At SUNY Press we are grateful to our acquisitions editor Larin McLaughlin and our production editor Marilyn Semerad for their support in bringing this book forward.

——

David Carey Jr.: I wish to thank Joe Conforti whose encouragement first got me thinking about the history and influence of Latin Americans and Latino/as in Portland, Maine. In turn, Zip Kellogg, Crystal Wilder, and Nicole Witherbee provided valuable research assistance on the introduction. *Finalmente, quiero agredecer a mi esposa Sarah por su constante apoyo y a mi hija Ava por tres años de sonrisas y pura alegría.*

Robert Atkinson: I am grateful for all those individuals over the years who have in one way or another guided or supported the efforts of the Life Story Center at the University of Southern Maine, allowing me to pursue my interests in the narrative approach, and in particular the life story interview. I am also indebted to Patricia Arredondo for her inspiration and encouragement. I would also like to thank Jen Meader, my graduate assistant, and Rose Mahoney, my administrative assistant, for their help, and, of course, Cynthia, for being with me always.

Introduction

Situating Latino Voices in a New England Community

David Carey Jr.

> At some point, on our way to a new consciousness, we will have to leave the opposite bank, the split between the two mortal combatants somehow healed so that we are on both shores at once and, at once, see through serpent and eagle eyes.
>
> —Gloria Anzaldúa, *Borderlands/La Frontera*

> *Hay tantísimas fronteras que dividen a la gente, pero por cada frontera existe también un puente.*
> (There are a great number of borders that divide people, but for every border there is also a bridge.)
>
> —Gina Valdés, *Puentes y Fronteras*

With the United States on the verge of claiming the third-largest concentration of Spanish speaking people in the world and the 2000 census indicating that nearly one in five inhabitants speaks a language other than English at home, learning about Latino plights, realities, and contributions is essential to understanding our changing nation and its relationship to the rest of the world. According to the U.S. Census Bureau, more than half of the immigrants living in the United States have come from Latin America. In light of the Census Bureau's declaration that Hispanics comprise the largest minority

(14 percent) in the United States, defining Spanish as a foreign language is becoming increasingly problematic.[1] Yet until Latino/as are recognized as citizens as well as immigrants (in contrast to Caucasians who are assumed to be citizens because of their physical features and [for many] their English fluency), Spanish is unlikely to gain broader acceptance here. Nonetheless, the increasing presence and influence of Latino/as is making the United States more like the rest of the Americas.[2]

These changing demographics have fueled a growing literature in Latino Studies that tends to focus on large Latino populations in major cities—Chicago, New York, Miami, Los Angeles.[3] While a small-town trend also is emerging in the literature, more research is needed in small cities and communities, especially since these kinds of places play a central role in the new Latino diaspora.[4] Latino voices from the whitest state in the nation (96.9 percent of Mainers identify as Caucasian) elucidate how Spanish speakers conceptualize and create community in places where they represent only a tiny (yet burgeoning) percentage of the population. By 2000, 9,360 Hispanics lived in Maine, representing only 0.7 percent of the population. By May 2008, they numbered almost 16,000.[5] The testimonies herein reveal why Latino/as leave predominantly Latino neighborhoods in large urban areas like New York or Boston for the safety and serenity of small cities like Portland despite the challenges of marginalization, racism, and isolation. By exploring the ways migration leads to residency, this volume serves as a model for the study of new and reemerging Latino settlements, particularly ones where migrants are so outnumbered that their communities are virtually invisible, even to other Latino/as.[6]

When U.S. Border Patrol agents in Portland raided Latino and Somali businesses, a homeless shelter, and factories that employed people of color on January 25, 2004, Latino and other community leaders responded by organizing meetings and a march, which city officials and other Portlanders supported with their presence. Though federal agents arrested only ten people for inadequate documentation, many more were harassed. Most were U.S. citizens or documented immigrants who caught the agents' attention because they looked like foreigners. In addition to targeting economically marginalized individuals, agents apparently were so blinded by their association of whiteness with U.S. citizenship that they failed to immediately release a Puerto Rican man who produced his voter identification card as evidence that he was a U.S. citizen. As a Puerto Rican who grew up in California and then made her way to Portland, Olga Alicea empathizes with this man's plight when she observes that even in places like California where so many Latino/as live, "the culture is still oppressively white."

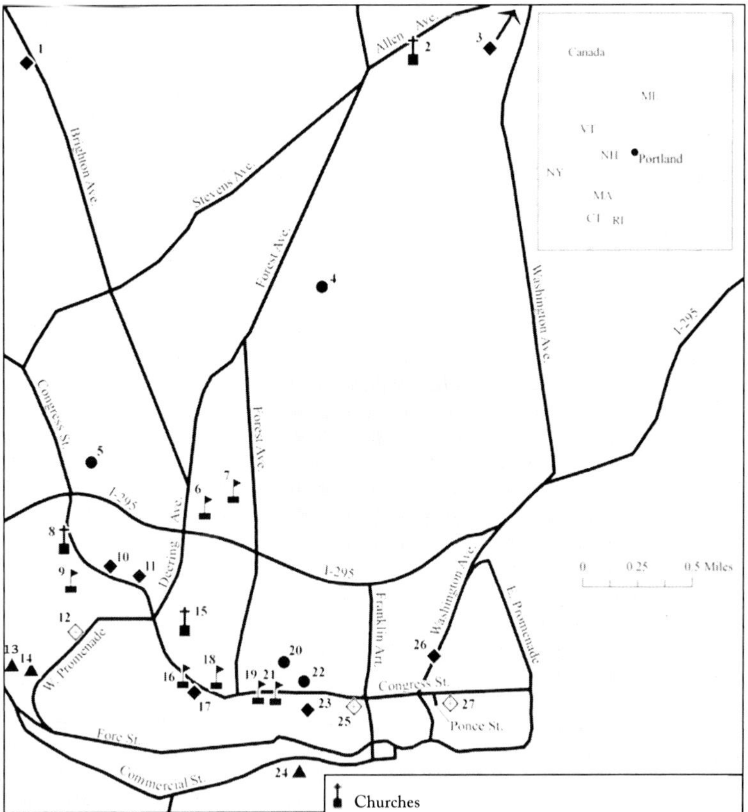

Map of Portland Latino Locations, by Rosemary Mosher.

Churches
- 2 White Memorial Seventh-day Adventist Church
- 8 The Deliverance Center
- 15 Sacred Heart Catholic Church

Historic Landmarks
- 12 Thomas Brackett Reed Statue
- 25 César Chávez Park
- 27 Ponce St.

Latino Businesses
- 1 La Familia Restaurante
- 3 Uno, 2, 3 Daycare
- 10 Lourdes' International Beauty Salon
- 11 La Bodega Latina
- 17 Bodega El Caribe
- 23 The Gold Boot Two
- 26 Tu Casa Restaurant Salvadoreño

Latino Social, Cultural, and Educational Spaces
- 6 WMPG Radio Station
- 7 USM Woodbury Campus Center
- 9 The Station (night club)
- 16 Center for Cultural Exchange
- 19 Community Television Network
- 21 Havana (night club)

Places of Employment
- 13 Barber Foods
- 14 Cozy Harbor
- 24 Portland Fish Pier

Services
- 4 Multilingual and Multicultural Center
- 5 Portland Adult Education
- 18 Tengo Voz
- 20 Preble Street Resource Center
- 22 Immigrant Legal Advocacy Project

Since immigrants of color are permanently foreign in a way that white immigrants are not, Latino/as can never fully assimilate (much less become white) nor do they necessarily wish to. They are perpetually foreigners within. In contrast, thanks to a skin color that has become normalized in the United States, white immigrants have the ability to immediately and then permanently disconnect themselves from immigration.[7] For Olga, "[D]iscrimination exists in not being able to see any representation of who you are in your environment." At worst racism dooms Latino/as and Latin American immigrants to marginal economic circumstances; at best it compels them to overcome additional obstacles to achieve their dreams.

In the aftermath of the January 2004 raids, businesses suffered because many Latino consumers refused even to leave their homes for fear they would be accosted.[8] As Ana Manza and Eliseo Brea, who hail from the Dominican Republic, note, the U.S. Border Patrol raids "affected all of us because we are all immigrants. We come from immigrant families and what happens to one immigrant happens to all of us." By identifying the way Latino/as and other U.S. citizens (with the obvious exception of Native Americans, Puerto Ricans, and many Mexican Americans) are connected through a history of immigration and discrimination, the Latino raconteurs in this book articulate a shared experience even for those who choose to ignore it.[9] Their accounts provide a window into the dynamics of community making.

Portland Latino/as and Latin American immigrants reflect the broader trend of a growing and increasingly influential Latino population in New England and the United States, but they also hold a unique position in this phenomenon.[10] Geographer Daniel Arreola's conceptualization of Hispanic/Latino community types (continuous, discontinuous, and new) is helpful in situating the significance of this study. Certainly, Portland is not a "continuous" community that was founded as and remains a Hispanic place, such as Laredo, Texas, or Las Vegas, New Mexico. Nor is it a "discontinuous" place that was originally founded as Hispanic but ceded this dominance at some point and is now becoming increasingly Hispanic again, such as San Antonio, Texas, or Los Angeles, California. Like so many other U.S. cities and towns, Portland appears to be experiencing the Latino diaspora as a pioneer Hispanic settlement where Latinos are making their presence known as a new group. Yet despite portrayals of the Latino presence as a recent phenomenon by informants in this book and despite the 2000 census (which estimated that one-third of all Latin Americans in Maine had lived in the United States for less than a decade), Portland is not a "new" Hispanic place either.[11]

Portland's Latino community points to a fourth category I call reemerging. Portland Latino/as and Latin American immigrants are reestablishing a

Martinez Auto Service (South Portland).

presence in a city that, unbeknownst to most Portlanders, was shaped by its nineteenth-century Latin American residents (some of whom became citizens). Small yet vibrant, the contemporary Portland Latino community both reflects and builds upon the legacy of its nineteenth-century counterpart and in this sense is putting down roots in fertile ground.

Though first populated by Wabanaki peoples,[12] Portland was founded as an Anglo city on July 4, 1786.[13] Shortly thereafter, due largely to a thriving West India trade and its demand for maritime workers, Portland hosted a burgeoning Hispanic (mostly Cuban) community, which thrived throughout much of the nineteenth century. Although most of these families and individuals had either moved away or assimilated (in one illustrative example Ramon and Juan Gutierez changed their surnames to Gardiner) by the early twentieth century, the current (and more diverse) Latino community has rich historical roots.[14] As such, unlike the Guatemalan immigrants who were the first Hispanics to arrive in Morganton, North Carolina, for example, today's Portland Latino/as and Latin American immigrants represent a second attempt at establishing a pioneer settlement.[15] The voices in this book contribute to a deeper understanding of these kinds of places. As a reemerging Latino community, Portland Latino/as and Latin American immigrants complicate conceptions of how ethnic minorities position themselves in new places.

But it is not just the relationship of Portland Latino/as and Latin American immigrants to their receiving community that makes their situation unique. Unlike many Latino communities that are dominated by one national or ethnic group, Portland's Latino/as are a diverse mix of peoples from such places as the Dominican Republic, Mexico, El Salvador, Puerto Rico, Guatemala, Peru, Colombia, and Cuba. As John Connors suggests in these pages, Portland's small size unites Latinos of different national origins. In truth, the diversity and fluidity of Portland's Latino community is both a source of strength and weakness. While the community displays formidable organizing skills during crises such as the 2004 U.S. Border Patrol raids, less sensational though no less important quotidian issues fail to ignite an united response. Unlike the aforementioned Maya in Morganton who predominantly hailed from the highland town of Aguacatán, Guatemala, and thus organized a union around this shared provenance, Portland Latino/as and Latin American immigrants do not necessarily enjoy such immediate and intimate connections.[16]

Though such organizations as Centro Latino Maine are attempting to remedy this reality, in general Portland's Latino community tends to be reactive rather than proactive. Given the diversity of Portland's Latino/as and Latin American immigrants, it is often a shared sense of marginalization that motivates them to come together as a community. Eliseo Brea, for example, expresses a sense of solidarity rooted in discrimination and persecution when he notes similarities between his experience and that of the undocumented: "We're people who are just coming here to earn our daily bread."

At the same time, the diffuse nature of the Latino community facilitates individuals' and even smaller groups' incorporation into Portland's social fabric. By this I do not mean assimilation (although that too is a possibility), but rather the ability to be present without attracting attention. Even Latino storefronts blend into the city's landscape to the extent that many Portlanders are unaware of Portland's Salvadoran restaurant or Dominican grocery stores. As a disparate community reemerging in a predominantly Caucasian city, Latino/as in Portland chart their lives as both outsiders and insiders, immigrants and U.S. citizens, Latino/as and Americans. The chameleon nature of such complex identities and imaginings allows them to connect with a number of different communities in both their sending and host countries.

As their ability to mobilize members of the larger community around a civil rights issue demonstrates, Portland Latino/as and Latin American immigrants are poised to face the increasingly complex and contested process of building bridges to connect communities instead of building walls to separate them. In many ways, Latino/as and Latin American immigrants ford frontiers both within Portland and between the city and state, the United States, and the Atlantic world. Modeling a commitment to Portland *and* their

The Gold Boot Two Shoe Shine & Shoe Repair. Portland Latino/as frequently consult the Cuban-American proprietor Armando Vives (shown on the right) for personal and professional advice.

sending communities, Latino/as and Latin American immigrants encourage native Portlanders to be more worldly and in so doing make the city more cosmopolitan. In her testimony, Victoria Chicón perceives a fundamental difference between people of the United States and Latin America:

> [I]n Latin America, in general we're aware of things. I mean, on a corner you see some old people or some kids at a bus stop and they're talking about what's happening in the world. But not here. I mean, here you know the news from here, but not the culture of the whole world. American culture, I mean, they're completely absorbed in that, but their historical past doesn't interest them. But we have so much of that, I think, right? The whole historical question, our heritage. *We have the advantage of seeing things more broadly.* (emphasis added)

Some informants, such as Laura Ochoa, go so far as to identify as the very interstices of immigration: "I *am* the middle" [between Mexico and the United States]. Many Portland Latino/as and Latin American immigrants are "on both shores at once."[17]

The hybridity of the Latino community and the individuals within it encourages us to reconceptualize the meanings of America and American. With the increasing influence of Latino/as and Latin American immigrants, perhaps contemporary Portlanders (and other U.S. citizens) will employ the rhetoric of their early nineteenth-century forebears who understood America inclusively as a hemisphere, not exclusively as a nation.[18] Whether through transnationalism, border-crossing, cultural transformation, or the economic forces that often set these trends in motion, boundaries (both real and imagined) between the United States and Latin America are breaking down and hemispheric connections are becoming stronger. For example, immigrants' remittances are a (albeit unequal) response to the foreign investment and free trade that extract wealth from developing nations and thereby compel people to emigrate. But as the multiplicity of the lives, voices, and identities in the following pages reveals, more than economics connects these regions. By adapting to the United States but not abandoning their culture and worldviews, Latino/as and Latin American immigrants both experience a transformation and transform their host communities.

This cultural exchange notwithstanding, the 2006 immigration debates revealed a wide gulf among U.S. residents. The proposed 700-mile-long wall on the U.S.–Mexico border in Congressman F. James Sensenbrenner Jr.'s immigration bill HR 4437 was emblematic of those U.S. citizens who were intent on erecting barriers instead of bridges. Furthermore, Representative Sensenbrenner's desire to turn undocumented immigrants (and those who aided them) into felons reflected a broader effort to criminalize immigrants and immigration. Gus Martínez, a Mexican immigrant living in Scotsdale, Arizona, noted, "They see you are Hispanic and call you a criminal, but we are not that."[19] Similarly, in her testimony, Blanca Santiago speaks of the tendency to associate Puerto Ricans with crime.

In response to these negative portrayals and legislative activity, Latino communities organized demonstrations that drew impressive numbers in Chicago (200,000), Los Angeles (500,000 to 1,000,000), San Diego (40,000 school children alone), Atlanta (80,000), Phoenix (20,000), Denver (50,000), and Washington, D.C. (30,000). Portland was one of over fifty cities that held rallies to recognize April 10, 2006 as a Day of Action for Immigrant Justice. Shortly thereafter, when activists organized a national boycott of work and commerce to recognize May 1 as a "Day without Immigrants," large numbers of Latino/as and Latin American immigrants again turned out and many businesses closed. Despite the exploitative living and working conditions and low wages that marginalize undocumented workers (as evidenced in

Adrian Bravo's testimony), these public protests point to the growing influence of the broader Latino community. At the same time, these events also speak to their invisibility. While the Latino media began covering these demonstrations before they happened, the English-speaking media was caught off guard. For example, in Chicago the English-speaking media failed to cover the largest demonstration in the city's history. As a result, to many English-only citizens, the rallies were surprisingly large and spontaneous.[20] By confronting the challenges of racism, economic marginalization, and invisibility, Portland Latino/as and Latin American immigrants are trying to build a more just and inclusive city. A flyer circulated by the Maine Immigrant Rights Coalition about the April 10 rally in Portland demonstrated that immigrants both deeply care about the United States ("the character of our nation is at stake") and conceive of it broadly: "No matter where we were born—WE ARE ALL AMERICA."

Latino Tales of the City

Rather than being exhaustive or even emblematic, this collection of narratives explores the ways members of a diverse yet intermittently united ethnic group reconstitute their communities and identities in a predominantly Caucasian city, and in turn how living in such a place shapes them. In an effort to reflect the diversity of Latino/as and Latin American immigrants in Portland and the United States, the interviewees include community leaders, religious leaders, students, factory workers, manual laborers, social workers, professionals, business owners, and the homeless. In addition to occupational and socioeconomic variety, these informants hail from nations as diverse as the Dominican Republic, Mexico, Venezuela, El Salvador, and Peru. Though all are migrants, not all are immigrants; some were born in the United States. All the informants are connected to Spanish-speaking places, though not all speak Spanish. Since gender balance was also a goal in the selection of informants, eight women and six men are included here. Their ages range from eighteen to sixty-two. Of course, no one raconteur should be held up as the voice of any one of these groups, let alone the Latino voice. Rather, the range of experiences and perspectives in the following pages speaks to the uniqueness of each individual and complexity of the Latino community.[21] As anthropologist Kay Warren observes, "The collage of first-person accounts, rather than a voice-of-God expository style, leaves more of the work of analysis to the reader and makes the collection all the more powerful for those who have not directly experienced" the ways migration, discrimination, and structural oppression fragment everyday life.[22]

The concern with diversity precluded random sampling. Robert Atkinson interviewed two English-speaking Latinos (John Connors and Laura Ochoa). I interviewed two couples I met through the Spanish service at Sacred Heart Catholic church (Ana Manza and Eliseo Brea, and Hernán and Marta) as well as Blanca Santiago and Adrian Bravo.[23] In an effort to avoid approaching Portland Latino/as merely as subjects, we invited Blanca Santiago to select and interview people. As a board member of Centro Latino Maine, Blanca had access to local leaders including members of the business community, but she also sought to interview people who lived on the margins of these social networks. In short, the guiding methodology for this study was network sampling, a process of arranging and developing interviews through personal connections.[24] The University of Southern Maine (USM) also facilitated these connections. For example, Robert Atkinson met Blanca Santiago through a course he was teaching at USM, and I came to know a number of Latino students (including Laura Ochoa) as the faculty advisor to the USM Latino-Hispanic Student Association.

In some ways, however, our methodology was not uniform. After meeting a number of times to devise and then fine-tune the project's goals and methodology, Blanca Santiago, Robert Atkinson, and I realized that our interests in the project were informed by our disciplinary and professional backgrounds. To explore the stories of Latino/as and Latin American immigrants in Portland, we needed an interdisciplinary approach. As a result, though the interview questions remained constant, the interview process did not. In general, interviews followed a format in which interviewers asked interviewees open-ended questions about what brought them to Portland and their experiences there. Though the distinctions are minor, they are worth noting. Oral history methodology guided my interviews. By earning interviewees' confidence and trust and conducting interviews in their native language, I sought to gain access to perspectives, insights, and empirical information unobtainable through traditional historical sources such as archival documents and newspapers.[25] In turn, Robert Atkinson employed his expertise in life stories whereby the interviewer guides the storyteller in recounting their lived experience.[26] Blanca Santiago approached her interviews from years of experience working with Latino/as with a particular focus on helping people articulate their needs and dreams.

Despite these differences and our role in selecting the questions and guiding the interviews, each of us was intent on allowing the people interviewed to

Sacred Heart Catholic Church where a Spanish language mass is offered each Sunday.

speak for themselves. But since "ethnographic and historical projects cannot be extricated from power-laden contexts," this objective was inevitably elusive.[27] For example, our positions as USM professors (and the economic, political, and social benefits associated with that status) affected Robert Atkinson's and my relationships with interviewees and thus the stories they told. Audience matters. At the same time, we should not underestimate the ability of informants to "negotiate the conditions under which communication takes place" and thereby direct, influence, and even control not only the information conveyed but also the topics addressed.[28] To ensure reciprocal text production, we asked interviewees to review the transcripts of their interviews and edit, delete, or expand on any aspect of them. In this sense, these Latino/as have framed their own histories. All but John Connors and Laura Ochoa were interviewed in Spanish. In the hopes of reaching a broad audience, the additional filter of English translations through which readers must sift became a necessity. Finally, while editing out the questions from the text eliminates the rapport and at times riposte between interviewer and interviewee, it also privileges the narrative flow of these accounts and thereby accentuates these Latino voices. So as not to obscure the process of negotiation that shaped these testimonies, we have included the interview questions in the appendix.

Catalysts and Cycles of Latin American Immigration

The voices in these pages are not emerging from a historical vacuum; on the contrary, they are building upon a Hispanic influence and connection in the city that dates back to at least the eighteenth century. The nineteenth-century West India trade, which made Portland a major Atlantic seaport, facilitated a close relationship between the Caribbean and southern Maine. As the focus of Portland's commercial ties with Latin America, Cuba in particular left a lasting impression on the city. Cuban planters sent their children to study in southern Maine, some of whom settled in Portland and left their mark on the city's landscape, architecture, economy, and identity. In turn, by recognizing themselves as international actors, many of Portland's nineteenth-century residents helped to create a welcoming environment for Hispanics by learning Spanish and trying to establish a library for Spanish literature and newspapers. After the Civil War, southern ports displaced Portland's position in the West India trade and the city's connection to Latin America waned. Even though a few Cubans and other Latin Americans continued to emigrate to

Portland into the early twentieth century, the city became more insular and less cosmopolitan as the twentieth century progressed.[29]

As is evidenced by the West India trade, Latin American immigration to the United States often was the result of larger forces, particularly U.S. investment and policies in the region. Of course, international relations also affected immigration. By the 1940s, the domestic labor shift (into defense-related industries) and shortage caused by World War II was a catalyst for increased interactions between Mainers and Latin Americans. Though they predominantly went to farming communities not cities, Mexicans (as part of the ill-fated *Braceros* agreement between the United States and Mexico [1942–1964]) arrived in Maine in 1944 to fill a labor lacuna.[30]

At about the same time, the Puerto Rican government initiated Operation Bootstrap, an economic incentive program aimed at industrializing the economy by attracting foreign investment—the first *maquiladora* model. Yet, the focus on capital intensive industrialization only increased unemployment and poverty, the very scourges the operation was trying to mitigate. Since the Puerto Rican government was simultaneously encouraging emigration, by the late 1940s and 1950s, Puerto Ricans (who of course were U.S. citizens) were migrating north in search of jobs; over three million currently reside on the mainland, nearly 40 percent of the island's population. According to the 2000 U.S. Census, 2,275 live in Maine.[31] As Blanca Santiago's testimony attests, Puerto Ricans' feelings and attitudes toward this program are complicated and conflicted. Even while she characterizes Operation Bootstrap as "a benevolent thing," Blanca describes the misery it caused her family. Since the government's economic policy and promotion of urban migration targeted females partly to control and discipline them but also to "modernize" Puerto Rico, women such as Blanca's mother were at the heart of this maelstrom. Portrayed as problematic on the island and largely left to their own devices once they arrived in the United States, the young women who migrated found few of the opportunities the government had promised.[32] As Blanca recalls her childhood, her mother's struggle becomes apparent. Yet in reflecting upon her past, Blanca highlights the role that such forces beyond her control had in allowing her to create a new life. Her oral history opens a window into Operation Bootstrap's complex legacy.

For other Latin American emigrants, the forces that pulled them to Portland originated in the United States. The flight of Dominicans provides an illustrative example. When the Marines occupied the Dominican Republic in 1965 to suppress a popular movement, capitalists from the United States soon followed with increased investments in the Dominican sugar industry.

Dominican emigration, almost 100 percent of which goes to the United States, increased almost thirteenfold immediately thereafter. Ironically, because foreign investment in export agriculture and manufacturing displaces small-scale enterprises (such as subsistence agriculture and textile production), the very measures commonly thought to deter emigration cause it. Dominicans did not necessarily resent this intervention, however. Partly because they seek to distance themselves from Haiti's history, fate, and people, many Dominicans are less critical than other Latin Americans of U.S. imperialism. In her interview, Ana Manza confides:

> We feel good about our country's history with the United States because they have always supported us. And when there's any problem, they're always there . . . to establish peace, so there won't be war, so there won't be problems in one's country. . . . That's why the Dominican Republic remains so stable. You don't see that it's like Haiti . . . because the United States gives it lots of opportunities for a lot of people. For professionals, too, they come here, work a lot, and a lot of opportunities are given to everyone. So, thank God, there are good relations between the two.

When the United States responded to a drop in international sugar prices by investing in the Dominican Republic's nontraditional agriculture, manufacturing, and tourism industries in the 1980s, emigration boomed again. Today the United States is home to about 10 percent of the Dominican Republic's population. Though few came directly from the Dominican Republic to Portland, many local Dominicans first emigrated to the United States in response to U.S. intervention in their country and the changing conditions of global capitalism—both forces beyond their control.[33]

Patterns of U.S. intervention and investment impelling immigration were evident throughout Central America and the Caribbean. As anthropologist Saskia Sassen observes, the United States "receives 19.5% of all emigration from Central America, but 52% of emigration from El Salvador, the country with the greatest U.S. involvement in the region."[34] Many Salvadorans who emigrated to the United States in the 1980s first worked on export-oriented coffee plantations in El Salvador. In fact, today so many Salvadorans are migrating to the United States (one out of every nine) that Hondurans are filling that tiny nation's labor shortage.[35] As one response to the drastic economic imbalance in the region, Salvadorans in the United States sent $2.8 billion to their families in 2005, which accounted for 17 percent of the Gross

Domestic Product in a nation where nearly 50 percent of the population lived in poverty.[36]

Though not the only factor, the stark economic inequality between developing and developed nations propels Latin American emigration to the United States. Like Laura Ochoa, many of the people intervewed "were raised in a poor family," and, like Adrian Bravo, they fled poverty. When viewed from extreme marginalization, the United States appears the land of plenty. The image of money being found in the streets "like leaves" that Lourdes Carpenter describes is common in the developing world. As anthropologist Roger Lancaster points out in his study of Nicaragua, "In a land of scarcity, the image of plenty is an absolute good in and of itself. . . . The glut of commodities on the developed side of the equation obliterates any system of reference, on the underdeveloped side, that might allow for an understanding of inequality, powerlessness, and relative poverty."[37] This myopia helps to explain why even Latin Americans who enjoy relatively comfortable lives in their countries, such as Lourdes Carpenter and Iván Cantor, migrate to the United States. Lourdes' transition from employing a servant in the Dominican Republic to cleaning a department store in the United States is emblematic of the disillusionment many Latin American immigrants experience in the United States.[38] Similarly, Iván's story typifies the experience of many Latin American immigrants who are struggling to build meaningful lives in marginal economic circumstances. He notes, "I've lived in Portland nearly eight years and instead of life getting better for me, it's the opposite."

Though economics is at the heart of immigration, U.S. foreign policy also looms over this phenomenon. Like Dominicans, many Central Americans emigrated to the United States in response to U.S. interventions. During the cold war, the United States often played out its preoccupation with communism in Central America, particularly Guatemala, Nicaragua, and El Salvador. The civil wars that engulfed Central America during the 1970s and 1980s can be traced in part to U.S. military aid and intervention. The United States tended to derail popular movements and democratically elected governments. The intensity of violence, which at times reached genocidal proportions (as in the case of Guatemala in the early 1980s), displaced many Central Americans. Like other Salvadorans and Guatemalans in Portland, Hernán and Marta fled their country to escape war. Yet despite (or perhaps because of) U.S. complicity in these civil wars, less than 3 percent of the Guatemalans and Salvadorans who have applied for asylum in the United States have received it. These examples reflect a broader pattern of developed nations' imperialist economic, political, and/or military interventions spurring emigration from the nations upon which they prey.[39]

Finally in 1990, Congress acknowledged the crisis and granted Salvadorans "Temporary Protected Status," which provided an eighteen-month stay from deportation for refugees who registered with the Immigration and Naturalization Service. Though Guatemalans never received deportation protection, an American Baptist Church class-action suit filed on their (and Salvadorans') behalf in 1985 gained them work authorization while their political-asylum cases were being reexamined. Remarkably, the cases of thousands who applied for asylum in 1991 have yet to be decided. Hernán and Marta are among the Salvadorans and Guatemalans in Portland whose asylum cases are still pending.[40]

Considering the historical forces behind their emigration, it is surprising that the Latin American immigrants in this book are not more critical of U.S. policy. Of course, for those seeking to earn residency or citizenship, criticizing their host country could be risky. But perhaps the very nature of living in the empire dampens criticism by making residents feel complicit.

In contrast to the hard-fought battles on behalf of Central Americans to gain asylum in the United States, after 1959 Cubans generally were welcomed with open arms. Ever since the United States rejected Fidel Castro's overtures of rapprochement, Washington has considered Cuba a communist threat to stability in the region. At one point, this dramatic shift in U.S.–Cuban relations renewed Portland's connections with Cubans. When President Jimmy Carter criticized Fidel Castro for refusing to allow asylum seekers to leave Cuba, Castro authorized the Mariel Boatlift in September 1980, which initiated a mass exodus of more than 125,000 Cubans to the United States; about one hundred of them arrived in Maine. Since some of the refugees were allegedly prison and mental hospital inmates, widespread panic and violence broke out where they landed. Cubans arrived in Maine amidst newspaper and television reports describing knife fights and riots in Florida. Consequently, in stark contrast to the welcome mat extended to their nineteenth- and early twentieth-century counterparts, these émigrés were so vilified that the Portland Refugee Resettlement Program had trouble finding sponsors for them. In response, the program opened a house on Danforth Street to provide temporary shelter and social services to refugees. More than half of Portland's Cuban refugees quickly emigrated south in search of warmer climates and Spanish-speaking populations. Those who stayed found work and in some cases married women from Portland, but racism continued to plague them.[41]

Portland as a Latino Place

While Latin American emigration to the United States increased after World War II, during the 1990s the national Latino population grew by nearly 60 percent. At first glance the meager 0.2 percent growth in Maine's Latino population during the 1990s appears to belie this trend. But according to the U.S. census, the Hispanic population in Portland nearly tripled between 1980 and 2000 from 355 to 974. And according to local leaders, these numbers were low.[42] Anecdotal evidence affirms this trend: Latino/as in this volume remark that the Hispanic population has increased significantly in the last ten to fifteen years. By meeting the demand for Latin American goods and services, Latino businesses have created the infrastructure of a Latin American community in Portland. Latino entrepreneurs of restaurants, grocery shops, and gas stations, civic leaders working for state agencies, notary publics, native Spanish speakers teaching in public schools, spiritual leaders, and musicians comprise an economic and social network that creates a welcoming environment not only for Latino/as but for other ethnic groups as well.

In turn, a nascent interest in Latin America continues to grow among non-Latino Portlanders. They enjoy Latin American music at local venues, pursue trade opportunities in Mexico, sell Latin American textiles in their stores, and study in the Dominican Republic, Cuba, Guatemala, Argentina, Chile. Maine's financial relationship with Latin America has grown considerably in the last decade. From 1996 to 2002, Maine exports to Latin America and the Caribbean increased 51 percent from $62 million to $93 million.[43] Frequent trade delegations such as the one Governor John Baldacci led to Cuba in December 2005 bespeak a growing interest among Maine entrepreneurs in Latin American markets. Some Portland businesses rely on Latin America products for their success. Expanding economic, political, and personal relations are strengthening Portland's ties to the rest of the hemisphere.

Originally the home of Wabanaki peoples, Portland has a rich history of immigration. Throughout the colonial period, European residents were mainly English with a few Scots and Scots-Irish. By the nineteenth century, Irish, Italians, Scandinavians, Armenians, Canadians (including Blacks), Greeks, Poles, Eastern European Jews, Afro-Caribbeans, Cape Verdeans, and Latin Americans had settled in the city. More recently, as a federal refugee center, this city of about 60,000 people is also home to immigrants from countries as diverse as Sudan, Somalia, Afghanistan, and Bosnia.[44] The oral histories of Latin Americans in Portland shed light on the plight and contributions of a small yet influential group of immigrants. Despite the

The Center for Cultural Exchange. Before it closed its doors in 2007, the center offered Spanish language programming such as dances and music.

presence of a handful of professionals, most Latino/as and Latin American immigrants in Portland contribute long, arduous hours of manual labor for low wages. Depending on the job, much of Maine's Hispanic population earns an average of $8.00–$12.00 an hour. For those from the Caribbean and coastal areas of Latin America, Portland's relationship to the sea and pen-

Adrian Bravo Chavez in front of the Hacienda Pancho Villa Mexican Restaurant and Cantina (South Portland).

chant for seafood have eased their transitions; for some, it is their source of livelihood. Many work in local seafood processing plants cracking sea urchins and peeling shrimp as Ana Manza once did. Others like Eliseo Brea, Hernán, and Marta work in factories, restaurants, and cleaning companies; some are domestic servants.[45]

Upon arriving in the United States, immigrants begin the difficult process of remaking themselves. Lourdes Carpenter's story of going from being a professional in the Dominican Republic to cleaning Macy's department store in South Portland and then through an arduous process of becoming certified as a beautician (while outperforming "almost all the Americans") and opening her own business is emblematic of this struggle. Yet many others who share her diligence and even fortuitous connections have been less fortunate. Iván Cantor, for example, went from a comfortable lifestyle in Venezuela and Colombia to living at the YMCA and becoming a client at a Portland area social services center. Like Adrian Bravo and Laura Ochoa, many Latin American immigrants seek to improve their lives through education.[46] Because of language and other barriers, many immigrants, such as Eliseo Brea, are underemployed and face perceptions that they are ignorant, even though they are highly educated. Coming from a world of "journalists, intellectuals, professors, teachers, cultural circles, museums" in Peru, Victoria Chicón admits, "The biggest challenge I've had [living in Portland] is achieving my own status." Adapting to their new home and nation requires altering expectations and self-perceptions. Through volunteering in various organizations, pursuing her film career, teaching Spanish, and learning English, Victoria proudly exclaims, "I made myself." Despite their absence in the historiography of Maine and their obscurity in Portland, Latin Americans have been and continue to be an important part of the city's economic, political, social, and cultural fabric.

Transforming Perceptions of Community

By highlighting the flow of people, the perspectives of Latino/as and Latin American immigrants help us to reconceptualize who and what is American. One of the common threads woven through the testimonies in this volume is a complex understanding of community that both incorporates and defies geographic, cultural, linguistic, national, and ethnic boundaries. Portland Latino/as and Latin American immigrants are building a pan-Latino community that is neither exclusive nor limited to Southern Maine. Nor is it united or universal. Some choose not to engage in the Latino community (a few feel marginalized by it); others are unaware of its existence. In their interpenetrating lives, most Latino/as and Latin American immigrants return to their native countries to visit family and friends; some like Ana Manza and Eliseo Brea, and Hernán and Marta plan to retire there. As one journalist noted of returning Salvadorans: "So frequent are their trips that many are as involved in the life of their native towns as they are in their adopted communities."[47] The fluidity of Latin American immigrants' lives points to the multidirectional character of migration. Even those who do not return to Latin America frequently or at all "live their lives in a transnational cognitive space" wherein they imagine, plan, and strategize based on transnational possibilities.[48] For instance, whether or not Ana and Eliseo, and Hernán and Marta retire in their natal countries, envisioning themselves doing so influences their decisions and actions.

Perceptions of community among Latino/as and Latin American immigrants extend beyond their national and ethnic identities to other areas of the world. In Portland, Latino/as have established relations and alliances with their non-Latino neighbors. As such, their imagined communities—national, Latino, immigrant, Portland, United States—are overlapping and

Juan González in front of his store La Bodega Latina, aka The People's Market.

concentric, not contiguous. As Olga Alicea explains, "I don't feel connected just to the Latino community. I feel connected with immigrant communities in general, because I feel that many of the challenges and many of the experiences are similar." To cite a few other examples of this amorphous conception of community: Blanca Santiago, a Puerto Rican woman who celebrates her ties with Latinos in Massachusetts, traveled to Guatemala with a medical delegation and in the process reignited her passion for serving the Latino community in Portland. When a Mayan shaman from Guatemala visited Portland, Peruvian filmmaker Victoria Chicón interviewed him for the local Latino television program, "Nosotros, We the People." Born in Peru, Victor Damian, whose photographs grace this book, returned to Bolivia to film grassroots movements there, which his mother Victoria Chicón then edited to produce a documentary that was screened at a number of venues in Portland; similarly, Laura Ochoa, president of the University of Southern Maine Latino-Hispanic Student Association (LHSA), returned to Mexico City to film and serve street children. Juan González, the Dominican owner of La Bodega Latina (aka "The People's Market"), and Lourdes Carpenter, the Dominican owner of Lourdes' International Beauty Salon, pride themselves on serving Portland's African, black, Asian, Anglo, *and* Latino communities. Similarly, John Connors proudly exclaims, "We have an event and half the people that show up are not Latino." The vivacity of Portland's Latino community is rooted in its ability to engage with other communities locally, regionally, nationally, and internationally. Their diasporic worldviews and lives make them Americans in the broadest hemispheric sense. At times Latino/as are comfortable identifying as U.S. residents and citizens. But they also tap into the political power of a Latino (or Latin American) identity when it suits them. At other times, their expressions of identity are local.[49] By seamlessly emphasizing his Dominican culture, leading local Latino movements, and participating in the Portland Rotary Club, Juan Gonzaléz demonstrates these fluid identities (as do others in these pages). For these raconteurs, the notion of community is fluid and often contingent upon how it can be deployed most powerfully. As such, the ways Portland Latino/as and Latin American immigrants organize are not reduced to class, ethnicity, national origin, race, or gender, but rather are complex and shifting combinations of these identities.

Because they are living at a nexus of cultures, their multiple vantage points simultaneously come from both within and beyond the nation's borders. If, as feminist author Gloria Anzaldúa argues, "The borderlands are physically present wherever two or more cultures edge each other, where

Tu Casa Restaurant Salvadoreño, a favorite among laborers who do not have time to prepare their own meals.

people of different races occupy the same territory, where under, lower, middle and upper classes touch, where the space between two individuals shrinks with intimacy," then La Bodega Latina, Lourdes' International Beauty Salon, and Tu Casa Restaurant Salvadoreño are borderlands.[50] And their owners, employees, and regular customers are among those poised to lead us through the labyrinth of increasingly connected and complicated relations between people from different and unequal worlds.

The experience of Maine's Latin Americans reflects that of many late twentieth-century immigrants who sustain connections with both their sending and host communities. Portland Latin American immigrants are participating in transnational processes that are "anchored in and transcend one or more nation-states."[51] As the voices in this book affirm, the nation as a unit and framework of analysis is increasingly giving way to approaches that capture a world in which the exchange and flow of people, commodities, capital, and cultures know no borders.[52] As a result, community, home, and place are becoming contact zones where the "endless process of comings and goings . . . create familial, cultural, linguistic, and economic ties across national borders."[53] Examining Portland from Latino perspectives provides a microcosm through which to conceptualize America as a place "always in process

Lourdes' International Beauty Salon, a gathering place for Latinas.

itself."[54] The incorporation of Latin American rituals and mores into U.S. culture is but one example of how the nation as an imagined community is constantly evolving and reproducing itself.[55]

In contrast to Portland's cosmopolitan nature in the nineteenth century, today the city betrays pockets of provincialism and insularity as evidenced by one store sign that urged customers to buy Mexican handicrafts to stem Mexican immigration. Though such conspicuous displays are not common, the proprietor's assumption that consumption would curtail immigration discloses an ignorance of the causes of immigration and the contributions of immigrants. The diasporic dimensions of Portland's Latino population connect the city to other parts of the Americas in ways that few Portlanders are even aware. As anthropologist Gina Pérez notes, "Invariably, migrants and nonmigrants alike are enmeshed in these transnational social fields, and over time migration becomes part of the fabric of places, as people begin to imagine themselves as part of a larger community that extends beyond their place of residence."[56] The very presence of Latin Americans in Portland and Portland's engagement in the Atlantic economy encourages local denizens to recognize themselves as global citizens even if they never leave Maine. An increased awareness of Latin Americans' lives, challenges, and contributions will enrich the way people experience Portland as a place and the way Portlanders conceive of their place in the world.

Bicultural Lives, Assimilationist Struggles

Despite the growing presence and permanence of Portland Latino/as and Latin American immigrants, their obscurity persists in scholarship and society.[57] Hernán from El Salvador notes, "People say there aren't Latinos here, but there are a lot." By way of explanation, his wife Marta adds, "One doesn't know them because one works in one place and another in another and they're not seen." Many Latino/as and Latin American immigrants in Portland live near their employment and get around primarily on foot. Such limited mobility further contributes to their invisibility in the city. Because they are undocumented and do not want to draw attention to themselves, some itinerant Latin Americans encourage this invisibility. Others prefer anonymity because they fear discrimination or simply want to focus on their work and return home without incident. Similarly, despite paying taxes and Social Security, many documented immigrants refuse to accept aid—food stamps, Medicaid, Children's Health Insurance Program—because they fear being judged public charges and therefore denied citizenship or refused permission to host a family member from Latin America.[58] Efforts to deflect attention from themselves have been so effective that some Latin Americans are oblivious to the Latino presence in their midst. A Hispanic janitor at a Portland high school, a Mexican woman in neighboring Westbrook (Maine), and a Peruvian teacher in nearby Poland (Maine) all were unaware of the Latino community in southern Maine.[59]

Some of those interviewed in this volume are eager to expand awareness of Latino/as and celebrate their contributions. Even those hoping to blend in are not necessarily seeking assimilation. Historically, for many Latino/as assimilation has meant downward, rather than upward, mobility.[60] And though scholars such as Samuel Huntington argue that resistance to acculturation undermines the melting pot regime, indigenous peoples in places like Guatemala and Bolivia have demonstrated that an adherence to ethnic traditions and languages can enrich nation-states.[61] Unlike Huntington who argues, "There is no Americano dream,"[62] many Portland Latino/as do not see ethnic distinctions, economic development, and social stability as mutually exclusive. In one sense, however, Huntington is correct: these Latino/as do not have an Americano dream; rather they engage in and contribute to the multiple layers of community in Portland and the Americas, not just their own Latino lives and communities. For instance, the founders of the USM LHSA wanted to give back to the Latino, University, and southern Maine communities.

Instead of isolating themselves, many Latino/as are integrating into society, but on their own terms. At the "'I Have a Dream . . .' A Latino

Perspective" panel at USM in April 2004, Leticia Foss, a Mexican teacher exhorted, "Don't treat us differently; treat us equally. Recognize our color and accent. It shocks me when people say, 'I don't see color in people.' I want people to see my color. We want to be productive members of society and live in peace and safety."[63] By saying they want their color to be seen and their language to be heard, they are challenging integrationist approaches to citizenship and belonging. At the same time, they are acknowledging a different type of American who is erased by Huntington's American Dream in which everyone is implicitly white. In so doing, they challenge notions of Americanness, Whiteness, and racial hierarchies in the United States. Diversity is part of what Latino/as and Latin American immigrants contribute to the city. And for many, these differences form important aspects of their identities. By celebrating her distinctions, Leticia resists assimilation to, but not participation in, Anglo society.

The tension between acculturation and cultural preservation is palpable in these testimonies, particularly for parents who want their children to do well in school without conceding their heritage. As most of the people interviewed in this book stress, speaking Spanish is important both for their self-esteem and to ensure that their children learn the language. Juan González explains, "It's important for me not to lose my language or culture. . . . Roots are important. But sometimes you feel pressure to assimilate. At first I did. . . . The only thing is that we keep our roots from our country. I mean, in my house, one culture rules, the one I brought here, as my parents taught me in Santo Domingo." At the same time, Juan is proud his children are "assimilating well."

As the stories in this volume attest, juggling two (or more) cultures can make people feel they are not fulfilling the expectations of either. Olga Alicea admits, at times "I have to prove my Latinohood." Similarly, Blanca Santiago confides that the Latino community shamed her for not teaching her children Spanish. Like so many of her counterparts, Blanca's identity is grounded in the liminal space between cultures:

> I'm like this little rural country girl and I get taken out of that and then told, "No, your culture is a bad thing, your food's a bad thing, you're not speaking that language, you're not going to marry a Puerto Rican man." And then all the fallout from that, just being separated from everything.
>
> I'm a real strange mix of a person. I don't think that I'm unique. I know that there are other people who have similar experiences to

> mine. But it is a strange mix. Usually you have someone who's got the stuff a little more integrated than I do.
>
> People say, "Where are you from?"
>
> "I'm from New England."
>
> I can actually answer like that. Where are you from originally? I'm from Puerto Rico and I'm a *jíbara,* but basically I'm a New England girl. That's also part of who I am culturally. I listen to all kinds of music. I really like the traditional Puerto Rican music. But I also grew up listening to the Rolling Stones.

As Anzaldúa observes, "It's not a comfortable territory to live in, this place of contradictions. . . . No, not comfortable but home."[64] Laura Ochoa concurs, "It's hard being here." She explains, "[S]ometimes I feel like I don't belong. I am the middle . . . because here I have an accent and I'm brown. If I go to Mexico they also think, 'Oh, you are losing your Spanish! Now you have a hard time speaking!' And they say, 'You changed in many ways. Your thoughts changed a lot.' Of course, I had to change! I'm swimming in a different ocean." Part of what makes balancing these cultures so difficult are the historical relations of inequality between Latin America and the United States. In her interview, The Reverend Virginia Marie Rincón laments, "I am often saddened by the fact that I assimilated too much. *I think I live in two worlds* and it sometimes makes me very sad that some people say, 'You don't even have an accent.' . . . I have given up a lot of my culture already." Being different contributes to notions of authenticity, but it also can lead to feelings of isolation and racism as Olga Alicea's testimony suggests. She often struggles "to be two things at once." Remarkably, despite discrimination, many Latino/as and Latin American immigrants want to retain the very differences that make them targets of racism instead of assimilating to the dominant culture.

Wherever they settle, transnational migrants often reconstitute certain practices and concepts from their home countries. At the aforementioned panel, Juan González explained, "I am making my own environment similar to what I had at home" [the Dominican Republic].[65] In this sense, Juan is building a bridge between the Dominican Republic and Maine, not just for himself but for Dominicans and Mainers. As anthropologist Nina Glick Schiller et al. note, transnational migrants' "complex activities across national borders . . . create, shape and potentially transform their identities."[66] In turn, their very presence alters the identities of their host communities by encouraging them to be multilinguistic, multicultural, and transnational.

Juan González is not alone in recreating aspects of his country in Portland. On a warm July afternoon in 2005, a few weeks before he was to visit El Salvador with his family, Hernán delighted in showing me his *milpa* (corn and bean plot) alongside his home as well as other parts of his garden where he planted cilantro and chiles. Glick Schiller et al. point out, "Many migrants persist in their relationship to their home society, not in contradiction to but in conjunction with settlement in their host society."[67] For many transnational migrants, creating a second home is contingent upon maintaining close ties with their roots. Sending remittances to their families in Latin America is another way immigrants such as Hernán and Marta solidify their connections there. Of course, remittances too exemplify the longstanding and unequal relationships between the regions. Naturally, part of what makes migrants transnational is travel back to their countries. These disbursements, gifts, and visits reinforce their family ties and strengthen their social relations across national borders.

Shifting Identities

The terms Latino/a, Hispanic, and Latin American immigrant merit discussion. Since Latin America includes South and Central America, Mexico, and the Caribbean, linguistic diversity ranges from Spanish, Portuguese, French, Dutch, and English to indigenous and creole languages. Consequently, although the preponderance of Caribbean and Latin American denizens are Hispanic, some are not. Diverse cultures, languages, ethnicities, and religions abound in a region that shares a history of colonization and, as Laura Ochoa's testimony reminds us, racism. Originally created by a U.S. federal order to define a person of Spanish cultural origin from Mexico, Puerto Rico, Cuba, and Central and South America, *Hispanic* excludes those who identify themselves as something other than of Spanish cultural origin. In contrast, *Latino* refers to people from Latin America or those who identify with their Latin American heritage, which is inclusive of indigenous, African, Asian, and Spanish Latin Americans (among others).[68]

The meanings and associations of *Hispanic* and *Latino* have changed over time. Prior to the 1960s, particularly with the first wave of Mexican immigrants and Puerto Ricans in the 1940s, Hispanics often attempted to assimilate into Caucasian society and culture. In the 1960s and 1970s, a significant shift occurred when Latino/as heralded liberationist views and identified as a colonized minority. As a politicized ethnicity, *Latino* denoted people from Latin America in the United States who developed a common analysis and consciousness based on a shared history of political and economic victimization. Emblematic of this change, Mexican Americans began identifying with a Chicano consciousness. By the 1980s, authors such as Anzaldúa articulated how Latino/as whose experiences were forged in oppression and marginalization were best equipped to address challenges of balancing cultures and unequal power relations.[69] With the attention to multiculturalism in the 1990s, Latino identity became sanitized in an effort to celebrate difference without criticizing imperialism, racism, or sexism. This next phase of Latino identity, in which distinctions among Latino/as fuels political activism, has yet to be defined. As the 2006 demonstrations over immigration reform attest, comprehending this movement is crucial to understanding not only Latino/as but also the United States. The testimonies in the following pages shed light on this new phase by articulating how people from Latin America (by birth or heritage) are celebrating and harnessing their interconnected, if not overlapping, languages, beliefs, worldviews, values, cultural traits, and traditions to inform and ignite their political power.

Naturally, Latin American immigrants contribute to this diversity and political power. During the 1980s, eight million Latin American emigrants arrived in the United States. In the 2000 census, 15 percent of Maine's Latino residents identified as foreign born.[70] Though determining when Latin American immigrants begin to identify and are identified as Latino/as is beyond the scope of this book, these testimonies point to a number of factors such as time, generation, racialization, assimilation, and political or community organizing that affect this shift.[71] In truth, this transition is not necessarily unidirectional or permanent. Labels and affinities (like the lives they represent) are dynamic. For example, even though these informants readily identify as Latino/a or Hispanic, they also find national designations desirable and useful. Taken as a whole, these testimonies speak to the possibility of unity in diversity as long as individual identities are recognized and respected.[72] Since no one national or ethnic group dominates the Portland Latino community, maintaining distinctions is part of their shared experience. Living in a predominantly Caucasian city and state underscores the importance of protecting and projecting difference. The way these informants tack between national and Latino/a or Hispanic identities is emblematic of how Portland Latino/as and Latin American immigrants both distinguish themselves as individuals and harness their collective power in moments of unity.

As the products of *mestizaje* (racial mixing), most Latin Americans are at least biethnic if not multiethnic and multicultural. In contrast, historically the United States has resisted interracial marriages and remains wedded to a small number of distinct racial classifications. For Latino/as who associate themselves with their place of origin or ethnicity, the complexity of their identities are seldom reflected in census categories.[73] John Connors explains, "It is not Latino-Hispanic. You're Puerto Rican, and you're Guatemalan, and you're Mexican, you're Dominican. Whatever it is, those distinctions are really important to us. It tells us what we're really part of, but we're very proud of being part of the overall group too, but respect the differences amongst ourselves."[74] Comfortable with differences, these informants eschew conceptions of collectivity that prescribe a singular subject as representative of the group.

As anthropologist Lisa Lowe argues, this approach produces multiple narratives and strategies of emancipation.[75] Identifying by country often indicates a resistance (even if unconscious) to the downward assimilation implied by taking on a U.S.-based identity, especially in the absence of a politicized Latino consciousness.[76] Since a national identity connects them to a world beyond the United States, it offers an escape (even if only imagined) when their Latino identity marginalizes them. Earl Shorris argues, "There are no Latinos, only diverse peoples struggling to remain who they are while becoming someone else."[77] Yet according to the people interviewed in this volume, there are Latino/as. Even though Olga Alicea identifies strongly with her Puerto Rican culture and heritage, she proudly proclaims, "I am Latina." She adds, "[T]o be Latino doesn't necessarily mean that we are all the same. We are all individuals." Ana Manza also finds solidarity in diversity: "We're very united, all the Latinos. I have a lot of friendships. It doesn't matter what country they're from; we all get along really well . . . the whole race."

Whether they use Latino/a or Hispanic (some such as Iván Cantor, Laura Ochoa, and Hernán use the terms interchangeably, further underscoring the mercurial nature of these identities), residents seek to be part of a larger Latin American community organized around a political agenda and analysis. Victoria Chicón, for example, went to the Center for Cultural Exchange and local churches in search of Latino populations. Efforts to develop Centro Latino Maine in Portland and the annual César Chávez celebration (in March) are evidence of a community that is conscious of its shared identity and seeking to unite, serve, and advocate for its diverse members. Even while these Latino/as affirm Benedict Anderson's notion of an imagined community (in part because of its political power),[78] they maintain national identities so as not to concede the rich distinctions that comprise the larger imagined Latino community. As such, they participate in a number of different imagined communities.[79] By celebrating both her indigenous and Asian provenience, Peruvian Victoria Chicón reminds us, "There is not just

White Memorial Seventh-day Adventist Church where some Latino/as worship.

one Latin America. It's really diverse." Similarly, Laura Ochoa identifies more with her Aztec than Spanish ancestors. The multiple layers of identities that both encompass and cut across ethnicity, gender, race, nation, and class influence how people position themselves in society. Such shifting imagined communities help explain how Latino/as can be committed to the United States *and* deeply connected to their natal lands.

Claiming a certain identity does not preclude being part of a larger group. Nor does being part of a larger group necessitate forfeiting ethnic or national distinctions. The perspectives in the following pages speak to the complicated and contested concatenations of identity, belonging, and community. Portland Latino/as and Latin American immigrants are creating communities that will both support their own ethnic groups and integrate into others. In this way, their interconnected imagined communities are both well defined and boundless.

Harmonious relations among Latino/as should not be overstated, however. Close friendships between Salvadorans and Mexicans at Sacred Heart Catholic church belie the tensions between these two groups that have erupted over competition for jobs in Portland. National differences often distinguish community members. Seldom do Salvadorans eat at the Dominican-owned La Bodega Latina (though some shop there). Similarly, few

Dominicans frequent Tu Casa Restaurant Salvadoreño. Differences do not necessarily result in dissension, however. As Ana Manza explains, "We've never been to Tu Casa, the Salvadoran restaurant . . . because . . . the custom of our country about food [is different] . . . A lot of Latinos go there and say the cooking . . . is really good." Except in times of crisis such as the 2004 U.S. Border Patrol raids, Portland Latino/as are seldom united.

Naturally, like class, ethnicity, and nationality, gender also affects relationships of Latino/as; accounts such as Laura Ochoa's recollections of family life in Mexico and her experience as president of the USM LHSA intimate the ways gender notions are maintained and altered in new settings. In a stark example of the sexual division of labor (and physical space) within families, Blanca Santiago recalls her childhood: "We [the women and girls] would make thermoses of coffee and huge hero sandwiches . . . and then we would send them [the men] off, almost immediately getting ready for them to come home for dinner. They would live over on that side [of the house], all men in our family lived over on the other side and we were all family together." Similarly, Ana Manza's descriptions of life in the Dominican Republic reveal social constructions that contrast women's domesticity with men's breadwinner roles. Yet her employment at a seafood processing plant in South Portland and relationship with her husband Eliseo belie that reductionist dichotomy. Eliseo notes, "In our countries, we're always very *machista*, but when you get here to the United States you have to forget about that, because here the first one to arrive is the one who has to cook or wash or always help the spouse."

Of course, in Latin America women like Victoria Chicón, Laura Ochoa, and Lourdes Carpenter broke out of traditional gender norms. As Ana Manza notes, the culture is changing in Latin America and often "the wife works as if she were a man." Even as women defy patriarchal norms, the male remains normative. When comparing his employment and education level to his sister's, Iván Cantor remarks, "Instead of it being the opposite as it should have been [because she is younger], she's the professional, the doctor." When personal interests, economic marginalization, and/or migration compel women to work outside the home, gender notions and relations change. Increased autonomy often affords women greater self-esteem. (Yet many female transnational migrants lose some of their independence upon returning to Latin America.)[80] The narratives in this book demonstrate how Latinas and Latinos manage these shifting relations.

Regardless of women's level of autonomy, gender relations can turn violent.[81] Through her story, Laura Ochoa poignantly identifies domestic abuse as an affliction in Latin America and the United States. Tengo Voz, an organ-

Immanuel Baptist Church, home to Tengo Voz, an organization that serves Latinas and their families.

ization founded by Reverend Virginia Marie Rincón to address gender-based violence and other problems in Portland's Latino population, speaks to these tensions. The following accounts from both men and women provide a window into the ways gender power operates and is contested in the Latino community.

As the distant and recent history of Portland's relationship with Latin America and Latin Americans demonstrates, such hegemonic contexts as global trade, government policies, ideologies, and wars largely determine the impetus and fate of immigrants. The aforementioned U.S. Border Patrol raids and the Central American Free Trade Agreement (which includes the Dominican Republic) are among the more recent forces affecting immigration and the lives of Portland Latino/as and Latin American immigrants. Yet even though such larger forces constrain their lived experience, immigrants and other Latino/as are not passive victims; in fact, they help to shape these trends.[82] For most people interviewed, Portland was not the first place they landed; they chose to relocate here. By creating a vibrant community in Portland and maintaining ties to their native countries and other areas of Latin America, these transnational actors model new possibilities for mobility and identity in an increasingly interconnected world.

Their migratory lives are partly a response to economic dislocations—such as those caused by large-scale agribusiness, export-oriented *maquiladoras*, and tourism—and physical threats: wars, genocide, crime. For some, such as Victoria Chicón, moving "seems to be one of the signs in my life." Because no one place is truly secure in a globalized economy, transnational migrants maintain connections to a number of different places.[83] While the peripatetic lives of these informants speak to this phenomena, especially in Adrian Bravo's story, their testimonies indicate that many Latino/as and Latin American immigrants are increasingly thinking of Portland as a home—evidence that even the most mobile transnational actors remain rooted in particular places.[84] Their commitment to Portland as demonstrated through their efforts to create vibrant, secure, and comfortable communities not only for Latino/as and Latin American immigrants but for people of color is an indication that they are both participating in the larger community *and* carving out their own space, autonomy, and identity within it.

Not surprisingly, Portland as a place appeals to Latino/as and Latin American immigrants for many of the same reasons it appeals to non-Latino/as. As these testimonies reveal, many moved to Portland because it had a lower crime rate, better school system and job opportunities, and more tranquil lifestyle than their previous residences. In short, it is a good place to raise a family. As John Connors observed, "'Why do Latinos come to Maine?' It's a beautiful state. Why does anybody come here?" At the same time, however, the resilience and perseverance that run throughout their stories also draw attention to the challenges of subtle and overt racism, which manifests itself, for example, in increased obstacles to obtaining a job, securing a loan, getting a driver's license, and accessing social services, and in being ostracized for being "too cultural" or not speaking English. Surprisingly, despite their articulations of individual experiences with discrimination, none—not even Adrian Bravo, who was deported—comment on discrimination against immigrants in broader structural historical terms. Though he is not an immigrant, John Connors comes closest to this kind of critique in his condemnation of racial profiling. As one labor historian notes, "U.S. policy attracts foreign workers but stifles them once they have arrived."[85] Even though this book seeks to, in the words of Reverend Virginia Marie Rincón, "give voice to their oppression," at times Latino/as and Latin American immigrants remain silent. Given their experience in the 2004 U.S. Border Patrol raids and 2006 immigration demonstrations, this silence is not likely a product of false consciousness. Rather it speaks to their vulnerability as individuals and motivation for uniting. Coming together as a

Immigrant Legal Advocacy Project, a resource for Latin American immigrants.

community allows them to criticize and counteract the forces that isolate and marginalize them as individuals.

Despite discrimination, in many respects Portland is tolerant and proactive. Founded in 1993 and supported by Maine foundations and individuals, the Immigration Legal Advocacy Project (ILAP) provides free legal representation to Latin American (and other) immigrants. In part thanks to ILAP's efforts, on June 2, 2003, the city passed an ordinance prohibiting police and other city officials from making gratuitous immigration status inquiries—an action that simultaneously pointed to the problem of racial profiling and Portland's willingness to address it. (But still, as Lourdes Carpenter and John Connors point out, as of 2008 Portland had no Hispanic police officers.) In 2006, Portland's Office of Minority Health and the MaineHealth hospital system targeted the Latino population for an asthma awareness campaign with advertisements in Spanish.[86] Reverend Virginia Marie Rincón suggests the 2004 U.S. Border Patrol raids had a silver lining: Latino leaders and their communities became more public and united, and, I would add, enjoyed the support of Portland's non-Hispanics.[87] As Peggy Levitt notes, transnational connections and communities are strengthened in "a social climate that tolerates greater ethnic diversity."[88] Though racism remains a problem, efforts such as these create a welcoming and secure environment for Latino/as and

Latin American immigrants in Portland. Juan González asserts, "I'm raising my family here, I'm proud to be here and I don't want that stuff that happened [the U.S. Border Patrol raids] to change the perception that Maine is welcoming to immigrants."[89] Like most of us, Latino/as and Latin American immigrants are actors in arenas they do not control, yet their cultural, social, and economic creativity influences and enriches the multiple places they live and work. Portland is fortunate to be among them.

In ways that both reflect and go beyond Benedict Anderson's theoretical framework of nation building and nationalism, Portland Latino/as and Latin American immigrants have imagined and created communities that are slowly altering the way other residents conceptualize the city.[90] These informants articulate a sense of transnationalism, of belonging and contributing to more than one nation. The very act of taking pride in and contributing to multiple places helps to break down borders between nations and barriers between people. Perhaps it is this theme more than any other in these pages that encourages us to explore the complex multiple meanings of America and American and, in the process, to expand our own imagined communities.

Notes

I wish to thank Joe Conforti, Avi Chomsky, Gina Pérez, Jo Radner, Blanca Santiago, Bob Atkinson, and the anonymous reviewers at the State University of New York Press for their critical comments on earlier drafts of this piece.

1. Hyon B. Shin and Rosalind Bruno, "Language Use and English-Speaking Ability: 2000," US Census Bureau Census 2000 Brief, October 2003; "Profile of the Foreign-Born Population in the United States: 2000," Current Population Report, U.S. Census Bureau, December 2001; "One in Seven in US is Hispanic," *Boston Globe,* June 9, 2005; George Lipsitz, *American Studies in a Moment of Danger* (Minneapolis: University of Minnesota Press, 2001), 10; Ilan Stavans, "The Challenges Facing Spanish Departments," *The Chronicle of Higher Education,* July 29, 2005; Samuel Huntington, "The Hispanic Challenge," *Foreign Policy* (March/April 2004).
2. Felipe Fernández-Armesto, *The Americas: A Hemispheric History* (New York: Modern Library, 2003), 172.
3. For some recent examples see Gina M. Pérez, *The Near Northwest Side Story: Migration, Displacement, & Puerto Rican Families* (Berkeley: University of California Press, 2004); Nicholas de Genova, *Working the Boundaries: Race, Space, and "Illegality" in Mexican Chicago* (Durham, NC: Duke

University Press, 2005); Gabriel Haslip-Viera and Sherrie L. Baver, eds., *Latinos in New York: Communities in Transition* (Notre Dame: University of Notre Dame Press, 1996); Ana Aparicio, *Dominican-Americans and the Politics of Empowerment* (Gainesville: University Press of Florida, 2006); Milagros Ricourt and Ruby Danta, *Hispanas de Queens: Latino Panethnicity in a New York City Neighborhood* (Ithaca, NY: Cornell University Press, 2003).

4. See for example Leon Fink, *The Maya of Morganton: Work and Community in the Nuevo New South* (Chapel Hill: University of North Carolina Press, 2003).
5. U.S. Census Bureau, "Profile of General Demographic Characteristics: 2000," Census 2000 Summary File 1 (SF 1) 100 Percent Data, Maine, http://factfinder.census.gov/servlet/QTTable?_bm=y&-geo_id=04000US23&-qr_name=DEC_2000_SF1_U_DP1&-ds_name=DEC_2000_SF1_U, (accessed October 25, 2007); Maine Center for Economic Policy, "Latinos in the Maine Economy," (unpublished draft, 2008).
6. One such place is Down East, Maine, where a vibrant Mexican and Central American community is establishing roots, see *Portland Press Herald,* April 11, 2006, C1, 6.
7. Ian F. Haney López, *White by Law: The Legal Construction of Race* (New York: New York University Press, 1996); Mae M. Ngai, *Impossible Subjects: Illegal Aliens and the Making of Modern America* (Princeton, NJ: Princeton University Press, 2004); David R. Roediger, *Working Toward Whiteness: How America's Immigrants Became White, The Strange Journey from Ellis Island to the Suburbs* (New York: Basic Books, 2005); Lisa Lowe, *Immigrant Acts: On Asian American Cultural Politics* (Durham, NC: Duke University Press, 1996); Yen Le Espiritu, *Home Bound: Filipino American Lives across Cultures, Communities, and Countries* (Berkeley: University of California Press, 2003); George Lipsitz, *The Possessive Investment in Whiteness: How White People Profit from Identity Politics* (Philadelphia: Temple University Press, 2006); Nazli Kibria, *Family Tightrope: The Changing Lives of Vietnamese Americans* (Princeton, NJ: Princeton University Press, 1993); Juan González, *Harvest of Empire: A History of Latinos in America* (New York: Viking, 2000), 88–94; Piri Thomas, *Down These Mean Streets* (New York: Alfred A. Knopf, 1978); Daniel Wickberg, "Heterosexual White Male: Some Recent Inversions in American Cultural History," *Journal of American History* (June 2005): 136–57. A recent report by the Pew Hispanic Center found that Latino/as' view of race and racial identity varies by region and economic security, see *Boston Globe* December 7, 2004.

8. *Portland Press Herald*, November 14, 2003; Meeting called by NAACP, January 30, 2004 (author's observation); *Portland Press Herald,* January 30, 2004; *Portland Forecaster,* February 11, 2004.
9. Indigenous peoples had migrated to North America thousands of years before European contact; northern Mexicans became U.S. residents when the United States usurped more than half of Mexico's territory with the U.S.–Mexican War (1846–1848) and the Gadsden Purchase (1853); and Puerto Ricans became U.S. citizens in 1917 nearly twenty years after the United States defeated Spain in 1898 to replace one colonial presence on the island with another. Of course, not being immigrants did not exclude these groups from discrimination.
10. For recent scholarship on Latino/as in New England, see Andrés Torres, ed., *Latinos in New England* (Philadelphia: Temple University Press, 2006); Aviva Chomsky, "Salem as a Global City, 1850–2004," in *Salem: Place, Myth, and Memory,* ed. Dane Anthony Morrison and Nancy Lusignan Schultz (Boston: Northeastern University Press, 2004); Aviva Chomsky and Claire Holman, "The Hidden Maine: Serfdom at DeCoster Egg Farm," *Maine Progressive* 6 (2) (December 1991):1, 4–7; David Carey Jr., "*Comunidad Escondida*: Latin American Influences in Nineteenth- and Twentieth-Century Portland," in *Creating Portland: History and Place in Northern New England,* ed. Joseph A. Conforti (Hanover, NH: University Press of New England, 2005); Ruth Glasser, *Aquí Me Quedo: Puerto Ricans in Connecticut/Los puertorriqueños en Connecticut* (Middletown: Connecticut Humanities Council, 1997); Edwin Meléndez and Miren Uriarte, eds., *Latino Poverty and Economic Development in Massachusetts* (Boston: Mauricio Gastón Institute for Latino Community Development and Public Policy, 1993); Miren Uriarte, *Rhode Island Latinos: A Scan of Issues Affecting the Latino Population of Rhode Island* (Providence: The Rhode Island Foundation, 2002); Eleanor E. Glaessel-Brown, "A Time of Transition: Colombian Textile Workers in Lowell in the 1970s," in *The Continuing Revolution: A History of Lowell, Massachusetts*, ed. Robert Weible (Lowell: Lowell Historical Society, 1991): 341–75; Eleanor E. Glaessel-Brown, "Immigration Policy and Colombian Textile Workers in New England: A Case Study in Political Demography," PhD dissertation, Massachusetts Institute of Technology, 1984; Aviva Chomsky, *Linked Labor Histories: New England and Colombia in the Long Twentieth Century* (Durham, NC: Duke University Press, 2008).
11. Daniel D. Arreola, "Introduction," in *Hispanic Spaces, Latino Places: Community and Cultural Diversity in Contemporary America* ed. Daniel D.

Arreola (Austin: University of Texas, 2004), 2; Terrence W. Haverluck, "Hispanic Community Types and Assimilation in Mex-America," *Professional Geographer* 50 (4) (1998): 465–80; Enrico A. Marcelli and Phillip J. Granberry, "Latino New England: An Emerging Demographic and Economic Portrait," in *Latinos in New England* ed. Andrés Torres (Philadelphia: Temple University Press, 2006), 26. For a far-ranging exploration into the Latino diaspora, see Héctor Tobar, *Translation Nation: Defining a New American Identity in the Spanish-Speaking United States* (New York: Riverhead Books, 2005).

12. A term meaning dawnlanders in the Algonquian languages, *Wabanaki* denotes the indigenous peoples of northern New England and the Maritime Provinces who shared similar languages, worldviews, and cultures; see Emerson W. Baker, "Formerly Machegonne, Dartmouth, York, Stogummor, Casco, and Falmouth: Portland as a Contested Frontier in the Seventeenth Century," in *Creating Portland: History and Place in Northern New England* ed. Joseph A. Conforti (Hanover, NH: University Press of New England, 2005), 1–8.
13. Baker, "Formerly Machegonne," 16; James S. Leamon, "Falmouth, the American Revolution, and the Price of Moderation," in *Creating Portland: History and Place in Northern New England* ed. Joseph A. Conforti (Hanover, NH: University Press of New England, 2005), 63.
14. Maine Historical Society (hereafter MHS) S-1026 43/9, Mary Lancaster Tompson Record of Students and Poetry Notebooks (see enclosed article "Children of Prominent Portland Families Attended Miss Tompson's Private School").
15. Fink, *The Maya of Morganton.*
16. Ibid.
17. Gloria Anzaldúa, *Borderlands/La Frontera: The New Mestiza* (San Francisco: Aunt Luke Books, 1999), 100–101.
18. For one example of such rhetoric, see MHS, *The Yankee,* July 9, 1823.
19. *New York Times,* April 17, 2006. For one Portland Latino leader's (Juan Gonzáles's) views on the immigration issue, see *Portland Press Herald,* May 16, 2006.
20. *Mexico Solidarity Network: Mexico News and Analysis,* March 20–26, 2006; *Denver Post,* March 29, 2006; *Portland Press Herald*, April 11, 2006; *Los Angeles Times,* May 2, 2006; *New York Times,* May 2, 2006; *People's Free News,* May–June 2006; United Farm Workers, "Strawberry Workers Shortchanged," unpublished document, circulated May 17, 2006; Carola and Marcelo Suárez-Orozco, *Trans-formations: Immigration, Family Life,*

and Achievement Motivation Among Latino Adolescents (Stanford: Stanford University Press, 1995), 35–50, 194.

21. The transcripts and recordings of all interviews are held at the University of Southern Maine Life Story Center in Portland, Maine.
22. Kay Warren, *Indigenous Movements and their Critics: Pan Mayan Activism in Guatemala* (Princeton, NJ: Princeton University Press, 1998), 128.
23. Hernán and Marta are pseudonyms. All other informants wanted to use their real names. All interviews were conducted between 2004 and 2006.
24. Lesley Milroy, *Observing and Analysing Natural Language: A Critical Account of Sociolinguistic Method* (Oxford: Basil Blackwell, 1987); H. Russel Bernard, *Research Methods in Anthropology: Qualitative and Quantitative Approaches* (London: Altamira Press, 1994); Dennis Tedlock, *Spoken Word and the Work of Interpretation* (Philadelphia: University of Pennsylvania Press, 1983).
25. David Carey Jr., *Our Elders Teach Us: Maya-Kaqchikel Historical Perspectives. Xkib'ij kan qate' qatata'* (Tuscaloosa: University of Alabama Press, 2001), 1–21; Daniel James, *Doña María's Story: Life, History, Memory, and Political Identity* (Durham, NC: Duke University Press, 2000), 121–56; Paul Thompson, *The Voice of the Past: Oral History*, 3rd ed. (Oxford: Oxford University Press, 2000); Paul Thompson and Hugo Slim, *Listening for a Change: Oral Testimony and Development* (London: Panos Publications, ca. 1993); Jan Vansina, *Oral Tradition as History* (Madison: University of Wisconsin, 1985); Joanne Rappaport, *The Politics of Memory: Native Historical Interpretation in the Colombian Andes* (Durham, NC: Duke University Press, 1998); Allesandro Portelli, *The Death of Luigi Trastulli and Other Stories: Form and Meaning in Oral History* (Albany: State University of New York Press, 1991).
26. Robert Atkinson, *The Gift of Stories* (Westport, CT: Bergin & Garvey, 1995); Robert Atkinson, *The Life Story Interview* (Thousand Oaks, CA: Sage, 1998).
27. Thomas Abercrombie, *Pathways of Memory and Power: Ethnography and History Among an Andean People* (Madison: University of Wisconsin Press, 1998), 20–21 (quote 20); Lynn Stephen, *¡Zapata Lives!: Histories and Cultural Politics in Southern Mexico* (Berkeley: University of California Press, 2002), 179; James, *Doña María's Story*, 137–41; Alberto Moreiras, "The Aura of Testimonio," in *The Real Thing: Testimonial Discourse and Latin America*, ed. George M. Gugelberger (Durham, NC: Duke University Press, 1996): 194–224.
28. James, *Doña María's Story*, 139.
29. Carey, "*Comunidad Escondida.*"

30. Manuel García y Griega, "The Importation of Mexican Contract Laborers to the United States, 1942–1964," in *Between Two Worlds: Mexican Immigrants in the United States*, ed. David Gutiérrez (Wilmington, DE: Scholarly Resources, 1996): 45–85; Manuel García y Griega, *The Importation of Mexican Contract Laborers to the United States, 1942–1964: Antecedents, Operation, and Legacy* (La Jolla, CA: Program in United States–Mexican Studies, University of California, San Diego, 1981); Ernesto Galarza, *Merchants of Labor: The Mexican Bracero Story* (Charlotte, CA: McNally and Loftin, 1964); Richard B. Craig, *The Bracero Program: Interest Groups and Foreign Policy* (Austin: University of Texas Press, 1971); Frances Turgeon Wiggin, *Maine Composers and Their Music: A Biographical Dictionary* (Maine Federation of Music Clubs, 1959), 109; Charles A. Scontras, *Time-Line of Selected Highlights of Maine Labor History, 1636–2003* (Orono: University of Maine, 2003), 53.
31. U.S. Census Bureau, "Profile of General Demographic Characteristics: 2000"; James Dietz, *Economic History of Puerto Rico: Institutional Change and Capitalist Development* (Princeton, NJ: Princeton University Press, 1986): 206–12, 240–55; Pérez, *The Near Northwest Side Story*, 8–9, 44–50, 56, 196–97; Gary D. Martin, "Industrial Policy by Accident: The United States in Puerto Rico," *Journal of Hispanic Policy* 4 (1989): 93–115; J. Jorge Klor de Alva, "Aztlán, Borinquen, and Hispanic Nationalism in the United States," in *The Latino Studies Reader: Culture, Economy & Society* ed. Antonia Darder and Rodolfo D. Torres (Malden, MA: Blackwell Publishers, 1998), 76; Peter Manuel, *Caribbean Currents: Caribbean Music from Rhumba to Reggae* (Philadelphia: Temple University Press, 1995), 51; Jorge del Pinal and Audrey Singer, "Generations of Diversity: Latinos in the United States," *Population Bulletin* 52 (3) (October 1997), 9, 15.
32. Pérez, *The Near Northwest Side Story*, 45.
33. Michael J. Kryzanek and Howard J. Wiarda, *The Politics of External Influence in the Dominican Republic* (New York/Stanford, CA: Praeger/Hoover Institution Press, 1988); Dan Kurzman, *Santo Domingo: Revolt of the Damned* (New York: Putnam, 1965); Abraham F. Lowenthal, *The Dominican Intervention* (Cambridge, MA: Harvard University Press, 1972); Saskia Sassen, "Why Migration?" *NACLA Report on the Americas* 26, 1 (July 1992), 15–16; del Pinal and Singer, "Generations of Diversity," 24; Silvio Torres-Saillant and Ramona Hernández, *The Dominican Americans* (Westport, CT: Greenwood Press, 1998), 61, 63; Patricia Pessar, *A Visa for a Dream: Dominicans in the United States* (Boston: Allyn and Bacon, 1995), 22.

34. Sassen, "Why Migration?" 16.
35. Hector Tobar, "Hurt by US Migration, El Salvador Looks to Its Neighbor," *Boston Globe,* February 12, 2006, A22; N.C. Aizenman, "The Emptying of El Salvadoran Villages," *Boston Globe,* May 14, 2006, A6.
36. *Boston Globe,* April 29, 2006; *Boston Globe,* March 19, 2006; Latin American and Caribbean Center, Florida International University, "Remittances Program," http://programaderemesas.org/paises/en/index_sal.html?c=1 (accessed August 7, 2008); Sassen, "Why Migration?" 15; Sarah J. Mahler, *American Dreaming: Immigrant Life on the Margins* (Princeton, NJ: Princeton University Press, 1995), 43.
37. Roger Lancaster, *Life Is Hard: Machismo, Danger, and the Intimacy of Power in Nicaragua* (Berkeley: University of California Press, 1992), 29. See his conversation with one Nicaraguan about the reality of migration to the United States, pp. 152–54.
38. Of course it also speaks to economic disparity in Latin America. Interestingly, despite struggles with manual labor and working for others, middle-class Latin American emigrants seldom express empathy for the plight of the domestic laborers they used to employ. Many Latin-American emigrants become so disillusioned they go home vowing never to return to the United States; see for example, Lancaster, *Life is Hard,* 162.
39. González, *Harvest of Empire;* Greg Grandin, *The Last Colonial Massacre: Latin America in the Cold War* (Chicago: University of Chicago Press, 2004); Matilde Zimmerman, *Sandinista: Carlos Fonseca and the Nicaraguan Revolution* (Durham, NC: Duke University Press, 2000); Timothy C. Brown, *The Real Contra War: Highlander Peasant Resistance in Nicaragua* (Norman: University Of Oklahoma, 2001); Thomas W. Walker and Ariel C. Armony, eds., *Repression, Resistance, and Democratic Transition in Central America* (Wilmington, DE: Scholarly Resources, 2000); John A. Booth and Thomas Walker, *Understanding Central America* (Boulder, CO: Westview Press, 1993); John H. Coatsworth, *Central America and the United States: The Clients and the Colossus* (New York: Twayne Publishers, 1994); Pérez, *The Near Northwest Side Story,* 13; Network in Solidarity with the People of Guatemala (NISGUA), "Resources on Guatemala and the Immigration Debate," April 26, 2006, http///www.nisgua.org.
40. "The United States Is Something So Big," *Maine Sunday Telegram,* July 29, 2001; Cathi Tactaquin, "What Rights for the Undocumented?" *NACLA* 26, 1 (July 1992), 28; NISGUA, "Resources on Guatemala and the Immigration Debate," April 26, 2006, http://www.nisgua.org.

41. *Portland Press Herald*, April 27, 1981; *Portland Press Herald*, August 29, 1983, 9; Michael Powelson, "Mariel Boatlift," in *Encyclopedia of Latin American History and Culture,* ed. Barbara A. Tenenbaum, vol. 3 (New York: Charles Scribner's Sons, 1996), 523–24; Vanit Sharma, "Fulfilling a Cuban's Dream: The Story of Lellany Castellanos," in *Maine Images of the U.S.: Essays of the Real World,* ed. Students of the Chase Smith House, 6th Grade (Portland, 2002).
42. U.S. Census Bureau, *1980 Census of Population,* vol. 1, Characteristics of the Population (Washington, D.C.: GPO, 1981); U.S. Census Bureau, *2000 Census of Population and Housing,* Summary Population and Housing Characteristics, PHC-1-21, Maine (Washington, D.C.: GPO, 2002); Marcelli and Granberry, "Latino New England," 31; Andrés Torres, "Latinos in New England: An Introduction," in *Latinos in New England,* ed. Andrés Torres (Philadelphia: Temple University Press, 2006), 4; Earl Shorris, *Latinos: A Biography of the People,* (New York: W. W. Norton & Company, 1992), 127; David M. Reimers, *Other Immigrants: The Global Origins of the American People* (New York: New York University Press, 2005), 101–56. The Maine Center for Economic Policy dated an increase in Maine's Hispanic population to the 1980s when migrants began arriving to work in the blueberry, broccoli, and potato harvests; see Maine Center for Economic Policy, "Study of Immigrant Population," unpublished report, Augusta, Maine, 2007. Community leaders argued that Maine's Latino population was grossly undercounted in the 2000 census. Some estimated that between 1480 and 1525 Latino/as lived in Portland in April 2000. "Hispanics Undercounted, Group Says," *Portland Press Herald*, April 3, 2001; *Portland Press Herald*, Jan. 15, 2003, 10A; John Connors, personal communication. In an inflated estimate, one journalist claimed Portland is home to 9,000 Latinos; see Trevor Maxwell, "Reaching Out on Health Care," *Portland Press Herald*, May 8, 2006. Similarly, Dominicans from Salem, Massachusetts, argue they were undercounted in both the 1990 and 2000 censuses; see Chomsky, "Salem as a Global City," 233; and Chomsky, *Linked Labor Histories*.
43. *GlobalView: The Newsletter of the Maine International Trade Center,* February 2005, 4 and April 2004, 12; *Maine Biz: Maine's Business Newspaper,* November 2001; *Portland Press Herald*, July 24, 2003.
44. Joseph A. Conforti, "Introduction: Placing Portland," in *Creating Portland: History and Place in Northern New England,* ed. Joseph A. Conforti (Hanover, NH: University Press of New England, 2005), xxiv–xxv; Baker, "Formerly Machegonne," 1–6; Maureen Elgersman Lee, "'What

They Lack in Numbers': Locating Black Portland, 1870–1930," in *Creating Portland: History and Place in Northern New England,* ed. Joseph A. Conforti (Hanover, NH: University Press of New England, 2005), 221–23; Eileen Eagan, "Working Portland: Women, Class, and Ethnicity in the Nineteenth Century," in *Creating Portland: History and Place in Northern New England,* ed. Joseph A. Conforti (Hanover, NH: University Press of New England, 2005), 193–98.

45. *Portland Press Herald,* July 29, 2001; Sharma, "Fulfilling a Cuban's Dream"; Joshua Vachon, "First Impression: The Story of Gustavo Parra and Monire Childs," in *Maine Images of the U.S.: Essays of the Real World,* ed. Students of the Chase Smith House, 6th Grade, (Portland, Maine, 2002); *Portland Press Herald,* Aug. 7, 1974; Scontras, *Time-Line of Selected,* 65; Maine Center for Economic Policy, "Study of Immigrant Population."

46. Acording to the Maine Center for Economic Policy, over 60 percent of the students enrolled in Portland Adult Education from September 2006 to July 2007 were immigrants. The 132 Hispanics who studied in the program comprised 12.4 percent of the immigrant students, second only to Africans. Similarly, across the state Spanish speakers constituted 491 of the 4052 immigrants formally studying English as a foreign language in 2007. As 12.2 percent of this student population, they were second only to Somali speakers; see Maine Center for Economic Policy, "Study of Immigrant Population."

47. N.C. Aizenman, "Big Returns for Salvadorans: US Immigrants Haven't Forgotten Their Hometowns," *Boston Globe,* March 19, 2006. Similarly for Dominicans, "migration appears more like commuting," see Chomsky, "Salem as a Global City, 1850–2004," 233.

48. Sarah J. Mahler and Patricia R. Pessar, "Gendered Geographies of Power: Analyzing Gender Across Transnational Spaces," *Identities* 7 (4) (2001), 447 (quote); Amy Kaplan, "Violent Belongings and the Question of Empire Today: Presidential Address to the American Studies Association, October 17, 2003," *American Quarterly* 56 (1) (March 2004), 12; Chomsky, "Salem as a Global City, 1850–2004," 231–37, 240.

49. Chandra Talpade Mohanty, "Feminist Encounters: Locating the Politics of Experience," in *Destabilizing Theory,* ed. Michele Barrett and Anne Phillips (Stanford: Stanford University Press, 1992): 75–90 (esp. 85).

50. Anzaldúa, *Borderlands/La Frontera,* 19. Marta's description of the Barber Foods Factory, where she estimates fourteen or fifteen different languages are spoken, reminds us that it too is a complex borderland.

51. Michael Kearney, "The Local and the Global: The Anthropology of Globalization and Transnationalism," *Annual Review of Anthropology* 24 (1995): 548.
52. Carolyn Porter, "What We Know that We Don't Know: Remapping American Literary Studies," *American Literary History* 6 (2) (autumn 1994): 470; Paul Lauter, "A Call for (at Least a Little) American Studies Chauvinism," *ASA Newsletter* June 1996, http://www.georgetown.edu/crossroads/AmericanStudiesAssn/newsletter/archive/articles/lauter4.html (accessed 16 March 2006); Shelley Fisher Fishkin, "Crossroads of Cultures: The Transnational Turn in American Studies—Presidential Address to the American Studies Association, Nov. 12, 2004" *American Quarterly* 57 (1) (March 2005), 21, 26; Pérez, *The Near Northwest Side Story,* 6, 11.
53. Fishkin, "Crossroads of Cultures," 24. See also Henry Yu, "Los Angeles and American Studies in a Pacific World of Migration," *American Quarterly,* special issue, 56 (3) (September 2004): 531–43.
54. David Palumbo-Liu, *Asian/American: Historical Crossings of a Radical Frontier* (Stanford: Stanford University Press, 1999), 389.
55. Homi K. Bhabha, *The Location of Culture* (New York: Routledge, 1994), 139–70.
56. Pérez, *The Near Northwest Side Story,* 14.
57. Almost invariably, the historiography of Maine ignores the contributions, even the very presence, of Latino/as and Latin American immigrants. See for example, Neil Rolde's chapter entitled "Ethnic Maine," which makes no mention of Hispanics, in Neil Rolde, *Maine: A Narrative History* (Gardiner, ME: Tilbury House, 1990), 260–94. Of the more than four hundred life stories at the University of Southern Maine's Life Story Center, prior to this study only five were from Latino/as.
58. David K. Shipler, *The Working Poor: Invisible in America* (NY: Alfred A. Knopf, 2004), 207; Maine Center for Economic Policy, "Study of Immigrant Population."
59. Patricia Pora, personal communication, November 2005.
60. Suárez-Orozco, *Trans-formations*, 13, 52–53, 66–67, 70, 189; González, *Harvest of Empire,* 92–94; Chomsky, "Salem as a Global City, 1850–2004," 237.
61. Huntington, "The Hispanic Challenge." Unsure whether Latin America constitutes a Western or non-Western civilization, Huntington fails to see a shared history in the Americas; see Samuel P. Huntington, *The Clash of Civilizations and Remaking of World Order* (New York: Simon &

Schuster, 1996). For a much earlier advocate of assimilation to promote stability and progress, see Robert Park, "Human Migration and the Marginal Man," *American Journal of Sociology* 33 (1928), 890.

62. Huntington, "The Hispanic Challenge," 45.
63. Leticia Foss comments at "'I Have a Dream . . .' A Latino Perspective," panel at University of Southern Maine, Portland, April 7, 2004.
64. Anzaldúa, *Borderlands/La Frontera,* 19.
65. Juan González, comments at "'I Have a Dream . . .' A Latino Perspective," panel at University of Southern Maine, Portland, April 7, 2004.
66. Nina Glick Schiller, Linda Basch, and Cristina Blanc-Szanton, "Transnationalism: A New Analytical Framework for Understanding Migration," in *Towards a Transnational Perspective on Migration: Race, Class, Ethnicity, and Nationalism Reconsidered,* ed. Nina Glick Schiller, Linda Basch, and Cristina Blanc-Szanton (New York: New York Academy of Sciences, 1992), 4.
67. Glick Schiller et al., "Transnationalism," 6.
68. Of course, the term Latino too can be exclusive. For example, Brazilians generally reject it as a label even though they are from Latin America. For further discussion of these identity politics, see Suzanne Oboler, "The Politics of Labeling: Latino/a Cultural Identities of Self and Others," *Latin American Perspectives* 19 (4) (Fall 1992): 18–36; Suzanne Oboler, *Ethnic Labels, Latino Lives: Identity and the Politics of (Re)Presentation in the United States* (Minneapolis: University of Minnesota Press, 1995), vii–viii, xiii, 1–16; David A. Hollinger, *Postethnic America: Beyond Multiculturalism* (New York: Basic Books, 2000), 19–50; Shorris, *Latinos,* xvi–xvii, 425; Rosaura Sánchez, "Mapping the Spanish Language along a Multiethnic and Multilingual Border," in *The Latino Studies Reader: Culture, Economy & Society,* ed. Antonia Darder and Rodolfo D. Torres (Malden, MA: Blackwell Publishers, 1998), 112; "A Look at How Latinos See Themselves," *Boston Globe,* Dec. 7, 2004.
69. Rodolfo Acuña, *Occupied America: A History of Chicanos* (New York: Harper & Row, 1981); Clara Rodríguez, *Puerto Ricans: Born in the USA* (Boston: Unwin Hyman, 1989); Lorena Oropeza, *¡Raza Sí! ¡Guerra No!: Chicano Protest and Patriotism during the Viet Nam War Era* (Berkeley: University of California Press, 2005); Anzaldúa, *La Frontera/Borderlands*; Felix Padilla, *Latino Ethnic Consciousness: The Case of Mexican Americans and Puerto Ricans in Chicago* (Notre Dame, IN: University of Notre Dame Press, 1985); Lisa Lowe, "Work, Immigration, Gender: New Subjects of Cultural Politics," in *The Politics of Culture in the Shadow of Capi-*

tal ed. Lisa Lowe and David Lloyd (Durham, NC: Duke University Press, 1997), 361–62.

70. William Robinson, "Why the Immigrant Rights Struggle Compels Us to Reconceptualize Both Latin American and Latino/a Studies," *Latin American Studies Association Forum* 36, no. 2 (Spring 2007), 21; Marcelli and Granberry, "Latino New England," 26.
71. For an exploration of this process, see Ricourt and Danta, *Hispanas de Queens*. Milagros Ricourt and Ruby Danta suggest that a Latino or Hispanic identity does not replace a Latin American immigrant's identification with a particular country but rather adds to it. The authors argue that language, geographic concentration, class, and gender are the crucial factors in this process. See also The Latina Feminist Group, ed., *Telling to Live: Latina Feminist Testimonies* (Durham, NC: Duke University Press, 2001).
72. For a cogent discussion of the idea of unity in diversity, see Patricia Zavella, "Reflections on Diversity among Chicanas," in *Challenging Fronteras: Structuring Latina and Latino Lives in the U.S.*, ed. Mary Romero, Pierrette Hondagneu-Sotelo, and Wilma Ortiz (New York: Routledge, 1997): 187–94.
73. Hollinger, *Postethnic America,* 19–50; Glick Schiller et al., "Transnationalism," 6.
74. For an exploration of the ways Latino/as both maintain their individual and group identities and come together for a common cause, see Nicolas De Genova and Ana Yolanda Ramos-Zayas's study of how Mexicans and Puerto Ricans in Chicago distinguish themselves from each other and enjoy moments of unity, *Latino Crossings: Mexicans, Puerto Ricans, and the Politics of Race and Citizenship* (New York: Routledge, 2003).
75. Lowe, "Work, Immigration, Gender," 368.
76. Mary C. Waters, *Black Identities: West Indian Immigrant Dreams and American Realities* (New York/Cambridge: Russell Sage/Harvard University Press, 1999), 24, 43, 48–49, 329–32. At the same time, Waters points out, "A regional identity as West Indian is a meaningful category of identity for people . . . because of the regency of nation-states in the Caribbean," (43).
77. Shorris, *Latinos,* 12–13.
78. Benedict Anderson, *Imagined Communities: Reflections on the Origin and Spread of Nationalism* (New York: Verso, 1991).
79. Kearney, "The Local and the Global," 558–59; R.C. Smith, "Los austentes siempre presentes': The Imagining, Making and Politics of a

Transnational Community between Ticuani, Puebla, Mexico and New York City," Ph.D. diss., Columbia University, 1994.

80. Helen I. Safa, *The Myth of the Male Breadwinner: Women and Industrialization in the Caribbean* (Boulder, CO: Westview Press, 1995); Pérez, *The Near Northwest Side Story,* 82, 104–7, 197–98; Sherri Grasmuck and Patricia Pessar, *Between Two Islands: Dominican International Migration* (Berkeley: University of California Press, 1991); Patricia Pessar, "Engendering Migration Studies: The Case of New Immigration in the United States," *American Behavioral Scientist* 42 (4) (1999): 577–600; Jennifer Hirsch, "En el Norte la Mujer Manda: Gender, Generation, and Geography in a Mexican Transnational Community," in *Immigration Research for a New Century,* ed. Nancy Foner, Rubén G. Rumbaut, and Steven Gold (New York: Russell Sage Foundation, 2000): 369–89; Patricia Pessar, "The Role of Gender in Dominican Settlement in the United States," in *Women and Change in Latin America,* ed. June Nash and Helen Safa (South Hadley, MA: Bergin and Garvey, 1986); Peggy Levitt, *The Transnational Villagers* (Berkeley: University of California Press, 2001); Pirrette Hondagneu-Sotelo, "Overcoming Patriarchal Constraints: The Reconstruction of Gender Relations among Mexican Immigrant Women and Men," *Gender and Society* 6 (3) (1992): 393–415; Pirrette Hondagneu-Sotelo, ed., *Gender and U.S. Immigration* (Berkeley: University of California Press, 2003); Marcela Cerutti and Douglas Massey, "On the Auspices of Female Migration from Mexico to the United States," *Demography* 38 (2) (2001): 187–200; Shawn Malia Kanaiaupuni, "Reframing the Migration Question: An Analysis of Men, Women, and Gender in Mexico," *Social Forces* 80 (3) (2000): 1311–48.

81. Pessar, "The Role of Gender in Dominican Settlement in the United States"; Pirrette Hondagneu-Sotelo, *Gendered Transitions: Mexican Experiences of Immigration* (Berkeley: University of California Press, 1994); Cecilia Menjívar, *Fragmented Ties: Salvadoran Immigrant Networks in America* (Berkeley: University of California Press, 2000); Grasmuck and Pessar, *Between Two Islands;* Pérez, *The Near Northwest Side Story*, 82.

82. For a cogent critique of the ethnocentric and imperialistic tendency in transnational studies that erases the agency of local peoples by assuming the West is the engine of change, see Terence Turner, "Shifting the Frame from Nation-State to Global Market: Class and Social Consciousness in the Advanced Capitalist Countries," *Social Analysis* 46, no. 2: 56–82 (esp. 62).

83. June Nash and María Patricia Fernández-Kelly, eds., *Women, Men and the International Division of Labor* (Albany: State University of New York Press, 1983); Glick Schiller et al., "Transnationalism," 12.
84. Pérez, *The Near Northwest Side Story*, 19, 198–99.
85. Fink, *The Maya of Morganton*, 199. See also Robinson, "Why the Immigrant Rights Struggle," 21–22.
86. *Portland Press Herald*, March 3, 2006. Health fairs also have been organized to address the specific needs of and reach out to the Latino community; see for example Trevor Maxwell, "Reaching Out on Health Care," *Portland Press Herald*, May 8, 2006.
87. The Reverend Virginia Marie Rincón, comments at "'I Have a Dream . . .' A Latino Perspective," panel at University of Southern Maine, Portland, April 7, 2004.
88. Peggy Levitt, "Migrants Participate Across Borders: Toward an Understanding of Forms and Consequences," in *Immigration Research for a New Century*, ed. Nancy Foner, Rubén G. Rumbaut, and Steven Gold (New York: Russell Sage Foundation, 2000), 461.
89. *Portland Forecaster*, Feb. 11, 2004.
90. Anderson, *Imagined Communities*.

Born in Puerto Rico in 1953, Blanca Santiago was five years old when her mother moved to New York City. Her mother later returned for her, and Blanca lived in New York and Massachusetts as a child. From that point on, she began the process of acculturation and assimilation that would bring her deepest regrets and insights. In 1987, Blanca moved to Portland with her three children and pursued a career in social work. She has continued her commitment of working with disadvantaged populations in Maine ever since. Though Blanca insists that for a long time she was on the outside of Portland's Latin American community, today she is one of its most important leaders. In 2004, she was awarded Portland's César Chávez Leadership Award.

Blanca Santiago.

1

Blanca Santiago

It's About Dream Building

My mother, Lydia, passed away when she was sixty-two, but I still hold on to a certain mythology about her, because of her story. She decided she didn't want to go to school, so she didn't learn how to read and write in Spanish. And it wasn't required to read and write. It wasn't required to go to school. It was great if the boys wanted to go to school, and really the only thing that was necessary for them to do was to learn how to read and write, and then they could come back and work in the fields and take care of the animals.

It was really a rural farm society there, but my mother decided that she didn't want to go that way, and as a result, for all of her life, she struggled with illiteracy. It was kind of a reality for her that she would have to get by on her charm, you know, her innate intelligence, which she certainly had. She was certainly innately intelligent, and creative, and resourceful.

I think it was 1958 when Operation Bootstrap came into play.[1] I've been fascinated by this part of history, you know, because I've been looking back at what was happening in the world that would make my mother leave a paradise. I went back to Barrio Cerro Gordo in San Lorenzo, Puerto Rico, and thought, why would you leave this for what you went to, which was the slums of New York?

After I researched it, I realized that Operation Bootstrap, called Operación Fomento in Puerto Rico, was basically the industrial age. It was a move towards industrialization, in recognition of the fact that the people in the hills were living with practically nothing, and that industry could really help these people. It was kind of a benevolent thing to think that people could really be helped by being brought to the cities to work.

So I think there was a recruitment to go to the United States as well, and a lot of promises, but with no real supports that were given to those people. And my mother at the time had me, and my little sister, and we were a couple of years apart. I was about five years old when she decided to go to the mainland, the United States, and she went.

She would send us back packages. We stayed with my grandparents. It was a big family compound kind of a thing. The houses were small, the outdoors was large, and the houses were close to one another, so we would all hang out together in one big space and kind of sleep in hammocks and things like that, and there was an outdoor eating place with a *fogón* [hearth]; my aunt still has her fogón there on her land next to her little house. We lived there, and I think that I probably lived there pretty happily all of that time, for a year and a half or so that I lived there by myself with my sister and without her.

But she [my mother] was very miserable in the United States, where she really had nothing. She was working in a factory job, basically making no money, having been separated from my father then subsequently divorced from my father, and by herself again. [She] just had her charm to go on. She met this man, and I didn't get to know about him, or really meet him, until my little sister passed away. My sister got very ill very suddenly, overnight, and there was no transportation to take her to the hospital in time and so she died. I don't know whether she died at the hospital or she died on the way. My mother came, and brought me back to terrible New York City, where it just was awful.

It was a culture shock that I stayed in for seventeen years. I say seventeen years, because it seems like I didn't really make any conscious decisions about my life until I was twenty-two. I'm sure I made decisions, but I was not awake.

We stayed in New York City with my stepfather in this one-room tenement where we shared the bathroom facilities with however many other people were living there. It was a terrible place. It was my first real taste of what poverty looked like, even though we had been living in this rural poverty in Puerto Rico, I was in a paradise just the same. I mean, you know, there were orange trees.

And the cold and the food, and everything, was just bad for me. School was very hard. My stepfather was an abusive man and an alcoholic and just a really bad person, not just to us, but also to my mother. When my sister was born in May of 1959, she, me, and my mother got into a public housing project in Brooklyn. We lived there for a short while. My mother separated from my stepfather. Shortly after that we went to live in Massachusetts with my aunts and uncles.

My uncles had come here as rural farm workers, basically working in apple orchards and landscaping. Mr. Bonilla had apple orchards and a landscaping company in Waltham, Mass. So we went to live with them for awhile. My mother had been working at this factory making toys in Maynard, and she used to bring back kaleidoscopes and things like that. She met this man there, and he was a Nova Scotian guy. She picked us up and moved us, I guess with his help, to Hudson, Mass., where we lived for a short while. I went to school there, and my sister was just a toddler. My mother ended up having to go to an institution because she had a nervous breakdown. I think she just couldn't bear it that she was so isolated.

She was no longer near her family. She had kind of alienated them, and at the same time said, "Okay, you're rejecting me, I'm rejecting you, I'm having nothing to do with you."

For a while we were totally separated from family. When I think about that family system and how everybody was together, and then to think, okay, now you're going to be totally separated from everything, you know, the pain is still very real.

There weren't very many other Latin Americans or Puerto Ricans in Hudson, Mass. at the time. But we didn't live there long. Shortly after that we ended up going to Marlboro, Massachusetts. We would always move a lot. We were in Marlboro probably the longest time, about eight years. I still have very fond memories of Marlboro. The school and the library saved my life. If it hadn't been for the library I don't know what I would have done, because I was there all the time. I would just walk down the street and across some lawns and I was at the library. When I wasn't there, I was in my room reading.

My mother ended up making some sort of peace with my Tía Tabita in Waltham. Not unlinked to being Catholic, we had a large family. My Aunt Tabita and my Tío Frankie had seven kids. I had five girl cousins, and two boy cousins, and many of them were right around the same age. My mother, having made this peace, actually would send me to them for the summer, and I would have a wonderful time.

But the best thing that happened as a result of that was that I started leading a double life. This double life, where I would go to my cousins' house and it would be total Spanish immersion, and then I would come back home, and everything was totally English. My mother didn't want us speaking Spanish. She would not cook Puerto Rican food, complained that it smelled up the house, that it was stinky and we wouldn't want to eat it. You know, Nescafe was the thing, no Bustelo for us, and none of the traditional foods. My mother discovered cranberry sauce and she tried it on everything. It was really kind of funny.

But my growing up years going to school and those formative years of language development and skill was really English language immersion. Mammy wanted it that way and really rewarded that. She really gave my sister and me the message that she really wanted us to have a different life, to have a better life. She gave us this sense that we were and could be better. I certainly didn't realize for a long time that we were living on welfare. I just had no idea we were living on welfare. I thought we were the family that had done well. It was the strangest thing, her mythmaking ability.

At the same time, I think that I had a really hard time with my mother, because my mother's boyfriend continued to be in the picture, and wanted me to call him Daddy, and I couldn't do that. My sister called him Daddy, and I knew that she wasn't his child. I had no contact with my father, and she had no contact with hers. Here was this man who we were supposed to treat as though he were our father. That was very hard as a reality.

When I would go to my cousins' house, it was just simpler. There was a Mom and Dad. There was this great big family on one side of the house. And on the other side of the duplex there were all these men, brothers of both my Tía Tabita and her husband Tío Frankie, who would wake up at 4:00 in the morning, and all the women would get up on the other side, including us young girls. And we would make thermoses of coffee and huge hero sandwiches from the bread that we would get from down the street, which was still warm, and cheese, and then we would send them off, almost immediately getting ready for them to come home for dinner. They would live over on that side, all men in our family lived over on the other side and we were all family together.

I started seeing the romance novels in Spanish and the comic books in Spanish and all of these things that I didn't have any access to during my summers in Waltham. Now I realize that I didn't have access to stuff in Span ish or in English either. The only kind of books that came into our home were books that were either from the library or textbooks. My mother didn't read or write, so she didn't bring books or magazines into the house. The fact that I had access to books in Waltham meant that I didn't have to stop being who I was, which was really a bookworm.

I didn't want to go outside to play. In the summer it was beautiful out, and I had all these cousins I could play with; I would play make-believe games with them, but I really just couldn't wait to get back to read in Spanish. I really learned how to read and write in Spanish by visiting my cousins in Waltham, Massachusetts. That's how I learned how to do it. I wouldn't speak it, though, because with the spoken language I felt too vulnerable. When I opened my mouth to speak, I thought that I would not be able to pronounce the words right. I was very shy about it.

I went to high school in Millbury, Massachusetts. There was another young girl, Lia Seaver, who was the only other person of Latin American heritage. Her mother was from Colombia and didn't want her with me, at least at first, until she met me, because, after all, "those Puerto Ricans were dangerous people." She had seen *West Side Story*, and also she watched television. She read the novel *The Cross and the Switch Blade* and heard stuff about the gangs in New York, and so she didn't know what to make of Puerto Ricans. But she met me and decided it was okay. Lia and I became good friends. Neither one of us spoke Spanish, so we had that in common.

When I was sixteen, I met my first husband. I met him at a party, and we started dating. He lived in Waltham and I lived in Millbury, and he'd come and visit me. At seventeen, I was a senior in high school. I became pregnant. I left school. Up until then I had been working at this town hall in Millbury. I didn't know that there was such a thing as college. No one talked to me about college. I wasn't tracked as a college kid.

My mother's dreams would have come true if I just could have gotten a nice office job where I could keep my hands clean, meet a nice guy who could take care of me, that kind of thing. That was her dream for me. But I got pregnant, and decided to leave school. I tried going to the School Age Mothers program, but I was really seriously depressed at that time; everything was falling apart for me. My ex-husband was also very depressed. We got married because both of our families thought that this is what you do; as a good girl it was what I had to do. I knew that my ex-husband wasn't happy with the situation but that he was being kind of pushed that way too, so we were there, the two of us, just sort of trapped. And I tried to say, you could change your mind about this, but we got married.

Four years and three kids later we ended up not together, after living with him unhappily, in a physically abusive relationship for four years. I had three kids, and I was twenty-two. I said to myself, "Wow, how did I end up here?"

When I realized he was having an affair it was really the best day of my life. It was just such a great thing. I remember saying, "I'm never living with you again."

I went upstairs, and got one of those great big Hefty trash bags and put all of his clothes in and put it on the door and said, "That's it, we're never living together again." And that was it.

Then my life began. It was just like that. Shortly after that, I found myself as a single mother with a seven-month old daughter who was very colicky, a two-year-old, and a four-year-old. We were all living in this apartment next to my mother-in-law, side by side.

Brandeis University used to run a social service center downstairs in a place that used to be a poolroom. One night the hallway filled up with smoke, after my sister had just finished dropping off her daughter for me to watch for a little while. I grabbed my little boy, who was up, and gave him to my mother-in-law to bring downstairs, and ran upstairs to get the two kids. The house was going up in flames. We rushed out, there we were, and I'm like, "Where's my daughter, where's my daughter?" This young Brandeis student said to me, "Is that your little girl there? Is there another little girl?" And I'm like, "that's right, I'm holding her." I'll never forget that bizarre moment when I just really didn't believe that I really had her. It just totally shook me up.

We ended up getting help—and I think this is probably one of the reasons why I'm in social services today—from the Red Cross, and from the Housing Authority we got emergency housing. We got all kinds of assistance from the social service agencies, and that's when I also became aware that I was eligible for all of these training programs. It was actually because I did learn Spanish while I was living with my mother-in-law and my ex-husband that I realized I could make a living helping people. And I said, "Wow, well, I've been doing it for family all this time. I certainly could get paid for it. That would be alright too."

I went to work for Programa Roberto Clemente, in Waltham, Massachusetts. In July or August of 1976 I decided that I just really needed to be closer to my mother, to get support from family, because I still was just too isolated, and it was my husband's family that was there. I got my GED when I was twenty-three,and then I started going to Quinsigamond Community College, I also took some courses at Worcester State [College] and at Clark [University] COPACE, the continuing ed program, and tried to figure out what I wanted to do for work. While employed through the New Careers CETA program, I designed my job at Worcester Youth Guidance Center so that I could work with kids and families. It was a really good time in my life, and my kids were doing okay.

But as a result of my acculturation and assimilation, and all of the things that I didn't know because I was busy surviving, I didn't pay attention to language, even though it had been so important for me. I didn't realize that it was bigger than just being important for me, and so my kids grew up not speaking Spanish. I didn't speak Spanish at home. It was a blind spot. I didn't have a lot of free time, raising three kids and going to school. I try to cut myself some slack, and at the same time look at it. It's a very criticized thing in my cultural circle. It's something that people will shame you about in a minute, that your children don't speak Spanish. It's really considered an embarrassment.

We've had lots of conversations about whose fault it is. And I have apologized and said it was my responsibility. I don't know if it was my fault and my responsibility. I'm just really sorry. That was a big one. What was I thinking? Where was my head? I really don't know. I feel I have a lot of regret about it. What can I do about it now except say that, yes, that was a mistake. It's something that I counsel people about. They may think that I say it because I might have certain judgments based on some high standard that I hold, but I have certain judgments because they're based on standards I didn't meet for myself. They're not about judgments that I have about other people and what they should do. I just like to point out that this has been my experience as a mother who did not tend to this important thing; this is what it's done here and this is what might happen later. My daughter, Melanie, went to Latin America, and her Spanish got pretty good; as long as she practices it she does okay. And both my sons, José and Antonio, have talked about wanting to learn at different times, but it's not the same as having it spoken at home. I should know.

I came to Portland in 1987. When I came here I worked at a Lee Jay's Bed and Bath for a while. It was the hardest physical work I'd ever done in my life. I didn't realize that folding towels and sheets could be so physically exhausting. And, boy was I miserable. I was making decent money, because I talked the woman into believing I really wanted to be an assistant manager. I know that's what I did. I just said, of course, I want management. Why wouldn't I want management? I think I could be a good manager, because I need $9.50 an hour, that's why. What I didn't say was, because I can't live on less than that. If I don't tell you that, then you're gonna give me $7.00.

But every day off I kept looking on the boards at the City of Portland, because since I had worked for the city before, I figured, well, another city job, at least they have benefits, it's 30 hours, I mean it's clean work. My mother would be proud. I'm not getting my hands dirty. I went one day, and they had a job for a Work Fare Coordinator. That's when I first started working with people with mental illness. It was fascinating.

Then I went to work with Catholic Charities Maine as a Shelter Outreach Case Manager. That was in May of 1990. I worked with them for thirteen years. About five years into the work I decided that I really saw a need to have a representative payees program at Catholic Charities Maine. I was really encouraged and supported to put together that program. But one day I realized that the part of the job that I liked is direct service work, and then there's this part that is about crunching numbers that felt really bad to me, and I don't see a time in the near future where that was not going to be part of my job. I was really unhappy, and I didn't really know quite what to do.

I remember one day being so unhappy that I came home to my husband, Jon, and told him that. That same day there was a message on the machine from Dr. Frank Reed, an eye doctor who needed an interpreter for a project that performs cataract eye surgery in Quiché, Guatemala. That was February 2003. I went and I had an incredible time. I was really taken by the people of Guatemala; I was just fascinated by the whole thing. I was using Spanish every day, and I was totally immersed, and engaged, and alive.

I said to myself, "Oh my God, there's this whole part of me that's not being used. I'm just not whole. I just don't feel whole, and this is why. Because there's other parts of me that are being engaged, but it's not this."

I went back to Portland and applied for a job with the Department of Labor. In May I was interviewed and they offered me the job the same day. It's really been a great experience, a lot more in keeping with who I am. I get to feel more a part of my community. And I think that that's always been a hard thing for me.

Look at where I started. Here I am, I'm like this little rural country girl and I get taken out of that and then told: "No, your culture is a bad thing, your food's a bad thing, you're not speaking that language, you're not going to marry that Puerto Rican man," and then all the fallout from that, just being separated from everything.

I'm a real strange mix of a person. I don't think that I'm unique. I know that there are other people who have similar experiences to mine. But it is a strange mix. Usually you have someone who's got the stuff a little more integrated than I do.

People say, "Where are you from?"

"I'm from New England."

I can actually answer like that. Where are you from originally? I'm from Puerto Rico and I'm a *jíbara,* but basically I'm a New England girl. That's also part of who I am culturally. I listen to all kinds of music. I really like the traditional Puerto Rican music. But I also grew up listening to the Rolling Stones.

I do get back to Puerto Rico. My Dad lives there. I made acquaintance with my father when my grandmother on my mother's side was passing away. She was in the hospital when I went and met him, and basically introduced myself to him, because he really hadn't shown his presence in my life up until that point. We still are sort of estranged. It wasn't a fairy tale ending. It didn't resolve all nicely like it does in a ninety-minute made-for-TV movie. It is more like a documentary.

I enjoy having that connection to the island and to my heritage, especially my Aunt Juanita. She lives there. She's just a really wonderful person, and her husband Victor. He's not just my uncle from having married my aunt, but he's also my cousin from being my father's nephew. Oh, so these are my first cousins, and their children are my first cousins and my second cousins all at the same time. And they still live in Cerro Gordo, in San Lorenzo. They still live right there, and my Aunt Fela, Tía Fela, still lives right there up in the hills. She still lives on our family land.

Some of what I've experienced in Portland in talking about this idea of "invisibility" earlier is I think that partly what happens is that people don't want to be seen. For some of them, it is because they don't have documents. That's a big issue here. There are a lot of undocumented citizens here. I also think that because of the status that many of them have, they can come and they can work in a specific job. It's a time-limited job, like they come here to work in agriculture as migrant seasonal farm workers. They're only here for that period of time to work in that job. When that job is done they go back. If they decide to stay, then they're not here with documents. Their documents aren't in order. But if they stay here, they can't use many of the services.

Then there are the documented workers, the people who have the visas for work, and they're afraid to use services that will make them public charges. A public charge is if you become a burden to the state. That's probably my way of putting it, but if you become a burden to the state you're considered a public charge. There are certain kinds of benefits that you shouldn't receive when you're in this status of being someone who can work here but aren't a United States citizen. Once you become a United States citizen then it's a different story. People are afraid of having their process of legal documentation jeopardized in any way. Sometimes it's because they are petitioning to bring a family member over. They're afraid that getting services like food stamps or housing might hurt their chances of having that family member come over, and in some cases I think it might. Each situation is unique. It's very important to know when it's okay.

Also there's the cultural value of humility. Help is best accepted when offered gladly. To be really, really in need before you go ask for help and then be humiliated is not what I mean by humility. Then there's the value of respect, which is something that even American-born people don't get at a social service agency. When you're not treated with courtesy the first time, you're less likely to want to go and put yourself in that humiliating position again, with someone who, clearly, might be younger than you, and doesn't respect you, doesn't realize that you wouldn't be there unless you absolutely had to be.

At the Career Center we saw eleven Latino people from Biddeford Blanket lose their jobs when the factory closed down due to overseas competition. There's one guy who's from Cuba. He's been here a long time, and he's always going to land on his feet, and always has, or at least in the time that I've heard of him he seems like he's done pretty well. But these are mostly women who are working. They are from El Salvador. They're not clear about the processes here. They've worked at all the seafood places. Their bones and bodies hurt from being in cold water and ice all of the time, working in the fish processing plants. They were happy to have this job at Biddeford Blanket. It paid well. They were coming from Portland to go to Biddeford, but it wasn't a bad commute. They were doing it together. They all spoke Spanish together and helped each other out with English. They were supporting one another. There was a community there, and then, you know, the company closes, and they're having a tough time just making ends meet. Many of them really have a hard time thinking about asking for help even during the holidays. "No, we'll see what we do." There's a lot of pride, a lot of pride in that community.

Not to say that there isn't a lot of pride in a lot of other communities. I'm sure that that's also the case. But there's a lot of pride in that community.

I asked one women I was doing some career counseling with, if she had thought about something that she might want to do.

"What do you mean? I've never thought about anything like that," she answered.

I talked with her about what she might want for herself, for her children, for her life. It was just foreign to her. So, I think that even to ourselves sometimes, we're invisible. And maybe I'm just putting that out there, because I know that I wasn't seen. As a child I wasn't seen. And certainly no one said anything about my future until I was in my senior year. Of course, it was a little late because by that time I already knew I was pregnant and probably going to be leaving school. Nobody really talked to me about it. It's important to see people.

Sometimes we just don't think about people and their dreams; we don't think about that. That's part of the invisibility thing. We know that people want a better life. Everybody wants a better life. And we know that people want a better life for their children. Who wants a worse life for their children? But are we really, really looking at what that means? What's underneath all of that? It's about dream building, aspiration. Is there an aspiration of yours? Is there some part of you that wants something really badly, or maybe some part of you that doesn't even realize that it wants something, that you should start listening to something deep inside you? I like to do that kind of work with people, which I think is about seeing them, or giving back. It doesn't have to be a big thing. It's just like, what are you thinking about? One step at a time.

I have faced racism in my own life, and I'm sure that I still do. In Portland I have faced a lot less than I did in Massachusetts. I think the sheer numbers is the number-one reason. It was comfortable for me to be around people who were not brown. Why, because I'd always been around people that were not brown, for the most part. It was not that different for me to feel different. It was definitely something I felt.

But I definitely felt singled out for discrimination and racist attacks when I was in Worcester, Massachusetts. That was because, in housing, people would take our mailboxes and write "Spic" on it. My kids faced a lot of hostility on the street. People were very upset that my cousins and people that I knew, my friends, were coming in and out of the house, and they weren't looking like everybody else in the neighborhood. The landlord basically asked me to leave, because he was afraid of the property damage and how his insurance rates would go up.

And rather than fight that I just said, "Yeah that makes sense. I don't think I want to be here either," and I left. I faced that, and I have faced discrimination from other people of color too when I was living in Worcester.

Maybe you want some more examples from Portland. I was down at WMPG, doing my radio show. Right after that comes the gospel show. This gentleman from the African American community was going to be one of the featured speakers or somebody was going to be interviewing him. We started talking a little bit while I was breaking down and while the DJ was setting up for the next show.

He said to me, "Oh, so you speak Spanish."

I said, "Yes I do."

And he said, "Oh, are you fluent?"

I said, "Yes I am."

He said, "My daughter really needs a Spanish-language tutor."

And I said, "Well, I'm really not a teacher. I don't really have that much patience."

He said, "But you speak it fluently and I'm sure it wouldn't be any trouble at all."

I responded, "Well, I really don't know, but I could probably give you some names of some people."

"Oh, well, your kids probably speak Spanish."

And I said, "No, my kids don't."

"How could you not have your children speak Spanish?"

I said, "Well, you know, it's a long story. Do you have some time? I could tell you." But you know it *is* a long story.

He said, "Well, that's terrible, that's just disgraceful."

It was only later that I thought to say to him, you know, you don't speak Swahili or, you know, you don't speak whatever your mother tongue was, your people lost it a long time ago.

If I were going to really speak my mother tongue, it would probably be some language that you wouldn't even recognize as Spanish, because the Taínos were the people that were on the island [they] called Borinquén when Christopher Columbus came with his men. So it's not like Spanish is my language either, so I guess that was lost too. And your language was lost too, and we're both oppressed here. Cut me a little slack. So I get that kind of thing.

I have witnessed other people be more discriminated against. I had gone to a client appointment with a young man who had been hurt at a job, and he was supposed to go to the Social Security office. I have had a longstanding relationship with the people at the Social Security Administration because of my work at Support and Recovery Services. We had an appointment. He got there first. I had told him that when you get there, you don't need to take a number; you just go and tell them that you have an appointment, and then you won't have to take a number. Well, the woman at the desk insisted that he take a number.

When I got there, I said, "Did you tell her that you were here?"

He said, "Oh yeah, but she told me I had to take a number anyway."

So I went up to the desk and I said, "He's here and he has an appointment."

And she said, "Oh, I'm sorry Blanca."

She was totally embarrassed and apologetic. I'm sorry, call me paranoid, to me maybe she treated him differently because she could and that's racist. It could happen anywhere.

I have seen people be treated with less dignity than is afforded me. And the reason why I would not necessarily feel that anymore is because I'm that much removed from where I was even when I was raising kids. You know, when I was raising kids I had to deal with people and their attitudes all the time, and I was discriminated [against] in housing. Now I have money to purchase a home. You know, people make assumptions. I have found also that there's a great number of people who have purchased homes in this Latin American community. I mean, they're homeowners, but probably people wouldn't look at them that way.

I don't know what the percentage is, but I am always surprised at how many people say, "I own my home." That's great, because they're doing it on $9 and something cents an hour, or $8, sometimes less than that. They've purchased homes.

Unfortunately all of the social service agencies are overwhelmed so they don't give people interpreters even when they know that they can't understand what the person is saying. And that's a real serious problem in this community. And then people end up having to take money out of their pockets to pay somebody to go and serve as an interpreter for them. I know that also happens.

I do think there's a sense of a united community amongst Latin Americans, particularly at the church. The Catholic church here is a big unifying force. There's also a big Seventh-day Adventist population. And then there are the Episcopalians. And each one of these has its own spiritual leader. The Reverend Virginia Rincón is a spiritual leader. The Latin American community's trying to get more organized now, and I'm on the board for Centro

Latino Maine, and we're trying to pull together an organization, basically to serve the social service needs of Latin Americans in Portland. I'm very excited about that.

At the same time, there's lots of other things happening, there's John Connors and the Latino Health Council. Manny Andrade has done a lot of AIDS prevention work specifically targeting the Latino community. The schools really pull people together. The Multilingual [and] Multicultural Program gets people to come out for stuff when it has to do with their children. And of course, Reiche School has a big concentration of Spanish-speaking families and kids. There's our bodega where I go often. Juan González is a great guy and has really established himself in this community. Lourdes [Carpenter] has her beauty salon on Congress Street now. It's right down the street from Juan's La Bodega [Latina]. She's Dominican too. When you start having centers like that where people can actually congregate and tell stories about what's happening in their lives, what's going on with who and what and all that, those are the things that are centralizing folks.

Preble Street Resource Center is seeing a huge influx of Latin American people.[2] The numbers change seasonally, but it's definitely on the rise. Every time I go there, I meet somebody new. And these are folks who have just had a really, really hard time of it in their own countries for a variety of reasons. When you add mental illness to being invisible, it's really quite a combination. Or add being gay, and being out. All of those things add to the difficulty of the individual situations.

The Center for Cultural Exchange does a lot of things.[3] Victoria Chicón of the Centro Latino is working on getting a collaborative needs assessment done of the Latin American community, and also identifying some artists and musicians. We would like to identify them as people that the community can use as a resource. They just finished doing Mundo Hispánico, which had a lot of nice events, and really tried to get the Latin American community tickets to those events so that they could be part of it. To some extent it worked. I think that more needs to be done to make things a little bit more accessible to the community. Certainly this community has been having some celebrations, along with having some tragedies, to unite it. Celebrations and tragedies are great unifiers, like they are in family.

Every once in a while I feel like visibly I get on a soapbox when I say this, but the Latin American community needs to be looking at what the spiritual needs are of our community, not just the religious needs, but you know, everybody's needs. *Se necesita alguien con quien desahogarse.* (You need to have someone in whom you can confide and trust.)

I know that right now the Community Counseling Center has only one woman, Blanca Gurrola, for all the need that exists. She wouldn't be able to handle [such] a full caseload. The need that I see is great. We need a mechanism that verifies our needs so that we can then say these are the services that are needed to serve this community. A lot of them are spiritual and psychological needs. That shouldn't come as a surprise. Everyone has these needs.

Our kids are having just as many problems in school as the general population. After all, each population is just a representation of the whole. They're going to be experiencing autism, and learning disabilities, and failure to thrive and all of these other things. We need services. We need culturally sensitive services for that. I think that we can't be humble about this and just wait for someone to realize our needs. We have that saying, *El que no habla, Dios no lo oye* (He who does not speak, God will not hear).

And so I try to use that whenever I have somebody who's saying, "I've got this problem, yeah, but I don't wanna do anything. I don't want to call attention to myself. I don't want to say I have a problem."

But at some point, somebody has to say, "Whoa, you know, there's all this need, this is a problem."

When the spotlight got put on Lewiston, when the needs of the Somali community got spotlighted, there was definitely an effort to address and do wraparound services for that community. And there's definitely a benefit to that, that is maybe not going to be seen today, just as the benefits that I received in 1977 weren't really harvested for another ten years, but that's what happens.

If we don't start somewhere, then there's nothing to harvest. I feel as if I've been on the outside for a very long time. I'm starting to get in slowly, partly because, *Uno no va si no lo invitan.* I always say it in English, too: If invited, I will come.

Notes

1. Operation Bootstrap began in 1947 when the Puerto Rican legislature passed a series of laws to develop export-oriented industrialization in Puerto Rico. See Pérez, *The Near Northwest Side Story,* 8–9, 44–60.
2. The Preble Street Resource Center is a social services agency in Portland.
3. The Center for Cultural Exchange was an organization that hosted cultural events—music, dances, plays, readings. It closed in 2007.

Adrian Bravo Chavez.

From his home in Chiapas, one of Mexico's poorest states, Adrian Bravo Chavez first migrated to the United States when he was barely fourteen years old. Escape from poverty and a desire to educate himself motivated his dangerous trek. His story reminds us that immigrants without documentation are among the most exploited people in the United States. Backbreaking work, poor housing and diet, debt, and low wages have marked his experience in the United States. Yet even against this backdrop, Adrian maintains hope that with an education in the United States he can fulfill his dreams of becoming a professional who can offer something to the community. For him, sharing his story is both cathartic and practical—he wants others to know the challenges undocumented immigrants face.

2

Adrian Bravo Chavez

I Wanted to Free Myself

My name is Adrian Bravo Chavez. I come from Chiapas, Mexico. I don't even remember what year I came to the United States, but it was a while ago. When I first came, I came illegally—"Illegal" as they say, because where I'm from, we, the poor people, don't have the money or the other things one needs to arrange to get a visa to come to the United States. There's no other recourse than for us to come as "wetbacks," or illegals, cross the border . . . desert and all.

I wanted to stay in Mexico, but the situation was so bad there, and I wanted to continue my studies. That drove me to come here to the United States more than anything else and to work and make money. Then I saw a way that I could go to school. It was like a dream come true for me, no? I said, "Wow, to be in the United States and go to school in the United States, with the gringos. Wow!"

I thought about many things. And finally I decided. I was working and I saved some money—I began to work when I was really young. I was outside of Tijuana working and with the money I earned in Tijuana . . . I had to pass myself off as older because the law there doesn't let minors work either.

I don't remember how old I was when I left Chiapas. It was four or five years ago. Now I'm eighteen. I was working there in Tijuana, Mexico, as a busboy and with those greenbacks—[laughs] greenbacks!—with that money that I saved, I went back to Chiapas to see my family, and since there was the chance to go to the United States, I came to the border at Sonora. I was there in Altar Sonora for about a week and I found the *coyote* [smuggler]. And the coyote took us through the desert and everything; they said many died along the way.

The coyote told us, "Get three gallons of water and enough food."

"And how long are we going to walk?"

"I don't know. We're going to walk about one or two days. It depends on whether or not you are all motivated to walk."

And we walked. In the beginning we were all walking well, given the high temperatures. There were probably seventeen of us. A woman came, her son, me, and my cousin, and some other friends. But the two of them were older; I was the only minor who went. I filled my backpack with about five gallons of water and a little bit of food, and off we went, and yes, we walked. We walked for nearly twelve days. And we had to sleep in the desert one night. Some had jackets, blankets, and I didn't have anything! So I had to put up with the cold all night long and I couldn't sleep because it was so cold in the desert. But then we arrived. We came to a place that they call Tucson, or something like that, in Arizona. That was where they picked us up. But when it came time for us to get in the truck, it's not like one rides sitting with a seat for each person. Instead they threw us [in], one could say, I realized that it was as if we were firewood. They stacked us one on top of the other. I was thrown to the bottom, and everyone was on top of me. I couldn't breathe in the truck. I felt like the pressure and the [lack of] oxygen was killing me.

Everyone said, "No . . . Try to breathe!"

I couldn't breathe. They tried to blow air into my mouth, but I couldn't. I was underneath and everyone was on top of me. I guess I cried or something. In that moment I felt like I was going to die. Finally we arrived in Chandler, Arizona, where we came to a house. We were there about a week. We talked to our family members, but I didn't. While I have family members—cousins—here, I didn't know their phone numbers or how to get in touch with them. That was why I didn't have anyone to help me here in the United States.

The coyote said to us, "Now you're all going to North Carolina. You're going to work off the cost of the trip."

We paid nearly two thousand dollars. Just to cross cost six thousand pesos; that's about six hundred dollars. In addition to that, we paid around two thousand dollars total. They took me to North Carolina to work off our debt in the fields. We arrived and the coyote, the owner, threatened us. He told us if we were to escape, he would track us down wherever we were and would do something to us. And we were scared, no? We tried to find a way to get out of there, out of that place, but we couldn't because we had to pay off our debts first.

That man brought us to another contractor. We began first to cut the *camote,* sweet potato, in North Carolina. We were planting sweet potato. And we planted tobacco and the man brought us to live in this old house. The contractor was back in the hills, and in this house there was power and water, but there weren't any beds or anything. Some [of us] slept on the floor. Some hit it lucky—we slept on old mattresses. They gave us each one blanket.

We worked from seven in the morning to six or seven at night, from Monday to Saturday, and we earned $320 dollars a week. And we had to pay the coyote every time we got a check. The contractor paid us our check. We cashed the check and then gave part of it to the coyote. We always had to give some to the coyote each time to pay off the debt. Some sent money home to their families. But I tried to pay off the debt quickly. It was sad because we lived some forty—I don't know exactly how many but there were many of us in the house—and we barely had pots and pans to cook with. We cooked our own food. We arrived, probably around seven at night. We left the bus running, and we raced for the pans and everything to cook the food. Some cooked dinner; some heated tortillas; others fried eggs to eat then and early the next day. We were all men. There was just one woman with us. She was from Veracruz, I think. We worked and the sun was very [hot]. Working in the fields of North Carolina planting sweet potato and you're on top of the machine, with the sun shining some ninety degrees—what do I know? [maybe] more than one hundred degrees—just dying of thirst and we wanted water but the owner didn't come to the fields. His son—he left him in charge—would go off to play with the truck and we would be there suffering from thirst with no water.

Then one day after I had paid off my debt, we decided to escape from the coyote. We went off with another contractor. They took us to pick cucumbers. It's hard work. You have to walk along with buckets on your thighs and pick cucumbers as fast as you can so you can make . . . because each bucket is a token. If you fill a bucket, then it's a token; you take it to the truck and they give you a token and those tokens are [worth] seventy or eighty cents each or something like that. You had to make as many tokens as you could in a day. There was one friend who would earn about eighty tokens a day. And I would go behind him and make about seventy or seventy-five. He would see the rest of my friends back in the field.

He said, "What's wrong with all of you? Put your back into it!"

"No, but we can't!" they would say.

Then they would grab his belt. Now realize that it was so hot in North Carolina, more than a hundred degrees. Your whole body would get soaked with water, but it was sweat—not water—sweat. I had to take off my shirt and wring it out and then put it back on and go back to work. My eyes were red and burning because the sweat would fall into them. So I would go along wiping my eyes and then picking, but trying to make as many tokens as I could.

The contractor who brought us said, "You're going to get more hours. Here we're going to pay you hourly and we're going to pay you more."

But it was a lie. Sometimes they wouldn't pay us what we deserved; they would pay us less. They brought us to live in an abandoned house near the road. But they say that in that house there were . . . . The story around those parts was that that the workers got assaulted a lot. We lived with that fear. One time we went to the gas station to buy a few things when the coyote approached us, the other one whom they had abandoned. I abandoned him, but I had paid off my debt.

He said to me, "You know your account is paid off. I've got nothing with you. If you want to come to the United States again, I'll bring you across again and I already know your name and everything."

But he caught the rest who had left before paying in the gas station and began to argue with them and pulled out a gun. They were all scared and everything. But after that he didn't do anything to them. Instead he went elsewhere. And we went back. He was from the United States.

After that, we went with another coyote—another contractor, who brought us and said, "I'm going to give you hours." The man had been in the army in Mexico, but for a long time he had been living in the United States. He was good people, you know?

He said, "I'm going to pay you hourly."

Sometimes he would take us to pick tobacco plants. In North Carolina, there are strong winds or rains and the plants fall. We had to take off or roll up our pants and go along standing up the tobacco plants in the middle of all the mud and water. Everyone was just covered in mud, your whole face. [Chuckles]

Sometimes I would start thinking. I would say, "God, when will come the day that I'll get out of here?" Or, "I wish I could go somewhere else; I wish I wasn't here."

But I had to put up with it because I didn't have anywhere else to go. I didn't have family. I didn't have anything here in the United States. Sometimes I felt very sad at night. Every day after work I would go off in the darkness to think.

I said to myself, "What could I do to get myself out of here? I want to get another job. Anything but this." But I couldn't. I didn't have family. And so it went.

We were there about three months, with the contractor. After that a friend of mine had a brother in Atlanta who knew a contractor that would come to pick blueberries here in the North of Maine. And he put us in contact with him.

Then he [the contractor] said, "After you finish the contract in the blueberry harvest, I can get you work in Boston." He said in the blueberry harvest you can make *good money* because it comes out to be like three dollars a box, but it depends on how many boxes of blueberries you make in a day. Sometimes it comes out to be three thousand dollars a month.

And we thought, "Wow! Let's go there!"

So we moved. From being many friends who came, there were just about four friends left. And those four friends came here to Maine. We didn't know where that state was.

"No, it's up above New York."

The four of us and other people came from Atlanta. The contractor was from Guatemala. We rode the whole trip in an old van. Once it broke down on the freeway outside of New York. [Laughs] We had to all get out and hide in the woods because if the police came they would be able to see us. They fixed the truck and then we all got back in again and went on our way. Then we stopped at a gas station to hide because they said that some patrol cars were following us. They thought we looked suspicious. So we tried to shake them. We kept traveling. We traveled, traveled, traveled, but we had no idea where we were until we arrived in Maine.

They said, "This is Maine. Here you're going to pick blueberries."

Well, we ended up driving around. We arrived in Rockland, I think. We ended up north of Rockland.

The contractor said, "You've got to get motivated, because here you can earn money. You're going to earn three thousand a month—*easy*."

"Oh—wow! That's great!"

We went to get an apartment. But since you rarely ever see a Latino around there, it's nearly all Americans, the people would call Immigration. Sometimes when we were at the gas station, twenty minutes after we left the gas station, Immigration would arrive. They were right behind us. . . . I realized that they were behind us, nonstop. They were following us.

The contractor said, "I'm sorry, but we don't have a room, an apartment where we can go to sleep."

What can you do? We went to sleep in a trailer, but the neighbors called the police to say there were Latinos there, "illegal aliens," as they say. So we had to leave the trailers. We went to live in the woods—there between the woods and the mountain, that's where we lived.

Afterwards the contractor said, "[There is] no other way. We have to live here because we've got no other option."

We had to buy some plastic tents and some tarps to stick under and sleep that way, and then jackets and blankets, no? We shopped at the store. We would go by two or threes to the store to buy supplies and return to the mountain and there we cooked. We made a campfire like they make in the towns back home, with a spit and everything. It was okay because to tell you the truth, I come from a poor family. There isn't anyone who would deny it. I didn't feel odd or like it was anything strange to be living that way. Sometimes it rained so we had to dig around the edge of the tent so that the water wouldn't run inside.

Picking blueberries was very, very hard. We had to be bent over all day picking blueberries from eight in the morning, or sometimes seven in the morning, until five or six in the afternoon. They paid us depending on how many boxes we made. But it wasn't what the contractor told us. Instead we earned maybe one thousand five hundred dollars per month. We were there two months. As they say, that's when the fall begins, no? Around then we were still up there. When the job was done, we would go swimming at the beaches and we would see nothing but Americans there. We would see them all there, all of them scared as if they were looking at monkeys, right? [Laughs]

And then right when we were getting in the water they would say: "No! Get out of the water!"

Or they would all come running because they would see that we were going to swim in the sea. Once a woman was there swimming. We arrived after her to swim at the same place and the lady said to us: "No! I don't want you here! Get out or I'll call the police!"

And she called the police. We had to leave that place running. Just imagine, to arrive really tired from the work that we did all day long with our backs in pain. We couldn't sit or sleep because our backs ached after being bent over all day long. On top of that, we had to cook. We had to make breakfast to bring to work the next day. It was really hard.

Sometimes at night, you hear the coyotes or wolves howling nearby and we would get scared. We said to ourselves, "We have to be on guard. If anyone sees anything suspicious at night, let us know. Don't let the wolves or the coyotes here eat us up."

We were there a while after the blueberry harvest ended. The man told us—he had promised, no?—that he was going to get us work in Boston. After that, he got angry with us because he didn't pay some of my friends the money he owed them. He stole hours from them. In addition to what he stole in hours, he stole in boxes of blueberries. We kept track of what we made in a day. At the end of the week we did a count. He kept his own count. And so we went. He sometimes stole from us. Since we didn't have papers or anything—wetbacks—we didn't have, how do they say, rights to anything. No one listened to us. And so there we were.

We said, "What's going on? Are you going to take us to Boston? Are you going to find us work?"

"No," he says, "Not now."

He had already brought us there, and we felt so bad. Then there were some friends from El Salvador. They did have papers, work permits. We met them there, all of us working together, and they invited us to come to Portland.

They said, "Why don't you come to Portland then? It's a city. You can get work in the fish companies."

I said, "What do I know? Wherever, just as long as there is good work there."

"Yes, they pay around eight dollars an hour, eight or nine dollars—it depends."

"Wow. Well, we want to go there."

So we came here but we weren't four anymore; now it was five of us who came here, five friends. Then we met a friend who was from the same hometown as we were, and he lent us his apartment. We stayed there about three days, but they drank too much. They smoked marijuana. They brought women back to their rooms and we lived with this shame.

We said, "The police could come here—What are we going to do?"

We left at night and came to wander around the park or wherever, and then later, much later at night we would go back to sleep because we didn't have anywhere to go. We didn't know where to go. It was scary. Until one day the owner of the apartment threw them out. That is to say, they also threw our things out in the trash. We tried to find our belongings, but they all got thrown out. We collected what we could and someone told us about the shelter. So we went there to live for about two months, I think. Around that time we met the social workers at Preble Street [Resource Center]. They helped us.

They spoke Spanish and said, "Don't worry. We speak Spanish. We are going to help you with whatever you need."

We wanted to rent an apartment, but we couldn't. We had the money from what we had earned in the blueberry harvest, but we didn't have papers. You need papers to rent an apartment and that was what we didn't have. So we had to sleep there and without work. We didn't know anyone.

We would find a Latino somewhere and we would say, "Hey, do you know about any work?"

"Oh, yes, yes!" they would say. "Oh, I'm going to help you."

They would just say it and then never return to help us. So we felt so bad. You see that one goes to bed at six at night, and at eight in the morning they're throwing you out, making everyone go outside. From there we would leave the shelter and eat at Preble Street [Resource Center].

We had dreams, too many dreams. We wanted to be in an apartment where we could rest, but no way. We couldn't. We tried to talk to the social workers about any help they could give us so that we could rent an apartment but that we were going to put up the money. In the end we didn't have it and we didn't know anyone in this place. This city seemed huge to us.

Sometimes we would go sleep in the park. When we were too sleepy, three or four of us would get together and go sleep there. Sometimes we would get hungry at midday and go to the store. Then we would go eat in the park—because we didn't have anywhere to live.

We didn't have work, either. Until one day, I think that it was someone from Cambodia took us to a place they call the Sardine Factory, some thirty-five minutes north of here [Portland]. But they paid very little. six-fifty an hour or six dollars—something like that. In addition to that, they stole from us. They didn't pay us. Since we didn't speak English, if we wanted to say something, they insulted us.

But then they said to us, "You don't have any reason to make accusations, blah, blah, blah, blah . . ." They said, "Shut up. Stop talking." Sometimes they would steal hours from us and not pay us well.

At that time I was going to the Adventist church. At the Bodega Latina, we met a man, and I said to him, "Excuse me. What's your name?"

"My name is Antonio."

"Where are you from?"

"I'm from Colombia."

"Hey—you don't know where there's an Adventist church here, do you?"

"Of course I do! I go to the Adventist church and I can take you there."

"Do you need a ride anywhere?"

"Yes, we want to go to the shelter," I said to him.

"Oh, you don't happen to live there."

And, so I began going to the church, and inviting my friends to go to church.

The man said, "I'm going to find some way for you to get an apartment or somewhere where you can live."

"That's great."

We had to get up at four in the morning, four-thirty, to go to work. When we got back here, we didn't have any place to go to rest, to sleep. [We were] terribly tired. We had to go to the park to sleep during the day. We didn't have anywhere to go.

Then the pastor said to me, "I don't want you to go anymore or for you to have to rent. I'm going to find a room just for you."

But I said, "I don't want to go alone. I want to take my friends with me. They should come too."

"No, because your friends don't come to church. Most likely they could lead you down the wrong path. I don't want that to happen. We want to help you because you go to church." Blah, blah, blah.

Finally one day a friend from church said to us, "Look, I have a room at my house if you want to go live there."

I said, "Yes, I would like to. We want to go live there, but all four of us."

He went and the room was big enough. He said, "It's fine. All four will fit."

It was a relief because within a week, it began to snow. [Laughs] Thank God! That week snow began to fall and we were in the apartment. It was such a happy thing for us. Around that time we were working at Barber Foods as temps and it was close, because the apartment was near the Greyhound station. It was such a joy to be in the apartment.

Around that time I said to the social worker, her name was Malvina, at Preble Street, "I would like to go to school."

She said, "Yes, you can go to school."

"That's great," I said, "But I don't know what to do."

She said, "You just have to sign yourself up."

In the end they took me to the Multicultural Office to see what level of English I had. They told me I was a little bit low on my English, that I more or less knew the names of things in English. They accepted me into Portland High School. I was in high school for three years and I graduated. I graduated. [Chuckles] I graduated from there and I was working. I studied in the morning and worked in the evening. I had to ask a favor of a friend of mine to give me a ride to work, so I moved to live along Cumberland Avenue.

I went to school despite the fact that many said to me, "You're going to school and working; it's too much for you."

It was something that I wanted. It was a special thing to me because I was going to school and to work. I wanted to get ahead. And I couldn't go to school in Mexico, you know. I think I got halfway through secondary school in Mexico. In the place where we are there isn't a middle school. We had to leave the city to study at the middle school. And that cost money.

I said to my dad, "I don't want to work. I'd rather not be an expense to you, but I have to do it."

He said, "No, it doesn't matter."

He rented a room for me. He paid for a room and he paid for food, but it wasn't much. I didn't have enough for the monthly expenses. Sometimes I didn't have shoes. I would go to school with shoes with holes in them. It was a city and I felt ashamed, but I said to myself, "What can I do? I can't do anything about it." So I began to work. Ever since I was little, I worked so that I could support my school but sometimes I didn't have enough time. I neglected my studies because I was working. After school I worked at night for a few pesos. The first day that I earned money there it was great because it was by my own efforts that now I was able to buy myself a pair of shoes. I could buy a pair of pants, a T-shirt, no matter how cheap it might be.

Then here in the United States it was different because there's more support. In the schools there you have to buy books, notebooks, and everything. Here you don't. Sometimes you go to those places and they give you notebooks or a pencil or pens. It wasn't anything out of the ordinary for them, but for me, it's a big expense. And there I was. Finally I was working at Barber Foods, but they didn't know my legal status. One day I talked to the boss, the supervisor, and told him that I needed to work at Barber Foods because I was in school and I wanted to support my studies. He said that was okay. They gave me a job with the company.

He said, "If you want to work for the company because you're going to go to school, what are your dreams?"

"Well, I want to go to college."

He said to me, "It's okay."

Then I told the social worker that I had a lot of dreams, like working in television or in radio, for example.

Then the social worker told me, "There is a Hispanic radio [program] here in Portland. Do you want to go see what it's like? The host's name is Rosita."

I said, "I'd like to go."

So we began talking. I talked to Rosita and she said, "If you want to come, you can come help me. I can teach you and whatnot." And so I began. By the end of the story, I had begun to do shows with her, talking, playing music, like a D.J.

[Then one day] she said, "You know what? On such and such day I can't make it to the radio station. I don't know if you can go in my place."

From then until now, that's how it is. I continue to go to the radio station. I have the show every Sunday, with Rosita at WMPG from 2:00 p.m. to 3:30 on Sundays. And the good thing was I liked it.

But I had a lot of dreams. Ever since I was a boy I had lots of things I wanted to do. I wanted to free myself to do many things, to learn new things. Channel 4, the public access [television station] also caught my attention. Supposedly they taught you how to use a camera. I paid for a class to get in there to study. I passed. I think it was a three-day class. They told me I could help them. Sometimes I have chatted with Victoria Chicón who does the Latino program. She asked me if I wanted to help them. They wanted fresh ideas from the youth to bring them together. But since I'm working, I don't have time. [Chuckles]

With regards to my sad life, what I don't want to talk about, but what I want you to know is that when I was in high school it was my last year and I was going to graduate. [Crying] Around that time I would always hang out with my friend. One day the police found us in a park. Realize that there were just three days left [to graduate]. We were all there. My teachers were happy. Many of them spoke a little Spanish. I got along well with them. They were all happy because I was going to graduate. And I was happy too. The time came for us to have the ceremony. I went to buy my clothes. They gave me the accessory, the one they use for graduation.

The teacher told me, "We're proud of you. You're going to graduate."

"Wow," I said to myself. "That's great."

They gave me invites to invite my family members. I went to buy the clothes that I was going to wear that day. I wanted something special because it was a big day for me, no? To graduate in the Americans' school was awesome for me. There were just two or three days until I was to graduate when I was in my friend's car, and they stopped him because he was driving with a suspended license. And that was when they stopped me too.

The police stopped me and called Immigration on me. They held me in the Detention Center. First they sent me to the County Jail. Then they transferred me to the Detention Center. I was sad, because Immigration was going to send me to Mexico. I couldn't be here. As much as I tried to tell them, to beg them to let me . . . that was a very sad story, a very sad time. I wanted to be in my graduation ceremony, of course. A week later—it was a Wednesday that Immigration took me—Thursday they took to me to Atlanta where they were going to hold me two or three days and then transfer me to Mexico. I didn't want that. I wanted to go back. I ran from the Immigration people in the Atlanta airport to try to come back here. Then he caught me and handcuffed me again. They transferred me to Pennsylvania where they stuck me in another maximum-security Detention Center. I was there for two or three months. I cried inside because never in my life had I gone through something like that. I had never had that experience. In that youth jail, they forced me to eat, just like in the military, you know? I had to eat. If I didn't eat, they sent a report to Immigration about me.

I said, "When are you going to get me out of here?"

"I don't know. Just tough it out," the Immigration people said. "In another three days we were going to Mexico, but you ran so I don't know when we're going to take you to Mexico."

I cried every time, and I prayed to God to get me out. Sometimes they treated me badly. I felt a little discriminated against. There were various people in charge there to see that all the inmates are in order, you know? But sometimes when we didn't do things well, they would bow our heads down on a chair or on the table for a half hour without being able to look at anyone else. And if we resisted anything, they would handcuff us and throw us on the floor. I asked the Mexican consulate to get out but they said they couldn't do anything.

I said, "No, please, give me some way to get out of here, a permit or something so that I can be here in the United States." But they never tried to do that.

"No. I'm sorry. You have to go to Mexico."

I said, "No, I don't want to go back. I want to go back to my school. I want to go to college." But they didn't understand that.

They said, "We can't do anything about that. You have to go to Mexico." Finally the day arrived when I could speak with my parents.

My parents in Chiapas said, "How are you, son?"

"I'm okay," I told him. Without showing all that I was suffering inside, I always said to him, "I'm fine. I'm fine, papa. Don't you worry."

And he said, "Yes son, you're okay, of course. We're just here in the consulate. When are they going to get you out?"

I said, "Don't worry. I'm going to get out soon."

They didn't give me any hope either that I would get out of jail soon. I was there about two months and then they sent me to the border in Laredo, Texas, where they turned me over to the Mexican Immigration agents who took me to a place in Mexico called "The DIF" where all the youths go. I didn't want to go.

On the bridge one of the immigration officers stopped me and said, "I know you can speak English and you can return to the United States whenever you want. You can say that you're American because you speak English, but come another day, come another time with a visa or a permit and you will be welcome here in this country, but like this as an illegal—no."

I said, "How should I do that? I can't get papers there."

"I don't know," he said. "We're not going to deport you this time. We're just going to give you voluntary departure. But at some other time we're going to deport you."

I stopped and thought on that bridge, divided between Mexico and the United States. I looked back and said, "God, my dreams are back there. What am I going to do? Just look ahead. Look ahead, and go. Look towards Mexico." [Cries]

It was a very sad moment in my life. And then I returned to Mexico. I returned to my home, like any other wetback with nothing more than a backpack and two hundred dollars in my pocket. My parents were crying, all happy to see me, that I had gotten out. That made me mad.

I said to my father, "Look, papa, I'm going to the United States again. I have to go again."

"No," he said. "Something else is going to happen to you. Don't go."

"I want to fulfill my dream," I told him. "I want to go there and I want to do it again. I want to go to school. I want to go back to do other things."

And you see that I came back again. I've been here barely a year, since I returned from Mexico, but in the end I feel happy. Sometimes I get angry because we don't . . . sometimes one wants to struggle for a better life and try to do some good things. They don't look at that and don't think about that. They think that you're an illegal and that you're committing a crime by coming to this country. But here I am again. Right now I'm going to school.

Right now I want to go to college. But sometimes I suffer because I don't have papers. There's no way to do it. It's not easy for me. It hasn't been easy. Sometimes I would like to have a car to get to school. Now I have to walk long distances to go to school. I have to work in places where you don't need papers even though they pay me less than the minimum wage because if I apply to a company, the first thing that they're going to say to me is, "Where are your papers?" And here I am again, back again. Sometimes I feel furious at myself and sometimes furious at others because it's not about being a terrorist. It's just about being a person who wants to get ahead. And who wants to show the rest of the world that one can give back more than one has. But lots of people don't think about that.

There's discrimination here in Portland, lots of discrimination at times. I've gotten used it with the amount of time that I have been here. I've gotten used to being here, not everything, but some aspects. I know many Latinos here.

I send money to my family depending on how much I have. When I have a little money and they need money, they call me and I try to save and send them money. Now I work in another restaurant Monday to Friday, Saturday and Sunday, too. I go to school on Tuesday and Thursday.

In the future I would like to be a normal person, free like an American citizen. Go to school and, for example, be a teacher, a lawyer, or a—what do I know?—but have a career. Sometimes I feel that I don't know how to get this all out. Telling this to another person is a way that I can get out all that I have stored up inside me. It helps the heart and soul.

Ana Manza and Eliseo Brea.

Born in the Dominican Republic, Ana, fifty-one, and Eliseo, forty-five, have lived in the United States for thirty-one and thirteen years, respectively, though they only arrived in Portland five years ago. They came largely to escape New York City and become part of the burgeoning Dominican population in Portland. After knowing each other since childhood in the Dominican Republic and living together for many years, they decided to marry in 2002. Though Ana is intentionally vague about the nature of her debilitating accident in 2001, it left her unable to work. Through their connections in the local Latino community, Eliseo has been successful at attaining gainful employment. They are devout Catholics who refer to their church as the United Nations because its congregants hail from many different Latin American countries. While they enjoy their lives in Portland, they hope one day to live again in the Dominican Republic. About a year after this interview, Ana and Eliseo purchased a home in Portland.

3

Ana Manza and Eliseo Brea

We're Very United, All the Latinos

Eliseo: We'll begin together.

Ana: Begin, my love.

Eliseo: My name, Eliseo.

Ana: I'm how old, fifty? Fifty-one. And my husband forty-five. I know what he is going to say.

Eliseo: Yes, I don't like younger women. I like them with more experience than me. I learn a lot from her.

Ana: We were born in the Dominican Republic. I've been in the United States for 31 years, and he's been here 13. We met in the Dominican Republic.

Eliseo: We've been in love a long time. Me after her, and she didn't want anything to do with me. She didn't love me. Until one day I won her. I don't like things easy.

Ana: So, he came over. I was here, he came and then we kept getting to know each other here. We met in Santo Domingo, but we continued the relationship; we got together in New York. And we got married.

Eliseo: We got married here in Portland, two or three years ago.

Ana: Just two short years ago. We were together before, but we weren't married. I didn't want to. I was really afraid, since he was younger than I, but when I saw how honest and good and gentle he was, then we decided to have a lifelong relationship.

Eliseo: I threw her the bait and she fell for it.

Ana: You know how sometimes someone can be scared, because he's younger. I'm five years older, but none of that matters to him. He respects me and loves me as if I were a young girl of eighteen, the respect that he has for me, and I have for him as well. We came to Portland because [of] my husband's cousin, Juan González, owner of the Bodega Latina.

Eliseo: He spoke very highly of this place here.

Ana: Of this state.

Eliseo: He said that here it was really peaceful, and that, since life was more difficult in New York, it's more dangerous. I like peace and quiet. And so, that's why we decided to come up here. It's gone well for us here, initially.

Ana: It was a bit difficult at first arriving from New York to Portland, but then we found an apartment and then we got jobs, but . . .

Eliseo: I started out, I was working in the Bodega Latina, with Juan, and I was the one in charge of the store.

Ana: It helps to be able to assimilate more easily here in Portland, to already have work. It helps to adapt a bit to the new place, to get adjusted a bit. Then, I got a job in something to do with lobster and with, what are they called, shrimp? shellfish, stuff like that, in South Portland. This was not with Juan's help, but with a friend who helped me get a job, but he died. He was Dominican.

Eliseo: Yes, there are plenty of Dominicans here in Portland. There are a lot of Dominicans who have companies. It's grown quite a bit. They've managed [companies]. There are a lot of people who know one another and have friends, and they help one another get jobs.

Ana: I was working there until 2001. Then I got sick and then I got a very debilitating illness, I caught asthma and then I had an accident with the Frosli which injured my whole body and since then I haven't been able to work and I've been disabled. Eliseo's still working. He works in a company . . .

Eliseo: First I worked in the Bodega Latina. Then I worked in a cleaning company about six months, and from there I went on to work at the company where she was working . . .

Ana: Where I was working. Then we were working together, and then he had a little difficulty, and they fired him from the job, and then afterwards Javier Valencia found him this job where he works now.

Eliseo: Javier from the church. Javier's my *compadre* [friend].

Ana: Yes, in 2001 he found him this job that he has now.

Eliseo: It's called Silver Company, in Westbrook. I'm in charge of a line of plating.

Ana: As I said, the only thing is that I lost my health. It's been very hard for me because in New York I was never ill. Then to arrive here and deal with so many chemicals and so much stuff, right away I got very, very sick. The climate bothers me because of the cold. Now that I have asthma, it bothers me quite a bit. When the snowstorm, the cold in January hit, I had something like an asthma attack. I had to go to the hospital two times. Now I'm quite debilitated. I take a lot of medications. I suffered a severe depression also. All of these things he's put up with together with me. He's had a lot of patience too.

Eliseo: With a happy face, but sadness on the other hand because . . .

Ana: Because I became ill. But our faith is so strong that we've never stopped going to church, and faith in God has always helped us to remain strong and always remain united and accomplish many things, and with justice we've accomplished it all.

There are a lot of connections here with Latinos helping one another. When Latinos arrive, right away they come to Sacred Heart, the Catholic Church, and immediately they ask for someone, and that person is ready to help them. We're very united, all the Latinos. I have a lot of friendships. It doesn't matter what country they're from; we all get along really well. We all share, Peruvians, Salvadorans, Spaniards, and the whole race. We call Sacred Heart Church the United Nations. We get along very well, and if there's some activity, some kind of meeting and if there's another religion, we share just the same. We don't have any difference about religion but just share the moment. They call me, when I'm ill . . . I have friends from another religion, when I was sick they were concerned, they called me, I mean, and it doesn't matter if they're not Catholic. We have a lot of communication with all religions.

Eliseo: The Bodega Latina is like a reference point, and a meeting place.

Ana: The Bodega Latina and the church are both reference places.

Eliseo: The church is the main place.

Ana: Not so much the Bodega but rather the church, because the church is where the whole race goes. Everyone meets at the church. There, after mass we have coffee and cake, where people share with other people, dialogue with people, and get to know one another. And so the connections get extended to all the people. We've been here five years; we'll have been here five years on April 14 and we like it pretty well. The only sad thing is that I got sick. We feel at home here. The people are really nice. The neighbors are very nice. The landlord has been very good to us, he's been very supportive, and he's given us a lot of opportunities. When only my husband was working, since we always keep his house neat and clean, we take care of the house as if it were our own, he gave us the chance for two years of not even raising the rent . . . because I wasn't working . . . He has a lot of respect for us, and we have good neighbors who we get along with pretty well.

Eliseo: The landlord is American.

Ana: It's a bit difficult to maintain the language, for the family, see, but always, they're always Latino. Whether they're from Puerto Rico or wherever, there's always their language. I say they always maintain their roots. They always speak to them in their language.

Eliseo: Other ways to maintain their roots are through food, living close together, fiestas, and Christmas. Those sorts of things help to keep . . . There are always ways of sharing, of, how do you say, of keeping the tradition. Go ahead, love. I let her talk, because she does it so well.

Ana: We have a daughter here. We also have other family here. I have my sister. My sister lives here and she has two sons. And the sons work and she does too. Right here in Portland. She came afterwards because of us. She talked to me, she talked to us, and my husband told her what the environment was like here for her sons, what it was like for young people being here, that it's a really good environment. So she came and got an apartment, and she works and both her sons work too. They've been here in Portland about three years now. They've been here two and a half, because in July they'll have been here four. I don't know if the sons went to school here. I think they're in high school or they finished, but, anyway, they're working. You know how when a boy . . . one is seventeen and he works and the other is twenty or nineteen and he works . . .

Eliseo: They're becoming independent.

Ana: They don't have their own apartment. They live with their mother. They work, but they live together with their mother.

Eliseo: It happens that way a lot, that someone comes and then other members of the family come. It's growing, yes, because someone starts talking to someone about how things are here, how to get along living here, and so because of that person then it starts growing and people start coming here.

Ana: The Latino community is growing quite a bit every day. When we came here in '99, in church we were 10 or 15 people. Now 110, 90, 200 people come, and if we do a celebration like the fiesta of Guadalupe, 250 people come. . . . A lot of Latinos have come here.

Eliseo: She has experience with this.

Ana: And also when the church started, when I was here, before [only a] few people came, and now all the people . . . come, all classes and races of people. Now you bring two cakes, and it's not enough. Before, with a package of donuts you had enough to share and that was it, but not anymore, now it's grown quite a bit. Yes, it's growing quite a bit. I'm a citizen, and my husband is a resident. He's going to be a citizen soon, God willing.

Eliseo: It's a rather difficult process for me.

Ana: Yes, it's hard for someone who doesn't know English. Because you have to pass a test, but the hardest thing is getting here, getting your residency and getting to the United States. Once you're here, if you really want the thing, it's easy, because they make it easy. The only thing is it's important to always keep everything in order and take care of yourself and behave well. There are a lot of opportunities here. We didn't have any problems when we came to the United States, because when I came here, my father was the one who brought me. He asked for me and he brought me as a resident and then, about ten years ago I became a citizen. I was fourteen when I arrived. I had finished school in Santo Domingo. He studied too. He went to the university.

Eliseo: I did high school in '78, '79, and then I did university schooling in '80, '81, and that was when I thought of coming here. So I left my studies and came here.

Ana: I didn't have the chance to go to the university, because we were fifteen brothers and sisters in my family, and so we were born out in the country where you had to go to town to finish the fourth year of school. So there was no possibility for us to be able to go to the university, because there were so many of us that, financially, it couldn't be done, but I did finish high school. But I came here and started working. Because I came here young, I didn't have a chance to do anything. I had to work continuously to be able to help my father. My father was already rather old then, and my mother didn't work, so I had to work to help my father pay the rent. So all of my life here in the United States I've worked, about twenty-eight years or so, until I got sick here, which was the first time I got sick. And now I can't manage working anymore and I won't go to work anymore either. With our free time when he gets home from work, I wait for him and we go to the mall.

Eliseo: To walk, to get exercise.

Ana: Because my back hurts a lot and stuff, and he always hunts for ways for me to feel good, for me to not get bored.

Eliseo: Then on Sundays . . .

Ana: On Sundays we go to church from 11:00 in the morning to 2:00 in the afternoon. Really, we're quiet types, and we've gotten accustomed to the environment here.

Eliseo: . . . to the peace and quiet. We like the tranquility quite a bit.

Ana: Last year we were in Santo Domingo because my mother died.

Eliseo: First we went just for a visit . . .

Ana: We were there for a visit and then we went back again because my mother got sick and died. So now after one year, we'll go back again, after one year, because it's a tradition among all Dominicans when a person dies, on the one-year anniversary, the whole family has to get together . . . It's like . . .

Eliseo: The end of a year.

Ana: As if it were the first day of her wake, when our whole family gets together. All the kids, all our husbands and wives, and we all get together, and there are almost two or three hundred of us.

Eliseo: We're planning to go this year, now.

Ana: There are many people because we have lots of friends, and our whole family gets together. Just imagine my father had at least, like, forty children. He had fifteen with my mother, that was, in marriage, and always since he was an able-bodied man from the countryside. He had seven kids with one woman as if it were nothing. Five, six, seven children. Can you imagine? I think that he had at least forty with one. Of course, it bothered my mother, but since she was the wife, she wasn't ever going to abandon her house or her things. Since it was the tradition of the family, and respect, you know, the wife was the wife. Of course, even though it bothered her. She was married to him, and she wasn't going to abandon her home, her kids for anything, you see. But it was hard for her, you know, for her and for us too. It bothered all of us quite a bit because we were the children of the house. But my father is ninety-five years old.

My father hasn't come to Portland but to New York. He was the one who brought me. He asked for me. He brought me as a resident, me and my mother together at that time. First my oldest brother came, and then my brother asked for my father. Then my father asked for me and my mother. Then, afterwards, Mom and I and Dad asked for three siblings, little by little. In that way we made a, how do you say, a moving stairway until everyone arrived and was here in the United States. Everyone worked, and many have gone into retirement already or others have gone back to the Dominican Republic to live quietly there. But everyone arrived here to the United States. And they've lasted fifteen, twenty years.

Eliseo: And they're exemplary.

Ana: Yes, everyone found work out there. I mean, life in New York is really hard; it's really hard because it's a world where corruption is bad. There are lots of bad things, lots of drugs, lots of everything. And we, all of my siblings and I, thank God, got here and worked and struggled honorably. They got ahead honorably, thank God. And we did too, we were fine until I got sick. We lived very well.

The hardest part has been me getting sick and it continues to be the hardest thing. Sometimes I have to get help, a counselor, to be able to accept all that's hap-

pened to me because [it is] such a quiet life. . . I used to do a lot of things with my husband. Now if I dance, I can't dance, because my legs hurt, my body hurts. It's all been a complete change in lifestyle, after that accident happened to me.

The biggest challenge here for the Latino community is not being able to speak English. It's the biggest problem, because when someone gets to a place and isn't understood, he feels so strained, he tries so hard and thinks that people are discriminating against him. When the person doesn't understand, they think that the person is stupid, and it's not that he doesn't understand. From my country and from all the other countries there are professionals who . . . it doesn't mean that these people are illiterate. They're people who've gone to school, but they don't speak the language. Many Americans, a lot of people misjudge them, because they think they're illiterate, and that's not how it is.

Eliseo: I don't think there's a lot of racism, a lot of discrimination against Latinos here in Portland, but there's a bit.

Ana: A bit. Because a lot of people say so, that there's a bit, yes. We find this in jobs quite a bit. At work it's very difficult.

Eliseo: It's at work that you see racism the most.

Ana: And especially when the person doesn't speak the language and doesn't understand how to say . . . My husband is the example. He knows his job perfectly, but he doesn't speak the language well and it's very hard to communicate, you know, but he knows his work, they gave him his line, he's in charge and everything, but if he needs to explain, he'd like to do it himself and not have to find an interpreter, you know. And that makes it hard for him. That's the hardest thing.

Eliseo: This aspect of life is very different from in New York. In New York we're all Latinos. In New York there are Latino grocery stores, Latino offices, Latino banks, we're all Latinos there. The majority of people are Latino. In New York it's almost 90 percent Latino, in the area we live in, where we used to live.

Ana: The best part of living here in Portland for me was when we started working and every path opened up for us and we were getting ahead, and our hope when we started to work was to buy a house. When I got sick, all of that fell apart. But we had a dream. When we had been working a year or two, our plan was to buy our house, but that couldn't be done. But we also felt very hopeful when at the end of all my illness I triumphed in something I wanted. We accomplished what we wanted, and that was a triumph over my illness and my pain. But we succeeded, because God in his mercy, and also the law.

Eliseo: Of course, there are other Latinos who also face discrimination here. There are three of us who don't speak English. It's not that we feel so discriminated against, you see, but if you think, because they don't understand you, and so at times you want to express what you're feeling, and when you bring in someone to serve as a translator, they don't say exactly what you want them to say. And you can't express yourself.

Ana: What pains them the most is that they want to express what they want, and with the person that serves as their translator, it's not reliable talking to them, because they don't trust the person, because he might say something else that isn't what they feel they're saying.

When immigration [U.S. Border Patrol] came to Portland, it affected all of us because we're all immigrants. We come from immigrant families, and what happens to one immigrant happens to all of us.

Eliseo: And we all felt it.

Ana: Sorry, my love.

Eliseo: It's fine. No, don't feel bad, my love. . . . Go on talking.

Ana: Yes, it was a hard time and they took a lot of people. And we all suffered a lot. But they say they're doing their job, but . . .

Eliseo: The Latino Committee [Centro Latino Maine] is working a bit to see if they can stop the reprisals against undocumented people. I mean, if they can stop pursuing them so much, because we're, we're people who are just coming here to earn our daily bread.

Ana: They leave family behind to come work hard here. The Latino Committee is a formal group. When I got sick, I felt that I couldn't continue working with them, but they have a really nice group. It's developing. It already has its name; it's already been approved by lawyers and all of that. It's all Latinos, the president and the vice president and all are all Latinos, but there are American people who speak Spanish or Americans and they come around, but they belong to the Committee. They're getting together, I know, on Tuesdays. The group is trying to build a building. We aren't very involved in the business of LULAC [League of United Latin American Citizens] or anything. Because the people who belong to the Latino Committe are from the church.

Eliseo: Some Latino people play soccer here in Portland.

Ana: Some people play, but since our sphere is so small, from the church to our house, because of my illness . . .

Eliseo: Yes, we watch our games. For example, when it's baseball season, which is our favorite sport, then we watch our games on television, but no, we don't have a formal team. At one time we thought of forming a team—a softball team, which amounts to almost the same thing, but with a little bit bigger ball. But I don't know what happened. The guys who were going to put together the teams never called me. I think they were afraid I would be too good!

Ana: Homeruns like [Sammy] Sosa. Of course, there are a lot of men here in Portland, enough Latinos to form a baseball team.

Eliseo: And we also go to the [Portland] Sea Dogs. I go to see the baseball games sometimes. There are Latinos, Dominicans who also play here for the Sea Dogs team. [They] are in the minor leagues to train, to get to the major leagues. We know the Dominican players from the Sea Dogs. When they arrive here and learn that you're Dominican they seek you out, and that's how we know them. Several of them gave me balls, pictures . . .

Ana: When he was working in the Bodega Latina he had a lot of contact with them, because that's the place they went to buy things and all of that. They stay in their own places in Portland with the team.

Eliseo: For example, that guy [in the photograph] is a friend of mine and is a player in the major leagues now. Pedro Almonte. He's a pitcher for the Boston Red Sox.

Ana: He played here, and he got along really well with my husband.

Eliseo: He was here two, three years ago, around 2001, around then. Now he's in the major leagues. Now he's playing with the Marlins. And that ball was given to me by one of those players from the Sea Dogs. And he signed it. And the manager of the Sea Dogs, who's Cuban, gave me this one.

Ana: This is our thing, because we have baseball in our blood. We love baseball a lot. From when they're small they always introduced the whole family to baseball and that's what we play the most.

Eliseo: I played baseball, but I didn't get anywhere. My Dad didn't let me play. I was a student then. I studied, so they didn't want me to give up my studies.

Ana: He was from the city.

Eliseo: Yes, I'm from Santo Domingo, the capital. And so one's parents always thought that if someone started playing baseball then they'd abandon their studies, and then everything would go to waste. However, look at it now. Being a ball player is a very good profession. No one knows if I could have made it. I was a pitcher. If I were like Pedro [Martinez], it would be great. Who wouldn't want to be like that?

Ana: Pedro's very famous.

Eliseo: They're exemplary.

Ana: He's very good to our country. He helps his country quite a bit.

Eliseo: They have foundations there, foundations that help . . . for example, Alex Rodriguez. They paid him 262 million and . . .

Ana: He's the best-paid baseball player and he has his foundations. He has his own foundation and he's helped; he's donated a lot of computers and stuff.

Eliseo: Sammy Sosa put up something like a mall and has helped the people by giving them jobs, so they can work.

Ana: As I said, Sosa was a simple man, a shoemaker; however, now he's a millionaire. Yes, baseball is the Dominicans' favorite sport, and where there are opportunities for a Dominican to make money . . .

Eliseo: There's no team in the major leagues that doesn't have a Dominican. All the teams have them, even if it's only one Dominican player. It's very unusual to find a team that doesn't have a Latino, especially a Dominican.

Ana: All the juice goes there, into baseball.

Eliseo: When September 11th happened . . . in jobs it hit too hard. And it was very hard because people that we knew worked there. People from our neighborhood that we knew, that were there and died, and also my niece's husband worked there. He worked at night and all his friends called him to work during the day, and the only one who was saved was him, because he didn't go to work during the day. It was a very painful blow. It affected all of us. Worldwide, it affected everyone. We all suffered a lot. [It was] a very difficult time.

Ana: It was a very, very difficult time.

Eliseo: And afterwards when the airplane crashed, there were lots of Dominicans on it.[1] Many friends of mine died. One who lived behind my house, from Santo Domingo, on the other street from where I lived, in the same barrio. We grew up together.

Ana: So many Dominicans died on that plane when it crashed, two hundred and some, and people we knew were traveling on it, who were from our neighborhood, and friends of his.

Eliseo: I don't think there was more discrimination towards Latinos after September 11th.

Ana: *What's most necessary we buy at the bodega, but not always. We go when we need some product from our country like he [Juan González] has. They sell yuca every place now. The Chinese sell yuca. All the places sell all the Latino products now. All the Chinese sell all the same products as Juan. But now that he put in that new bodega . . . Did you see the new bodega? He's already moved it.*

Eliseo: It's on the corner now.

Ana: It's beautiful.

Eliseo: Very nice. And he's planning to put in a restaurant, a little restaurant, probably in the not too distant future. What we call a *fritura*.

Ana: But it's going to be a "fritura" restaurant because he's going to put in tables, I think, and a Dominican woman is coming from Lawrence [Massachusetts] who's going to cook the food, and his business is going to be good. He's gone a couple of months without doing it because he has to renew his things now, but that's his plan. We've never been to Tu Casa, the Salvadoran restaurant that's on Washington [Avenue] because as you know, since the custom of our country about food . . .

Eliseo: If the food is different than [what] one eats from other countries, one always limits oneself most to one's own food, the way one likes it best.

Ana: But they say that a lot of Latinos go there. What's the tortilla called?

Eliseo: The pupusa.

Ana: The pupusa, exactly. A lot of Latinos go there and say the cooking . . . is really good. They make pupusas that are great . . . and roast beef, and I know them, yes, but we never go to the restaurant.

Eliseo: We almost always prepare Dominican food, and sometimes we go to eat Chinese, at the Chinese buffet. They have good food, too.

Ana: We go pretty often on Saturdays. He likes their food. Since my back is so weak and since he's free on Sunday we prepare food for the week. We prepare it together; he helps me. He washes, he does all that stuff, because here it's very hard for me since I can't handle chemicals or anything. He takes care of all these things.

Eliseo: There's no machismo here, okay? It's not just men who wear the pants. Of course, it's the way it should be. In our countries, we're always very machista, but when you get here to the United States you have to forget about that, because here the first one to arrive is the one who has to cook or wash or always help the spouse.

Ana: In our countries the wife almost never works, she always devotes herself to her house and her children. So, the man who's well off, the man is the only one who works, and has to be attended to, you know. And so the wife takes care of everything and when the husband arrives home, everything is already done, all the food is prepared, but not here. Here the couples always work, both of them. Of course, this part of the culture is changing a bit. Because now the tradition is so socialized there that the wife works as if she were a man there. There it's the same, but sometimes when there are three or four kids they can't do that because the family's too big. There in our country you experience machismo more, of course.

Eliseo: They say that the man is the one who wears the pants. I'm the man of the house because I wear the pants. But I'm not it today. No, I'll never ever wear a skirt! I'll always wear pants. No, now women wear pants, too. Of course, it's fine that way. Our thought is to someday return to our country. First you make the base here, the future here, and then go to wherever one is best off. Right now life is very expensive in Santo Domingo and possibly we'll stay and live here in the United States.

Ana: We also maybe have plans that if my health continues this way, since I'm so ill, maybe to find a state like, perhaps, Florida, Atlanta, where one can . . . where the environment is better.

Eliseo: Where it's not as cold, a warm climate.

Ana: The change of climate, you see, because the colder it gets here, the worse I feel. And I know that the cold's never going to change. I'm very afraid of the cold, very afraid because I know that every time it gets cold my health always gets very fragile, very bad. So this is our plan, God willing.

Eliseo: I like it quite well here in Portland.

Ana: We like it, if we didn't have this problem of my illness, the problem that in the future I might get sicker and sicker and sicker because of the cold. For that reason we might have to move to another state, otherwise we'd stay here forever because everyone treats us well. We've faced a lot of hard times, quite a lot, but not everything has been difficult in life. It's improved here in Portland. I know that several years ago we went to a meeting and the first thing they talked about was that César Chávez, that he was someone, very . . . He's Mexican, right? Yes, Mexican, exactly. That he was like an example, no? And they wanted to put up like a . . . Something like that, I don't know, like, someone very important to Mexicans, César Chávez. I heard that several years ago. But since we don't know much about the things of Mexico or anything like that because we don't have much communication to talk about these things. . .

Eliseo: He's a hero for the Mexicans.

Ana: Yes, like Juan Pablo Duarte is for us.[2]

Eliseo: The father of our country, because Duarte, Sancho, and Mella were fathers.

Ana: In our history this is very . . .

Eliseo: He freed us from slavery.

Ana: Yes, he is a hero of independence for the Dominicans.

Eliseo: Independence from Spain.

Ana: It was in 1492, when Columbus . . . and independence is the 27th of February.

Eliseo: No, independence was in 1844—February 27, 1844. And Columbus discovered America in 1492.

Ana: We feel good about our country's history with the United States because they have always supported us. And when there's any problem, they're always there . . .

Eliseo: They're the first to put in their grain of sand . . .

Ana: To establish peace, so there won't be war, so that there won't be problems in one's country.

Eliseo: They help quite a bit.

Ana: Quite a bit. That's why the Dominican Republic remains so stable. You don't see that it's like Haiti, or like other countries, but always stable because the

United States gives it lots of opportunities for a lot of people. For professionals, too, they come here, work a lot, and a lot of opportunities are given to everyone. So, thank God, there are good relations between the two.

Eliseo: Thank you at least for sharing a moment here in our house. We're always at your service.

Ana: We're at your service. And we've been talking honestly about who we are, and all the experiences we've had, the ups and the downs.

Notes

1. On November 12, 2001, an American Airlines flight leaving New York City destined for Santo Domingo crashed, killing the 260 people on board and five people on the ground.
2. Juan Pablo Duarte (1813–1876) was a leader of Dominican independence from Haiti (not Spain) in 1844. Along with Francisco de Rosario Sánchez and Ramón Matías Mella (1816–1864), he formed *La Trinidad* (The Trinity), a secret society with the purpose of overthrowing Haitian dictator Jean-Pierre Boyer (1776–1850).

On a vacation from her native Mexico when she was twenty-seven, Laura Ochoa vsited Newburyport, Massachusetts, "and I just loved New England." It was there that she met her future husband and began what would be a transformative journey. From a poor family with six children, raised in the suburbs of Mexico City, by parents who did not teach her the richness of her own indigenous heritage, she discovered her Aztec roots on her own and now feels "really connected" to this side of her family's ancestors and their rituals. Yet she also witnessed the discrimination indigenous people face when they go to Mexico City from the rural towns. In this country, in her bicultural marriage, she not only struggled with learning English and a very long and frustrating immigration process, but also domestic violence, such that she and her young daughter sought refuge in a shelter. She eventually found a welcoming community where she now feels very much at home. Laura Ochoa has a warm, engaging, and grateful spirit, as she now carries out her life as a single mother and student leader with much hope for the future.

Laura Ochoa, and her daughter Diana in their home.

4

Laura Ochoa

Swimming in a Different Ocean

My name is Laura Ochoa, and I'm thirty-eight years old. I was born in Mexico City. I have a lot of memories from early in my life. I come from a big family. We are six children, my dad and my mom, living in the suburbs of Mexico City. We were raised in a poor family. My dad was a worker. My mom was at home taking care of us six children.

I grew up in the typical Mexican family where the dad had to go out and bring [home] the money and my mom had to stay at home, cooking, cleaning, taking care of the house in general. We have a lot of traditions and celebrated the Mexican holidays, of course. Independence Day is a big, big celebration in Mexico, which is September 15th. But personally, for me, I like more the Day of the Dead. Even though I'm not totally indigenous, I feel more indigenous in my heart than Spaniard. So I feel really connected with the Aztecs, who are my ancestors, and their rituals. I love the ceremonies and rituals that they did, because they are so rich.

My favorite state in Mexico is Oaxaca. It's a very poor state, but it's so rich in history, in food, in art, and they celebrate that Day of the Dead with a big, *big* party. They cook food, *mole*—which is the sauce—and chicken, and a lot of typical food from Oaxaca. They bring flowers and incense. They use this flower that looks like the marigold but it's so aromatic. It's bright orange. It smells good. Still, I can smell it now! [Laughs]

And they celebrate dead people. They believe that they come from heaven or maybe somewhere else to celebrate with us. [Laughs] Sometimes people go to the cemeteries, which is kind of bizarre for some people, and bring the food and alcoholic beverages; they use crepe as a tablecloth and they eat. And, of course, they bring music, *mariachis*. It is kind of interesting, and it is fun because historically the indigenous people didn't cry. That comes from the Spaniards. So there's a celebration about death because it's another step or stage of humanity.

Well, to be honest, I think that my parents didn't accept their roots, being indigenous. A lot of people don't realize, to be called indigenous, or *indios*—like we say—is a derogatory word. So it is not acceptable. However, when I started to study, I had the luck to get more education in Mexico and more here. And eventually I will get my bachelor's degree. When I learned more about my own culture and the richness that it has, I kind of liked it—I love it. And I feel proud to be indigenous, even though I'm not 100 percent. But in my heart I am! My father looks more indigenous. My mother is kind of more white, but neither of them taught me the richness of that. In Mexico City when we see somebody coming from rural towns they are discriminated [against]. They are indigenous and we look at them like they're weak. But we don't realize we come from them! We don't realize that they are rich in their blood. They are carrying strong blood, I call it. [Laughs]

How I came to this country is a very long story. I was working in Mexico as a private nurse, working very hard, twelve, sometimes twenty-four hours a day, because I wanted to be self-sufficient, and I was. I rented my own place, which was not okay for my family, it didn't look good. You have to be married, because that's the typical Mexican woman that they have to be. [Whispers] But I didn't do it. [Laughs] So I got my apartment and I worked hard. I wanted to pay my bills, to eat, and have freedom, so I had to work hard.

But also I wanted to travel. I always loved traveling. Because I didn't have a lot of money, of course, I couldn't travel to anywhere but the Republic of

Mexico. But, when I was twenty-seven years old, I came to Newburyport, Massachusetts, for vacation, for one month. I visited friends there, so I didn't have to pay a hotel. And I just loved New England. I still love it.

At that point, I met my now my ex-husband. He was working in a restaurant where I went to have dinner. I saw him, he's very cute, so charming. So we went out for a couple of months and then suddenly we moved together. That was too fast, probably. But my immigration status was as a tourist. So I had to go to Immigration and ask for an extension of another three months to stay here. So I did. In total I was allowed to be here six months. During that time I got pregnant and he asked me to marry him. It was really fast, I have to admit it. However, I was thinking, "What am I going to do with this baby?" I was twenty-eight years old, I just didn't know what to do. I was thinking, "Okay, probably this is a good thing."

But, he is an American, and I was—honestly—just here for vacation and I wanted to go back to my job as a nurse and be in my own country. I didn't plan the pregnancy and all that stuff. He asked me to marry him, and I accepted, but I was thinking that he was not the right person for me. But I wanted a dad for my daughter. I was thinking, "Okay, probably this is good. Probably this is not good. We'll see." I traveled back to Mexico, and we got married there. My daughter, she's now eight years old, was born in Mexico City. He met my family, and I was happy during the pregnancy.

But after we were in Mexico, he started to show signs of controlling my behaviors. He was so slow in this that I just didn't realize, or probably I tried to shove that down and say, "Okay, everything is fine. Everything is fine."

He was saying, "I am here in this country, this crazy city . . ."—Mexico City, and of course it's crazy! [Laughs] It has twenty-eight million people there. I agreed it's crazy. But I think that he was using that excuse. He was telling me what to do, how to cook, what to eat, how to clean, how to take care of Diana—everything! Of course, very soft, Okay?

He would say, "No, you shouldn't do that . . . Why don't you just . . .? " Like, you know, manipulating. I didn't realize because he was so nice. We had great moments. So this was just nothing. And, at that point, I probably just lived with that without any problem. The problems started when Diana was born in Mexico. Then he just started to be more controlling and yelling. Yelling, and yelling, almost every day.

He would apologize to me, "I'm sorry . . . I'm not going to do that again. What happens is that I don't have any family here. You have to understand I am alone and it's so hard to—I don't speak the language. And I don't have anybody, and the food is terrible, and everything is terrible. You have to understand me."

And I would say, "Okay. Yes."

"But you know that I love you."

"Yes, I know that."

It was like every time I go to talk about this violence, and talk about my experience, I tell everybody that I felt like I was trapped in a circle, a motion circle, because it was moving constantly. On one hand he was telling me, "I love you. You have to understand . . ." But then—switch—and he was yelling at me, "You don't know how to do it! You have to be more careful with the baby!" That circle was in constant motion. It didn't let me get out of there.

So, he was very abusive. In fact, one day I was moving my stuff, and I have this organ, this beautiful organ that I worked hard to buy. And he was—my parents were there—he was yelling at me in front of my parents, and it was so embarrassing for me. My dad said, "Are you Okay?"

I said, "Yeah. Nothing is . . ." I think that I was kind of rude and said "It's not your business" or something like that. "I'm strong. I'm fine. This is my life."

He said, "Okay." My father was a controlling man, a very typical macho man, but he would never yell at us. He was very protective, and my mom too. So, I didn't see that. But I was in that with Matthew.

One day was the worst thing that made me leave. I used to write in Mexico, because I had my freedom, my apartment. I love writing and it took me like six months to write that story, and Matthew was mad at me because I was talking on the phone with a friend of mine. He was jealous about everybody! He didn't want me to go to see my mom. But he didn't want to come with me! [Laughs] I have friends, of course—guys, males—and I was on the phone talking to them in Spanish. So he was saying that I was flirting with them, because I was laughing. I am usually a happy person and I love jokes and everything, but he didn't like that because he thought that he was my lover, and he was saying, "I know that"—Can I use bad words? [Laughs] He was saying, "Just because you want to go and sleep with him . . ." And all that sort of stuff.

I said, "Come on! Stop it! I just had a baby and they are my friends!"

"No, I don't believe it!" And he took the phone and hung it up.

And I said, "Okay, that's it. I'm leaving."

"Yes, you're leaving. But you are leaving without Diana." And so, he took Diana. He locked her in the room. At that point he was mad and I could see fire in his eyes.

I was afraid for my baby, and I said, "Give me Diana, because I'm leaving!" I don't know how I did that. I pushed so hard on the door. He put a bed against it! But I just wanted my baby. I said, "Give me my baby!"

So he gave her to me, and I went to my mom's. I think that I just took a couple of things with me, like Diana's medicine and diapers. I ran really fast. First, I wanted to call the police, and he just pulled the phone from the wall and I was scared. I went to my mom, and told her what happened and I said, "Can I stay here?" I was thinking, "I don't have anything. I have a baby. I don't have a job. I don't have money. What am I going to do?"

So my mom said, "Well, we're going to support you. You can stay here. You can get a job, and I'll help you in taking care of Diana." My mom is such a wonderful woman. She has her moments, of course, and I tell her that. But I love her. She's kind of like a role model for me. She also had the guts to leave my dad when he became very abusive to her. So it's like a chain, you know, which is not good, and I'm trying to break that circle of violence.

But then I realized that I was home and I didn't have clothes or nothing, so I came back to the apartment. And Matthew was not there, but I just realized that my story was ripped up. It was in the trash. I don't know if he knew that, but it was so important for me. And I just couldn't put it together, and of course, I didn't have a computer in Mexico to save it or anything. I didn't have a copy of that, so he destroyed what I worked so hard for. He just put it in the trash. So I was very, very sad at that point. I went home, and he called me so many times. He was sorry and . . . [Sniffles] I'm sorry, but it has been many years and still when I think about it, I get emotional.

But he called me, and told me, "Come back. Come back. I love you."

And at that point I was figuring out what to do. I had a daughter, and I did not have money. My mom also, she's a janitor, and she didn't have a lot of money. She works so hard for herself and now it's me and my baby!

So Matthew told me, "I'll be fine after I come to New Hampshire. I promise, I'll be fine."

And I believed him. [Laughs sadly] I don't know if that was a good thing or not. We came to live in New Hampshire, and at that point he was telling me, "I'm going to help you to get your permanent residency," because again, I was traveling with a tourist visa.

Diana was an American and a Mexican too, because of him, but I was just on the limb. He was giving me excuses every time I asked him, "We have to get my papers, because after my visa expires I'm going to be in trouble."

He said, "Oh, well, I don't have time. I don't know how to do that process."

I was the one who was trying to do something. Well, actually I didn't know because I didn't have money at home. We didn't have a telephone. We came to New Hampshire, and he was working, and the first two weeks he was fine. After that he became very abusive again and probably it was worse, it escalated more. He was yelling at me in my face and I was here and he was punching walls beside me. He was destroying my things, my pictures, and throwing things at me. It was pretty bad. He didn't bring any food home. We had cereal, crackers, cookies, sometimes milk. That was the food. He was working in a restaurant and he ate in the restaurant. So it was his way of punishing me.

I decided not to eat. "You are just giving me crackers, I'm not eating anything." So I just didn't eat. But my daughter was there; I was breastfeeding, of course. And I think that she was the one who made me have more strength and stay alive, probably. [Laughs]

One day we went to the pediatrician's office for her shots and I saw something about domestic violence and I read it and I said, "Wow. I think that I am in that position." I took it, with fear that Matthew would see me, and hid it in my clothes. I was shaking!

But I always was like that. He'd say, "What's the matter?"

"Oh, nothing. I'm fine."

"Oh, you are so crazy—like always!" I think that he said something like that—really mean. And I just didn't answer anything. When he went to work, I read it, and I was thinking so many questions. At that point I think I was illegal because my visa had already expired. I had been there almost two months. So I was very, very worried. First, because he constantly would tell me, "If you don't do what I say, I'm going to move your ass back to Mexico, and I'm going to keep my daughter."

That was the biggest fear that I felt, because I wanted my daughter. I love her more than anything, and I wanted her with me. So I did everything that he wanted. Turn down the TV! Don't watch it! Just like a robot. And even with that he was never happy. So I was questioning, "If I call this place, what is going to happen with me? And if he calls Immigration, I'm going to be deported and lose my baby!"

But I was so depressed. And angry. I was just thinking, "If I stay here, I'm just going to die or I don't know what. So I better get out of here and see what's happening."

So I called the domestic abuse line. I remember it was winter, snowing. I didn't have a phone in the apartment. So I took Diana, wrapped with a lot of blankets, and went to the public telephone and called.

They said, "What can we do for you?"

I said, "I need you to help me." At that point I think I just started to scream, "I need your help! I can't take this anymore!" I was just very desperate.

So they said, "What do you want to do?"

I said, "I want to leave. Please take me away from this because he's going to take my daughter away. He said that."

They gave me a plan. I had to take everything, all the important documents and baby's toys and everything. And I packed everything. I went to the police station and waited for them there. That was—oh—that was hard! I think that was the hardest thing that I have ever done. But I did it and I feel proud about that.

They called me, actually. "We wanted to tell you there's no room for you in the Portsmouth shelter. But we were thinking to take you to Sanford, Maine."

I said, "Where's that?" I didn't know where Maine was.

"Is that okay with you?" they said.

I said, "Listen, I really don't know where that's at. But take me anywhere. It's going to be better than here." So they did. I went to that shelter in Sanford.

They told me all the rules that I had to know. They provide me with food, diapers, everything that we needed, they gave me. They showed me the refrigerator, and they said, "Here you have the food. Here you have your drinks and everything."

And [laughs] I said, "But I don't have any money to pay for that." And I started to cry.

They said, "You don't have to pay for this. It's all free." And then I cried more and more!

I stayed in the shelter for one month. It was a very, very tough month for me because I was just allowed to be there for one month. I got a protection order. You have to deal with the court, which was very scary for me. But I got custody of my daughter. Matthew could visit her. I had to be in court many, many times because he came and abused me verbally. One day he tried to kidnap my daughter. Many times we had to modify that.

The immigration issue was another thing and was the longest, longest, tedious, painful thing. It took five years to get my permanent residency. Meanwhile I was poor. I had to go visit the pantry kitchens and my lawyer. Finally after knocking on so many doors, one day I had to go to Boston with the baby and wait there for three hours to see the lawyer and explain my case. She said, "I'm sorry but we can't help you here. You have to go to Maine."

Oh! [Gasps] So I came back, very, very depressed. Then a lawyer gave me the number of Peter Darwin, an immigration attorney, and I went to visit him. At this point I didn't have a car, right. I didn't have money. I was getting food stamps and benefits, but just for my daughter; for me, nothing, because I was not an American citizen and I didn't have a residency card. I'm illegal.

I went to see Peter, who told me, "Yes, I'm going to help you, but it's going to take a while because your case is pretty hard. But I think that we have a pretty good chance to get it." So he gave me a list that I had to get: proof of domestic violence, letters from witnesses who saw the domestic violence, everything, translate everything. It was like putting a puzzle together, but with one thousand pieces, every piece. I didn't even have the pieces. I had to get them from somewhere, and put them together. It was just unbelievable.

But then with the terrorist attack [September 11, 2001], things were slower and slower . . . [Laughs] So after five years, finally I got my permanent residency. At that point, I was free. I got my Social Security number, got my license, I could work. So that was pretty important for me. That's a summary of how I got here.

Eventually, somebody told me, "You should go to Adult Ed, and learn more English." So I did. I would take high school [classes], which was for me good so I could learn more. And then my teacher told me, "Wouldn't you like to go to college?"

I said, "No! I can't do that! I'm stupid!" Because my ex-husband always told me, "You are stupid." "No, I can't do that," I said. "That's for smart people and I'm not."

So she said, "Stop that. You have good grades!"

"But I don't have money."

"You can get financial aid, you can get scholarships, I think that you'll do fine."

I just didn't believe it. But I filled out applications and wrote my essay and sent it. But I was thinking, "Nah, that's not for me."

But the good thing is that I got the letter, and they said you've been accepted to the university. I said, "Wow!" The first class that I took was free, because I got a scholarship. I was scared. [Laughs] I was very scared! "How will I be in college with all these white people?" I mean, in Adult Ed it was ESL [English as a Second Language], there were a bunch of people from other countries, from Cambodia, Hispanic, and so. But college, with all the white people, was intimidating!

I said to my teacher, "I can't do it! I think that I'm not going to go."

"You have to go," she said, "Because you'll do fine."

"But sometimes I cannot pronounce well. I don't understand . . ."

"Just go!"

And I did. [Laughs] So the first class, I was just sitting there all nervous, and yes, I saw a bunch of white people. [Laughs] I had this nice teacher, and the first class we talked about cultural differences and all that stuff. And I was thinking, "This is not bad." I was very happy. I just took more and more classes until now. And here I am. I am going to get my bachelor's degree in nursing, hopefully in two years.

I've gotten some very good support, mostly my teachers, and also I had to see a counselor, for two years, because I had very, very low self esteem. So a lot of people helped me out. Of course, Caring Unlimited, the domestic abuse agency, they are the place where I got more support. Now I have this very good scholarship from the Social Lady Foundation, which is mainly for women who have been victims of domestic violence. So they pay all my education, because I couldn't afford it. I am very happy because I have a lot of support. I still have too much to do.

I don't know [about discrimination]. I honestly haven't noticed that. Probably because I'm a nice person [Laughs], and everybody loves me! [Laughs] Of course, I have differences, but this is part of the Latino-Hispanic Student Association. I'm the president, and I'm working with a lot of guys who are Latinos, too. I'm in the position sometimes—which is kind of hard, because I'm Mexican and not in my country—of being a leader in this country and dealing with the guys from my old culture who have a lot of the typical Latino values. It's kind of hard. So not discrimination, but more than that is trying to balance and understand and be a good leader. Sometimes I get really frustrated and say, "No, okay, you shut up!" [Laughs] "I'm not taking that!"

I think the right word [for what I've gone through] is transformation. I was very trapped, and now I'm just like a butterfly. I'm flying. In fact, I have my daughter who is doing excellent. She's a beautiful little girl who is just so happy. She does so good in school. She does good in sports. And she's just amazing! I love her! But also I think that I am doing good as a mom and as a friend and as a leader. Also, I am trying to give more to people because I got so much.

Now I am feeling good. I think that I've recovered my self esteem, that I have so many projects in me that I really want to do them. I know that I am going to accomplish them. One of the projects that we are working now—the

Latino-Hispanic Student Association—is helping children in Mexico City who live on the street. Last Christmas I went to Mexico and I was doing that project. It's like a documentary, you know, of my life. I heard that somebody says I have, not an obligation, but because I changed my life and now I'm whole, and I'm reaching new capacities, that I can change other lives, and I will. So it is hard, but with patience and hard work, I think that we can do it.

First of all, I need to finish my education, and I will. I think that it is so hard, my courses are so hard. [Laughs] But I'm doing fine, except for Chemistry—I hate it! But the others, I'm fine. I think that I can do it. When I have something in my dreams, I felt a long time ago like I wanted to be a better educated woman, and I was trying to figure out, "How can I do that?" "How can I finish school and know more English?" That makes me just be more focused in what I really want. Now I have a lot of dreams, but the main dream that I have is finishing my education, being a nurse, working in a hospital, raising my daughter—a healthy daughter—and doing something else for the community.

I'm taking five courses and working at the [USM] Language Lab fifteen hours a week, working with the Latino Student Association—I don't watch TV! [Laughs] I don't chat on the Internet! I'm a runner. I run when I have a chance, of course, not lately. I haven't even cleaned my house! My life is studying, cooking for my daughter, and taking care of her, her homework, and her clothes, and seeing that she has everything that she needs, my school, doing my projects, and trying to do meetings and everything that I need for the Latinos, and also work on the other projects. I think that if I organize myself I can do that, but I'm not sleeping well, of course. [Laughs] But I'll have time when I'm older to sleep, when I retire—but probably not. I'm going to be doing other things!

My daughter's in second grade in Sanford. We live in Sanford. So that's another thing, I have to drive forty-five minutes. She feels so proud to be Latina! [Laughs] She doesn't have a lot of Mexican things here. She just has me. I try to teach her that she is part Mexican and Mexico has a lot of good things, and is rich in history and everything.

Every year we have La Posada at USM, and it's just a very, very nice party because we dress in our colorful Mexican dress and she comes so proud with her little dress, and she dances. She appears all the time in the newspapers, and she brings that to her classroom to teach them, "Look at that. Do you know how to say something like apple in Spanish?" she says that. I think that she's very, very proud to be not totally Mexican, [laughs] but part.

My daughter's bilingual. For me it was kind of hard. Even though I did learn in Mexico like six years of English, it's hard. You think that you know, okay, six years studying English, "Oh, I know a lot. I'm ready. I'm going to the U.S. and speak." Then I came here and tried to speak and people didn't understand. I didn't understand them. "Too fast! Please, I don't understand!" [Laughs]

When I was in high school it was also hard, especially the writing, and all the grammar, it was hard, but I did it. Diana knows; we speak Spanish at home and she does pretty well. But in front of others, she speaks English of course, at school with her friends. But when she's at home, I try to have her speak Spanish with me.

I don't call myself very religious. I'm not even Catholic. You might be thinking, "From Mexico? Okay, she's Catholic." No! My mom is kind of like Christian, Protestant, but she's very fanatic and I don't like that. I never went to church in Mexico. But I think that inside of me, I always believed that there's a God. I think that I forgot that part.

When I was in Maine, after I left the shelter, I had this necessity of a spiritual something. I really wanted to talk to a religious person. So I went to this church, a Unitarian church and I said to the pastor, "I really need to"—because at that moment I didn't have insurance for counseling, and I was getting crazy, and I wanted to talk to somebody. I mean, I had the support groups in Caring Unlimited, but I really wanted more like spiritual relief, so I went to this very nice, kind man from my church and I said, "But I'm not from your church. I don't know what this is about. I just want to talk with somebody."

And he just said, "You're welcome. Everybody's welcome in my church."

And I said, "Oh, thank you!" I was talking and crying and he was praying for me. And I felt so much better! Eventually I would go and see him and sometimes he didn't have the right answer to my problems but he would pray and just his voice, his kindness, I felt much, much better. I became a member of that church. Now I'm also the treasurer of the church. [Laughs] I forgot that. So I've been there, at the Unitarian church for seven years. It's a great church. I don't go very often—[whispers] no time. [Laughs] I attend meetings sometimes and take my daughter. She used to sing in the choir and she has a beautiful voice. I think that this is important for her, that she has a little piece of that spiritual thing which has to be with morals, honesty, and all those important things.

Sanford is my new home, and my family too. In Sanford, I have a lot of people who know me there, because it's a small town. I do a lot of community things there. We have Caring Unlimited, and it's kind of close. It's my family, because I have my friends here and all the people that I know. I can go out to the supermarket and meet a lot of people who know me, "Hi Laura! How are you doing?" And just talk to them. In fact, now I have a friend who lives across my street and she is like my second mother. My daughter calls her *mémé* [grandma], because she said, "Oh, I'm going to adopt you." I met her when all these things were happening and so I got a lot of support from her and her family. She's a French-Canadian lady, and she's just unbelievable.

Portland I like too, because this is the area of my school. Again, if I go out here probably I would meet some student or somebody from the school, because also I meet a lot of people. I love people! This is kind of like my work, study area. And Sanford is my home. So I travel almost every day, Sanford to Portland. [Laughs] This is my second family.

I miss my family in Mexico, of course, a lot. And it's hard to go there and stay with them, and eat the Mexican food, eat my mom's beans—best beans ever!—and see my sisters and brothers. Everybody's just amazing when I go there. I get crazy, I get like, oh! I'm the center of attention and talking to everybody! And eating! I just wish that the time stops so that I could stay more with them. But, sadly, I think that now here is my home and my dreams are here.

Eventually I could go back . . . but [sighs] I have to stay here and do my education, and my daughter's life is here too, her school and . . . But my heart is still in Mexico [laughs sadly]. My dad, and everybody is there. But sometimes I feel like I don't belong. I am the middle. Where do I belong? Mexico or the United States? It's kind of weird, because here I have an accent and I'm brown. If I go to Mexico they also think, "Oh, you are losing your Spanish! Now you have a hard time speaking!" And they say, "You changed in many ways. Your thoughts changed a lot." Of course I had to change! I'm swimming in a different ocean. [Laughs]

When you come back to your native ocean it's just like—we were reading this amazing allegory of the cave in a philosophy class—it was unbelievable. Have you read it? When I was reading that, I felt like that prisoner that went out of the cave because that was what he was used to seeing, but when you leave and you learn other stuff and you get education, and you try to go back to the cave and teach your people, "Okay, this is what it is. This is what respect is. This is what domestic violence is." This is what I felt. They look at me like, "You are crazy." [Laughs]

I understand that it is the way they want to be, because my family, and the collective society in which Mexican people live, don't allow them to fly.

They are all together, which in some things are really good because the family keeps them all together, and mom wants them all here! But on the other hand, they have some times when somebody flies away, and it's that they are weird, or the black sheep, like me. [Laughs] They call me that. I don't think that I am the black sheep.

So if this is going to show people the way Mexican immigrants come and all the obstacles that we have to pass, I'm more than willing to share my life and my experience with other people, because I think other people in this moment are facing domestic violence, and other people already have a real past with domestic violence. It's hard being here. Any time I have a chance to express my life and how Latinos are here, I will do it.

John Connors.

Born in Portland, John spent his first few years growing up in a very ethnically mixed New York City neighborhood. His grandmother was from Puerto Rico, and the rest of his family is Irish. He speaks about the culture and traditions of his grandmother, "Those roots go back a long way and are very deep." He moved back to Portland at about age eight, where he soon learned that "you didn't want anybody to know you were Puerto Rican." He graduated from high school in 1960, went into the Air Force, came back, experienced racial profiling, helped bring a League of United Latin American Citizens (LULAC) chapter to Portland, and began a life of activism for health and civil rights issues, including being president of the Maine chapter of the Labor Council for Latin American Advancement of the AFL/CIO. In his more than sixty years, "Things have changed quite a bit," he says, and, though there is still a lot of work to be done, "Portland is beginning to feel like home."

5

John Connors

It's About Community Building

I'm Irish-Puerto Rican. My grandmother was from Puerto Rico. I was born in Portland, but we spent my first few years in New York City, and I remember that you didn't want anybody to know that you were Puerto Rican. I was not allowed to speak Spanish as a youngster. My grandmother would get very upset. I had to comb my hair like a gringo. I wasn't sure what those terms meant but I knew that it wasn't something that you should be proud of at the time. I really get a big chuckle out of it now, because the biggest parade in New York is in early June, Puerto Rican Pride Day, which is bigger than Saint Patrick's Day now, with over four million people on Madison Avenue, which is more people than we have on the island of Puerto Rico. And besides that we have almost 200,000 people in the parade.

Over sixty years, things have changed quite a bit. Right now it's cool to be Puerto Rican, at least in New York on the first of June. I remember when I first visited the island of Puerto Rico. The only thing that I could say was, "I'm finally home at last." And my daughter was already there, and before I left the airport, I said, "I never want to leave; I'm home."

She says, "You haven't left the airport, Dad."

It's something in the heart. Pretty much the feeling, it is like being home. I felt like I belonged there.

I went back to Puerto Rico after I got married and had children. It wasn't that long ago that I first had an opportunity to go. I can't wait to go back. I hope to go back for the election this year. I had the good fortune of meeting Pedro Rosselló, who was the governor then and I hope that he'll be reelected to the governor this year of Puerto Rico. This will be his third term.

It was just my grandmother that was from Puerto Rico. As a child, I learned some important things from her, that it's okay to have opinions, it's okay to have emotions. It's very okay to be who you are, even though on the outside we had to be quiet, that it's okay to be Puerto Rican, it's okay to be Latino. And it's okay to be Irish. I believe that very strongly today. Two island peoples come together, there's something kind of magical about that.

I remember my first trip into Old San Juan, the very first street I crossed was O'Donnell Street, so I go, "There's got to be something natural there." Then one of the first early great heroes of Puerto Rico is a guy by the name of Alejandro O'Reilly, so I go, "Yeah, we've been here a long time." So it really was fun. It's a beautiful place. I loved the spirit, I loved the food, I just loved the feeling of family, music, and a lot of pride. There's a lot of history in Puerto Rico that people don't really understand.

The cultural tradition that my grandmother passed on was Three Kings Day, when children will put a little box of cookies, and a little grass or something in a shoebox under the bed, and of course, mom and dad do their magic overnight. It was to feed the wise men and to feed the camels that came to visit the Christ child. That was pretty important. My first visit to Puerto Rico was on that day. I remember the celebration in the square in Old San Juan, it was really kind of pretty. And I go, "Yeah, that was what Gram was talking about." It's nice to hear the stories, but it's really nice to go back and be in the same place, the same footsteps as people before you were. That really convinced me that I needed to become more involved and more active in the Latino community overall.

I was about three when I moved to New York, for probably about five years, from three to eight. We moved to a neighborhood in Brooklyn, not particularly Puerto Rican, it was quite a mix at that time. It was close to Ebbets field, and I remember the building that we lived in, there were Italians, Jewish people, and Polish people, and it was like the United Nations. I didn't know there was a whole lot of difference for a long time, until I came back to Maine eight years later, and "oh, everybody's separate here." I missed that. I had the run of the building.

I had more grandparents from more different places than anybody ever met. I think that it probably opened me up to be a little more sensitive to that, you know, that we're not really all that different, but we think we are sometimes.

Of course, nobody's more passionate or loves music more than Puerto Ricans do, but, you shouldn't say anything about the Irish too, so I guess it's pretty close. It's kinda fun to have the mix, I think.

The thing about Portland and all the Latinos who have been here a long, long time is that we are still treated as though we got here just yesterday and are leaving tomorrow. If anybody had the chance to go up to the old cemeteries in Portland, they'll find back at least in the 1700s, early 1800s, grave markers with Latino surnames on them. There were even cigar stores on Exchange Street. We have a very Latino street up on Munjoy Hill, it was really Ponce [*pon.se*] Street, but everybody calls it Ponce. I think that we don't know our history. It's been a while, and a lot of what were Latino names and families have become Anglophiled over the years. I hope our job in the next ten years is to let them know that, yeah, you're part Latino too, and that it's not just a new experience here in Maine. So, we're making a lot of progress.

Some of the reasons for the invisibility start with: What does a Latino look like? For other people, it's somewhat obvious. But Latinos can be any color, any size, any shape, any combination in the world, and it doesn't always stand out. I mean, we don't walk around with blankets over our shoulders leading a donkey down the street. We have Asians and Muslims and Irish that have red hair and blonde hair and black and brown, and every color of the rainbow. It's kind of neat. I don't think that people understand that in Maine yet, that there's really a wide variety. Puerto Rico is probably the most stunning place in the world to see that contrast. I mean, we have a lot of people from Korea that are Puerto Ricans now, and Middle Eastern Puerto Ricans. There's such an international flavor.

I think in Maine it's going to take a little bit of time. There's a lot of history to learn here in Maine. We had a teacher at Portland High School—which I don't think that we have today—in 1847, he graduated from college here in Maine. He was from Cuba. There was also an early architect here in

Portland. So those roots go back a long way and run very, very deep. I think it's exciting, when people find this out.

I was about eight when I moved back to Portland. I remember that very well. I remember the first other people that I met that were Puerto Rican. I was looking out the window, and I told Gram, "I want to go down and say 'Hi' to those people." I wasn't sure what the difference was, but it was a rhythm of speaking—because a lot of them were freshly from Puerto Rico—and there was an energy that you didn't always see elsewhere. I just thought they were fun people and I wanted to go down and be with the fun people. Most of the other people I knew in the building just came over from Europe right after the war. They were nice people, but they weren't the same energy. I just wanted to be part of that.

I mixed in pretty well in school when I came back here. It was neighborhood schools back then, which made it very nice. I went to my first school in New York; it was a parochial school, run by the Jesuits, which was an interesting introduction to education. Then I went to local grade schools here in Portland. There was no diversity in those schools at the time. Everybody looked and sounded exactly alike. I didn't realize that we did have a history here. I knew that things Latino were exciting to me for some reason.

I remember when I was a little bit older talking to my dad about César Chávez and the work that he was doing. Being a strong AFL/CIO guy, "We couldn't organize 'em," he said, "I don't think that the Mexicans are going to organize anybody."

And I said, "Don't be on it, Pop."

There was always that kind of feeling and connection somehow, that kindred spirit going on between those things that I read. I did a lot of reading about Latino history and both sides of the question of the war. An interesting part of the Mexican War was the St. Patrick's battalion, young Irishmen that came over and joined the U.S. Army who deserted to fight on the side of Mexico when they found out how badly the U.S. troops were treating the men, women, and children of Mexico. A lot of them joined the Mexican side to fight what they believed was the moral reason to fight, not for land, but for identity. That to me is a very important story and lesson, and one that I still think about a great deal today—trying to put your values first. And I think that sometimes we don't always do that enough. So it's part of the things that I was interested in doing, kind of shaped my warped mind to be what it is today.

Kids in grade school were aware of what neighborhood you were from. The biggest one was probably Deering Center, and there's people from downtown Portland and Oxford Street and Morrill's Corner, but that was basically the breakdown. Even into high school, I think at Deering we had three black children and one mulatto, and we all knew each other growing up.

I didn't experience any discrimination then. That's only happened later in my life, actually, especially when I travel. The first time that I really got a good, clear dose of it, was a few years ago when I came back from Guatemala, I had darkened up pretty good and we were pulling into a terminal. I remember when I was going to switch planes; I was waiting for my luggage to offload. I had about ten customs agents with their dogs surrounding me. There's seventy people in this airport, but a lot of them real young people that had come back from partying down there, right? And I'm surrounded by these people. I'm going, "They're going to tear every little bit of my luggage apart. I'm never going to make my connection."

But somehow I looked a little bit more stereotypical Latino at that time, so the combination that "Oh, there must be drugs involved." Of course, all the people on the plane with me are all stoned. But, you know, I fit the profile a little bit better. The good news was when I got my bags and started walking really slowly and unlocking it toward the counter, the guy at the counter was a Latino and he just waved me through. But the idea of being surrounded by people and those dogs was frightening.

I've worked a long time and I've known other people and have seen that. When it first happens to you, it gets a little scary. Sometimes you get pulled aside and get a little lecture or screening at the airport these days. But a lot of my discrimination comes because I've got a big mouth and I walk in it pretty hard, but I ask for that a little bit too, so I don't equate that quite the same way, but we'll see what happens.

An example would be federal law enforcement, especially racial profiling. I've had a running conflict now with the Border Patrol for about five to six years in Maine. We now meet with them every couple of months and a U.S. Attorney, who basically tells me, "Stop lying about the Border Patrol and quit talking to the media." And I go, "I'll be very glad to when they stop racial profiling." They deny it. They just think they are doing good police work.

But I go, "We know better. This is what goes on." I'm always the bad guy trying to cause trouble. And we sit in a room full of federal agents, and you're going "No" and there's no one else there to get your back; it's not always a comfortable feeling, but you learn to talk to people in a nonthreatening way and try to point out and educate why it is indeed profiling.

I was in the middle of a car, and we were pulled over because it had out-of-state plates and a lot of people. Well, if it's on the 4th of July in the State of Maine during vacation month, it represents about half the cars on the road. When you stop fifty out of fifty and they've all got brown-skinned Latinos in them, you're profiling, buddy! You're not stopping anybody else. But the good news is that every time they think about doing that, they think of me first, and back it up a little bit.

There's always other ways of doing good police work besides profiling. Profiling, to me, is really a lazy, sloppy way of doing it. It's not very effective. For two hundred dollars we can change our entire appearance to be anybody in the world, with a cheap wig, a pair of contact lenses, and a little bit of body makeup; I mean, we could be anybody in the world, that quickly. So you're basing it on skin color and stuff like that, then you're not doing a really good job of trying to do the things that you need to do. And if you're persistent, you can joke with them a little bit, and you know, try to break some of the tension and try to get people to look at things from the other side of the table. It helps.

If you go, "Put yourself in the other person's shoes, if you could for a minute, how would you feel and react?" Especially if it's a war-torn country, like maybe Guatemala or Honduras, where you see everybody showing up with a gun and a uniform on, you know it's not good news. You're probably not going to have supper that night. And so if you're acting nervous and fidgety, it's not because you're trying to hide something; you're scared!

We try to get people on that committee to understand when an officer comes up to your car because you just did something dangerous or stupid or your car is really not safe, and they don't know who you are, and they might raise their voice, it's just to get you to pay attention. Maybe they don't understand what you're saying, and so they're not responding; it's not because they're asking for you to shoot them, it's because they really don't have a clue what you're saying. We try to bring people closer together.

We did that the other day at the University of New Hampshire when we talked to their chief there. I said, "How can we get better understanding? I'm sure that at a university of this size, you must have a number of student organizations from different countries, you know, of different nationalities. Ask them if you can go to their meeting, invite them to yours. Get to know each other."

"Well, we have 25 percent turn-over every year."

"Yeah, but the other 75 percent after the first time or two, will do most of your job for you."

But the idea is to go out and meet people, and find out there's no difference, that when all your relatives came here they all had accents and talked different languages, too. It's nothing new. So embrace it, and go, "Okay." Learn from it.

Spanish is a beautiful language. I mean it's the second most popular language in the world. The only one that's used more in the world today is Mandarin. Not English. English is only number three. So get a little bit more progressive and then broaden what you're doing. You're going to hear more and more Spanish just in Maine.

The question I get a lot is: "Why do Latinos come to Maine?" It's a beautiful state. Why does anybody come here? We have a lot of people that come here in the military and they serve a couple of years and then get ready to retire and say, "This is where I want to spend the rest of my life." People come up on vacations, or business trips, some of us have family who come up here and visit and go, "This is a nice place. I can get a job." There's some stuff going on now, we have churches, Latino, Spanish-speaking masses now, and we have stores where we didn't have any a few years ago. We have business people, and people in other professions. We never had these things before, so there's a sense of growth now finally.

I just turned sixty-two, and for most of my life there was no growth in my community and now it's going on. Now we're looking at doing books, and we've got a little bit of stuff on the radio, and we're looking at doing a TV show around Latino health, and you know we've got several organizations going, we've got different events happening. We're building a community within the State of Maine.

We've got people coming from Peru and a lot of people from Puerto Rico and the Dominican Republic, and from Mexico and Honduras. It's just a great mix. The thing about Maine is that all the communities come together; we're not separated like we are in other bigger cities, the Puerto Ricans over here and the Mexicans over here and we never talk to each other. So that kind of building is a kind of energy that a lot of people have. If we can keep that as we get bigger, it's going to be exciting.

There's going to be a lot of chances to do a lot of things. It gives us a chance to learn about each other. There's no such thing as a place called Hispanic or Latino; there's twenty-something-odd countries and cultures and different backgrounds and histories and food and music. When it comes together there's an energy that's exciting to all of us. I mean, it's not all about events and salsa anymore. There's so many new energies coming in, and there's so much for us to learn about each other.

We consider it critical that we're reaching out to some of the Native American communities here in Maine. We've got some good relationships now with Penobscot people—we've worked very closely with them, because we think that indigenous people are really important too. We never talked to each other before in this state. The great news is we talk to other people in other states about what we're doing, and we get a reputation for being a pretty good place.

That doesn't mean that we don't have problems, but when you get some numbers and get some stuff going, then all of a sudden you can make some changes. Example, I don't know how many Latino youth we have in the University of Maine system. A couple years ago, we didn't have any. There were several that were nontraditional students. We have a lot of bright youngsters in this state that should be going to college straight from high school. We need to work on that harder. The City of Portland has hardly any Latinos working for the City of Portland. We need to change that. We have never had a Latino reporter or newsperson in the State of Maine yet! The most popular show we have is the one on Sunday afternoon that Rosita does on WMPG. We need to get more out there. We need to build on these things, because it's about community building. It's about sharing history.

We have an event at the church and we have a hard time fitting in because everyone else wants to come in and join us, which is tremendous. We want to learn, we want to share, we want to be part of what's going on. I mean, we have an event and half the people that show up are not Latino. We did the census, and I think the breakdown was about six hundred different geographical areas of Maine, and we had Latinos living in four hundred and fifty of them. That's a pretty big chunk of the state of Maine. It's not just in Portland or Lewiston. It's up in Aroostook County, it's up in Kingfield, it's on Beal's Island. We need to communicate. It's not new, but it's fun.

When we did the census, I talked to the lady up in Bangor. I go, "Are you all set to do the Latinos? Is there anything that we can help you with?"

"Oh, we don't have to worry about it, Mr. Connors. All the Latinos go home after Christmas, and they don't come back until late April."

I says, "Well, I've got a few places that you might want to check and find out."

She calls back a couple of days later and says, "My God, it's like half the Latinos in the world are living up here now."

Every community called her, "Oh yeah, we've got a community over here." We've got a little community in Milbridge, we've got thirteen hundred people in the community, but more than one hundred Latinos. They've got their menus in Spanish, even in the restaurants.

This is fun—and exciting! Not only are people working for Decoster [Egg Farm] and raking blueberries and working in fish processing, we have engineers, we have business managers, we have store owners, we have teach ers. We got almost every profession that you can think of in the community, but it's a well-guarded secret right now. Yeah, Portland is beginning to feel like home.

There's more stuff going on now that makes this place feel like home. We're feeling a little bit more comfortable with it. There's still a lot of things that we need to do. We need to look at higher education. It's considered that if you're Latino you don't go very far in school. One of the greatest engineering school in the country is in the island of Puerto Rico: the Mayagüez campus. It had the first five-year engineering program in the country. The good news about that is that 20 percent of your students are female. You don't think about Latinas being engineers, particularly, but we have Latina engineers here in greater Portland, and it's not new—there's been several in the past few years. We don't think about those things because people of war and poverty didn't always have the chance to go on to higher education— but given the opportunity there's an awful lot of untapped potential and talent there. We have to remember that [we] wouldn't have computers today if it weren't for Mayan Indians who came up with the concept of zero. They also came up with an astrology map that we still use today, over a thousand years later.

There's a lot of potential that when it's tapped into and allowed to expand, is really overwhelming, and we need to do a better job in that. I just found out today that a Latina is doing some recruiting for the University of Southern Maine, and I think that's great. It's a great first step. So there's a lot of hope out there, but there's a lot of things we need to put in line and develop and not go, "Oh, you're Latina, so that means you've got to learn how to go and peel shrimp, or that you've got to go rake blueberries." It's just bizarre, we need to get beyond that thinking.

I know of people from Guatemala that live in Vermont, that came here as refugees about 18 or 20 years ago now. Mayan Indians from way up in the countryside. Their five children went to school, all went to college, and now all have doctorate degrees. The capacity is there, [but] the opportunity is not always there. We don't have police officers that are Latino. We do have some teachers in quite a few of the schools around in Maine now. But we need to grow those things so that our youngsters know that "Yeah, I can do that."

I went to a great thing that they did for some kids from Portland High School a few years ago. It was the first time they did a self-improvisation play about themselves. The good news is that they all wanted to go to college. The sad thing is that they all thought they had to go on sports scholarships. I go, "No, the brains are there—use them." When people found out, "Yeah, I can do that," all of a sudden the lights started going on, the energy started to flow. That's a part of an educational process and an exposure process. I think that we're going to be able to do that.

We've got some people here that are pretty outspoken too. Some of us are pretty comfortable and we speak up for those people that are new, that are probably on asylum or they haven't got their green cards yet. Some of them may not be here with their papers at all, but you know, we can speak up for the people that can't. We've made a lot of progress in the past few years. We've pulled together. We've got an open-door policy with the governor now. We've got a pretty good working relationship with the City of Portland. We work a lot with the University of New England on some health issues, initiatives. We've been part of the University of Maine. We've got some good friends there, but I'd like to see it expand a little bit. We want to get our numbers up, and make sure that it's always seen.

There's a little bit of pride, and a little bit of belonging. Back in the '70s, we had a large Puerto Rican community that moved to Portland, but they only stayed here a little while because there was nothing here that felt like home. And back in the '80s we had a lot of people from Cuba; many of them stayed for a while and then left because there was nothing to feel like they were anchored. And we lost a lot of people in coming and going. Now people are coming and are staying, they're getting involved in the community, in business, in education, and they're getting involved with the schools. You know, groups are intermarrying. People say, "Why should I come to Maine?" and I go, "Well, you can go to California or you can go to New York and go to Boston and become part of what's going on, but if you come here now in this point in history you can help shape what the community's going to look like five, ten, fifteen, twenty years from now." To me that's exciting, that I can be part of what happens.

I meet once a year to have breakfast with the Secretary of State. I know the City Manager of Portland. It's fun to be able to come up and say, "OK, we have a problem, and this is how we want to help address that problem." It's important what we do. We've been here a long time, and I think that it's important to talk about the issues.

We had a César Chávez thing at Lincoln Park a few years ago and the local newspaper didn't cover it. I called and asked why.

"Oh, we decided it was a nonevent." We had over three hundred people. That's bigger than most of the events in Portland. The guy says, "Oh we're busy and it's a nonevent in Portland."

They go down there the next week in Boston and cover the Greek Parade down there. It was a lot of fun, but you can't cover something a block from your window? César Chávez is one of the most important men of the twentieth century in this country. He changed a lot of what we did, and how we think, and how we feel. He learned from Martin Luther King. When they were in jail together for speaking up for what they believed in they wrote to each other. There's a natural thing when you take these things together and bring them together and talk.

I was here when Chávez came to Portland in 1974. It was great having him come here, but he wasn't exactly kind to Maine, and I think that people may not realize that one of the things he said is that Maine is a paper plantation, that a lot of the workers are not treated very well. It took quite a few years after that, about twenty years after that, for some of that to turn around. Unfortunately today, because of government cutbacks on a federal level, we're starting to see some of those things happening again.

I'm very concerned about that auto crash that we had that claimed fourteen lives a few years ago.[1] We've worked for quite a while to get the wives of them to come here and testify in court. The State Department said no. Between the women they have sixteen children. Wage and Hour and OSHA have had their funds cut by this White House, so when there's things going on that should be investigated, they're not. It doesn't take long for that to get out and for people to learn about those things and start taking advantage of people that are very honest, simple, hardworking people.

I get very angry that we can't do more about that. We've still got those vans running in the Maine woods, and it's only a matter of time before it kills more people. We've had two horrific accidents—since 1998—with those vans, but nothing has been done to get them out of the woods or make them safer. I get very angry with that stuff. I get very angry when you disrespect the value of an Indian or a Latino life.

Our border policy in this country is a disgrace. I remember when President Reagan went to Berlin and asked them to tear down the wall. A few years later we built a wall across the southern border. It has claimed over three thousand lives, of men, women, and children. It's a very painful death and when I tell people what the death is like they get very angry at me. This could ruin your supper, but you know what? That's what the people are dealing with. That's what we allow to happen in our name. If it's happening in our name, by our government—it's *our* government, then it's up to us to speak up to get them to change the rules. Now we talk about terrorists, but we're talking about people that come here and risk their lives to work at some of the worst jobs that nobody else wants to take to support their family. The very same person that is now president said at one time when he was governor of Texas, "Any man that would walk four hundred miles to take care of his family is the kind of man that we need in Texas." Well, you know what, your actions and your words don't match, because right now we have more people dying on that border every year that want to come here and feed their family.

I don't think any man or any mother worth their salt would take the risk of your child going hungry or going without. We treat them like criminals, and that's a crime. We want to change our immigrants—people coming across that border? We need to use our influence; we need to use our bully pulpit to change the conditions that people live in in this hemisphere, our next-door neighbors. We were upset to have to rebuild Iraq because they have 60 percent unemployment. There's 60 percent unemployment in southern Mexico, in Guatemala and Honduras. We think that's acceptable. Not to me, it's not. We need to be very voiceful about that. It's our right as U.S. citizens to object when we think they're doing something wrong. I think that we have up to seven hundred deaths every year from people crossing that border. That means because of our policies, people are dying. That is beyond belief. We are a better country than that.

One of the very first men to die in Iraq was a man named José Gutierrez, he was an orphan from Guatemala City. He came here at sixteen years old, crossed the border by himself. He was eventually adopted, became a U.S. citizen, and died as a U.S. Marine. That man should be honored. And he's not the only one; it happens every day. And people come here to do what they're supposed to do.

We don't talk about the history of my beautiful Puerto Rico. We talk about the men in Somalia that they dragged out by helicopter, but we don't tell anybody that one was Puerto Rican. We don't talk about the people that were killed even in the Marine barracks explosion. Well, many of them were from Puerto Rico. We don't talk about the forty U.S. Congressional Medal of Honor winners that were Latino. We don't talk about, back in the 1930s, when U.S. citizens were deported back to Mexico—U.S. citizens, and they were not allowed to come back until we needed them to serve in the war. We don't talk about half the Mexican men in the United States who at that time served in the United States military. We don't talk about the Latinas, the U.S.

citizens in Puerto Rico, who were forcibly sterilized under U.S. Government contracts. We don't talk about these things, not because it's evil. We don't honor the people that we abuse.

I get very angry about that. We're better than that. We need to talk about it. It's a secret that we had a Latino teacher here over one hundred and forty years ago. We don't talk about the things that are important. We don't talk about the service to this country. The first young lady that ever died in U.S. combat in Iraq was part Native American and part Latina. Those are important parts of who we are, and it's a shame that we don't have that because our children need to have heroes that aren't sports stars and music stars only.

We need people that are teachers. We need people that are engineers. We need people that are doctors. Our youngsters need to know that "Yeah, going to school means that there's something for you on the other end." We need to invite more of our Latino youngsters to come over and have a day of school at the University of Maine and hook up with somebody and drag them to the classrooms and show them what it's like. We need to do that more and more. The first Latino I know in Maine that actually got into the University of Maine system, her dad was one of the people doing the sea cucumbers, and she got a scholarship to the University of Maine at Machias. Nobody else in her family ever went to college. Nobody else in that community got there, but she did the work and got there—on her own merit. She did what she needed to do to get there. And believe me, this is not an exception, we need to do more recruiting.

The one thing that absolutely, *really* makes me angry—and I get it every year—I get somebody who'll call, "Oh, I want to help those poor Hispanics."

I say, "What do you want to help them do?"

"Well, I'm going to Puerto Vallarta, and I want to practice my Spanish."

I go, "Well, yeah, they teach Spanish classes, but its sixty bucks an hour."

It's like, the perception of Latinos, because they speak a different language and take a job rather than going on the dole, that people aren't educated and not intelligent. Now that's B.S., big time. And that really, really pisses me off. I think that gets me more angry than anything else. The assumption—people you know nothing about—that they're not capable of doing anything they set their minds to, because history—the record—shows you're wrong. In Atlanta, Georgia, the five largest corporations are run by Latinos. You'd like to be able to run Coca-Cola, wouldn't ya?

I graduated from Deering High School in 1960, and then went into the Air Force. It was the best opportunity for me at the time. I knew with a big family and so forth that I wasn't going to go to college. It was a chance to go and I got involved in electronics pretty early on. I kind of enjoyed that. It was pretty good. I had the chance to get to know a lot of different people. I had the chance to go to Mexico quite a few times. It was exciting. I got out of it, but I went back into electronics, as a biomedical electronics technician here in Portland. That was pretty interesting. So I came back here after the Air Force.

I started getting involved in organizations a little bit before LULAC was here. There were some Puerto Rican issues here in Maine—probably in late '95, early '96. In '96 I went to Puerto Rico, and that was the absolute commitment then. We really got involved and brought LULAC here. We were hoping to get a little bit more support on the local issues, but basically we found out that we were probably better equipped to deal with issues locally and develop on our own. I think that health is a very, very important issue for the Latino community of Maine right now. There are a lot of similarities and there are a lot of differences in Latino health issues. I'm trying to develop some of the ones that are fairly unique to Latinos.

The number three cause of death among Latinos is accidents. They want to talk about tobacco here, but that's a very small issue overall in the Latino community, so we're trying to get our priorities lined up and develop some programming around those and do some education and stuff. We did a health fair this year. We did our first needs assessment. We collaborate with the City of Portland, with the Bureau of Health also, and with some agencies outside of the state of Maine, and some others inside the state of Maine. We're going to be doing a collaborative on asthma. Also on diabetes, which is very important. Adolescent obesity is another very important issue in the Latino community, too. We're able to take the national numbers and show how it affects the people in Maine. HIV/AIDS is a bigger issue here than it would be in California because the makeup of the communities is a little bit different.

We're pretty fortunate to keep a pulse on what's going on across the state of Maine. We've got groups up in Aroostook County, and we know who they are, and what they're doing. And people Down East and what they're up to. Sometimes the employment opportunities change too, and we can track that fairly well. We've also developed with the State of Maine Department of Labor an excellent relationship—and the Director of the Governor's office and some other people like that. So we're able to work on some good issues. One that I'm proud of is that we've finally convinced the governor's office to start putting together a driving manual in Spanish. We're only going to be able to get it on the Internet, but that's better than nothing.

I have not held any public offices. I have tried to run a couple of times, but I didn't play politics all that well. I figured you got to be nice to everybody, and that's a choice more or less, so I think sometimes to be effective as an advocate or as a community activist, you got to be able to speak and not worry about who you offend or don't offend.

All of my activism has been as a citizen. It's more effective that way. I just did several months for the Portland Health Department on some HIV stuff, but I feel really nervous because you can't be blunt. You go, "This is what we're talking about. This is what works. This is what's going on." And not worry about, "Well, you're not going to renew my contract." I've seen people over the years who have become very effective all of a sudden walk into this marvelous job that is basically a very expensive gag to shut your mouth. I really would rather talk about fixing the issue.

This year I was given an award by Maine Migrant Workers Advocacy Group. And last year, I got one from the City of Portland, an award in honor of César Chávez for some of the work I was lucky enough to be able to do. It's when you've got a guy like César who grew up poor and he didn't have a whole lot going for him, as privilege goes, and he was able, by his conviction and his hard work and his faith, to change what went on in this country. It's a pretty amazing story.

I see people out there that tell me, "Well you've got to do this," and "You've got to do this."

I go, "When I stopped doing it my way and I looked over and saw how César become so successful, I started seeing a little bit of progress, because what he did was not have great big groups and tell them, 'This is what you've got to do.' He would just meet with people and talk with them about whatever they wanted to talk about." We call it "five cups of tea," you know, you meet with somebody five times and you talk about family, you talk about your job, you talk about whatever sports thing you might be interested in, and eventually they know why you're there, and they'll probably bring up the issue and then sit down and have a little chat about it. Then they'll bring a few people in, and then a few more people in. After a while, you've got a movement going, but it's not by running around dictating to people.

Religion has always been important to me in my life. I think it is to most Latinos. It may not be going to church all the time, but my sacred ground is in the office next door. This is why I invite people in here, I've got César Chávez on the wall, and I've got a picture of the Virgin of Guadalupe. It's very important. I go to church almost every Sunday. It's also an important social piece too. It's like the priest who happens to be Irish Catholic, this boy from South Portland that speaks very good Spanish, is a priest, and he's part of the family. He's earned our respect because he's been there for us when things have been tough, and he's pitched in and he's worked with us. We have a lot of respect for him for that. So there's a growing awareness of what's going on. If you want to have a party and have a lot of people, you go to the church and you have a little bit of music and some food, and you'll have a full house. It's really neat.

My hopes and dreams for the future? I think that in the next ten years you're going to see some of the things that I'm concerned about change pretty quickly. I think that they will through evolution, not through threatening and screaming and hollering, but I think it's going to take a little bit of pointing out the facts to people. We need to do better. Like with the University [of Southern Maine], with Rachel Morales now, she's doing some recruiting. So I'm sure she's going to try to work on getting some Latino youngsters prepared to get in. I think that's a really important first step. We had, at one time, a lot of people from Puerto Rico and Mexico here, then Central America, the first-generation immigrants, a lot of them with not a whole lot of education, but their youngsters are coming along now, and a lot of them are going on to school, looking at other careers and professions.

Recently, the change in the country around immigration has become very nasty. A lot of this is due to fear, what we see and hear daily. Each year the number of people that die on the border grows, and now we see more women and children that die. We see families living in fear, and we hear gut-wrenching stories of parents and children being ripped apart and deported. The real fear is that when a loved one leaves they may not come back but be deported.

In just about every community there are businesses that need the workers, and the workers need the jobs. The enforcement of the immigration laws often target one group. The fallout reaches far more than the undocumented; it touches families and the community.

Our community here is getting a good reputation across the country as a place to come. We're growing. It's painful, but we're doing it. The dynamic is big, and I think the next census that we organize is going to shock people out of their socks. I know our population is much larger than the last census said, and I hope we get it organized well this time—it's going to be shocking. We know that because we see people every day. We meet new people every day. We get calls every day from new people. We get calls from people that plan to move here. People are bringing families, some of the working men that came here four or five years ago are now bringing their families here, so that whole thing is changing. The dynamic is changing pretty rapidly. We're getting a little bit organized. We're talking to each other, and we're getting some plans going.

La Bodega just expanded there. Now Juan's got a restaurant as well as his little Bodega. I know that the pupusería—Tu Casa—is now looking for a bigger space. There's a lot of changes going on. We've got barber shops. We've got a young lady that's a glass artist up here on Congress Square. There's a lot of stuff going on, nice and quiet and peaceful. It's not always getting in the newspaper. We know the community by word of mouth, and that's kind of fun. That's more like back home. You talk to your neighbors, you talk to your friends, and you go to church. There's always something going on.

It is a strong, close-knit community that's growing. There's some people that are outside, but it comes together. We get mad at each other, but it's like family. You get mad at each other today and you forget about [it] tomorrow. It's really exciting that overall there's an intermixing of the groups. It's not Latino-Hispanic. You're Puerto Rican, and you're Guatemalan, and you're Mexican, you're Dominican. Whatever it is, those distinctions are really important to us. It tells us what we're really part of, but we're very proud of being part of the overall group too, but respect the differences amongst ourselves.

Note

1. On September 12, 2002, a van packed with fifteen migrant workers—ten Hondurans and five Guatemalans—veered off a bridge on a remote lumber road in northern Maine into the Allagash Wilderness Waterway; only one man survived.

When The Reverend Virginia Marie Rincón came to Portland in 1999, she saw the need for Spanish language ministry. As she stayed on, she realized it was a place where she could pursue her goals: "When I can help people get a bag of groceries or fill out applications to get food stamps or to get a job or to enroll in a university, to better their lives, to give voice to their oppression, or to give voice to what they see about themselves, it just helps me feel like I'm answering the Call." In response to these and other needs, she founded Tengo Voz (I Have a Voice), an organization that provides social services to Latinas and their families. Following in the tradition of the grandmother who raised her, Reverend Rincón is a spiritual guide, interpreter, and activist.

The Reverend Virginia Marie Rincón.

6

The Reverend Virginia Marie Rincón

Answering the Call

My name is The Reverend Virginia Marie Rincón. I'm fifty-two. I'm originally from Houston, Texas. I was born in Lafollette, Tennessee, and three days after birth my mother took a train and went back to Houston, Texas, and so I was raised there.

Well, there is a story to it. Apparently my mother married my father and immediately he joined the armed forces and was stationed in Lafollette, Tennessee. He didn't come back to my mother at any point. So, in the ninth month of her pregnancy she sought to find out what was going on. So she managed to get to the station where he was, and found out a lot of things about why he hadn't come back to his commitment to the marriage and to the pregnancy. So, she went into labor [because] she got so upset about some of the issues she found. I was born while she was visiting Tennessee. The day I was born, it is said that it was such a little town they had never even seen Mexicans. And so I was a headline: "First Mexican Baby Born" in this little town near Lafollette, Tennessee. [Laughs]

I was raised in Texas. I was basically raised by my grandmother. My grandparents were migrant workers. One of my creation stories is that we came from corn. When a child is born, we put a kernel of corn in the palm of their hand to give thanks and to acknowledge that they will have to labor to survive in this world. The second is the Christian version, which was very strong in my family.

We lived in what we call the Port of Houston. This is a very poor part of Houston. I grew up in an area that is *very* much gang-infested, and with lots of social-economic stuff going on around there. I think it definitely made me who I am today.

Growing up, there weren't the best schools. There was a lot of poverty and a lot of violence around me. It wasn't unusual to see people shot in your front yard. People *dying* around you . . . When I was little, the police beat my father close to death. All of us kids were in the car. It was like a crazed exhilaration, like, "It's on."

It wasn't all bad though. There was a lot of community. My grandmother was very much a community activist of her day. She was a shaman and a healer, so lots of people would come to her to talk about what was going on with their daily lives. I think her journey definitely affected my journey. She made it very clear that of all the grandchildren that she had, I was the one that had the gift to heal. So she trained me in what people will say is the "knowing" of being able to heal people.

It's very interesting how I came to Portland. This was back in '99 going into 2000. I had a nice little church and a nice little job in the South End of Boston. I graduated from seminary in '97, and I was the lay-pastoral associate of Saint Steven's Episcopal Church. At the time there were a lot of issues there because they were losing their funding and I was kind of looking at the possibility of going to Los Angeles, California, because my beautiful daughter lives in Los Angeles, California.

Also, at the same time, a seventeen-year relationship suddenly ended. And I decided that I would come and visit a dear friend who is a priest and just spend the weekend here in Portland. As I arrived, I was asked to do a reading in Spanish at one of the small missions in the Bayside area, which no longer exists, that was Saint Elizabeth's Episcopal Church. And I decided, "Yeah, sure, I can do that." And the next weekend, it was, "Well, can you preach bilingually?" And I said, "Yeah, sure, I can do that." Then Latinos started coming, and one thing led to the next and I stayed! As a result, a ministry kind of emerged out of that and because I have a strong activist gene in me, I think that Portland was the perfect place for me to kind of expand on that.

My beautiful daughter lives in Los Angeles, California. But I do feel like I have family here. I have met some incredible people that I feel are like my family, one of which is Blanca [Santiago], and other people that are activists in the area. I also live with a family that I met while I was a minister at Saint Stevens in the South End of Boston, and they're very much my family. I live with a set of twins—they're sixteen years old—and their mother. And it's always an interesting day. You never know from one minute to the next.

I was raised Roman Catholic. There's a funny story, and I don't know how significant it is, but I think that it kind of was the beginning of the Call. I was in parochial school. My grandmother wanted the best kind of education for me, so she enrolled me in the little parochial school down the street where she would walk me to every day. And every morning, it was convenient for her because we prayed the rosary every morning at the Virgin de Guadalupe statue that is outside of the church. So she would ask me to pray the rosary and then she would take me to school.

And one of the things that happened was that I really didn't cooperate with the nuns. They had a very difficult time with me. I was always questioning everything. [Chuckle] And I must have been about seven or eight, I was trying to get ready and be prepared for my first Holy Communion. So, I was always being punished, and what they would ask me to do was pray the rosary an *ungodly* amount of times. Almost every day I was asked to pray the rosary. [Laughs] And one day, I was taken to the altar rail to pray the rosary and the nun left. And I jumped the rail and I went back into the sacristy area where the priests keep their vestments. So, I curiously opened the drawers to the vestments, and put the stole over my head and vested myself, came out to the front altar, and said, "The peace of God be with you." And the other kids that were also at the altar rail being punished, praying the rosary, thought it was hilarious, and at that very moment Mother Superior walked in, and didn't think it was funny. I no longer went to parochial school after that.

They had to enroll me in public school. [Laughs] That's the funny side, but the more sincere and serious is that I've always had a call. I've always felt very different. At the age of thirty I left the Roman Catholic church, after years of leading spiritual retreats and formal conversations with monsignors and all. I decided that my call meant ordination. And as we know, the Roman Catholic Church does not ordain women. So, I was received in the Episcopal Church in 1984, and immediately began the pieces of education that I needed to apply to seminary. I applied in 1993, and graduated in '97. So I consider myself still a Catholic—once a Catholic, always a Catholic. But I'm definitely an Anglican Catholic. I was in Austin, Texas, when all this was happening.

In '84 when I was received, I still had a Roman Catholic monsignor who was my spiritual director and who said, basically, "You're too much of a feminist, and I think that you're not going to last in the Roman Catholic Church very long."

And so, in '84, around that time, I switched into the Episcopal Church and came to the Episcopal divinity school in New England in 1993. I've been here about twelve years now.

I like Portland a lot. I like the water around me. I like the people. I just like it. In some ways, and I think that some people may get offended at this, but in some ways it reminds me of Austin, Texas. It's just progressive, but not too progressive. I keep hoping that we can get more progressive.

This ministry has been my work. I can't explain it. You can't even articulate it. But maybe in the simplified form it's simply all by God that I should be in Portland doing this work. I love it. I feel that when I'm doing it and I can see people smile, or when I can help people get a bag of groceries or fill out applications to get food stamps or to get a job, or to enroll in a university, to better their lives, to give voice to their oppression, or to give voice to what they see about themselves. It just helps me feel like I'm answering the Call. I don't always know why; there's some days that I question why I do what I do, because I don't get paid for the work that I do. And I'm very tired at the end of the day sometimes. But it's just awesome to me to be able to help somebody.

Gosh, there have been so many good memories in Portland. I was a nurse for twenty years. Because of that I'm able to be in certain situations that other interpreters may not be able to be in. I help deliver babies a lot. I've delivered at least—or helped deliver—four babies in the Portland area and I just love it. It's just totally awesome to me to be able to interpret and help and be the coach for my sisters.

Probably other activists in the Portland area would feel like it was the best thing that ever happened when we marched on Congress Street, and gave voice to our concerns about how Immigration does, or doesn't do, their job. It's deep within me. I'm definitely an activist. It's ingrained in me. My grandmother did it every day of her life, and it's just a part of me and it makes me happy. I'm not always sure how to do it, but the Holy Spirit always leads the way.

Violence is never the answer. There is no rational reason to make war. Not a lot of words are needed. I'm not much of a black and white person. How could there ever be only two sides to an issue. War is never the solution. I don't believe in war.

The day the Immigration officers came to Portland [January 25, 2004], there was a brilliant blue sky and temperatures below freezing. When they got to the Greyhound Bus Station, several buses were loading and unloading. They came on board, shut the doors behind them, and told everyone to stay where they were. No one knew what was happening. Maybe they thought they were being hijacked. They staked out La Bodega Latina, too, stopping everyone going in, coming out, and passing by.

Right after the terrorist attack, I was leaving a restaurant run by a Salvadoran family in town. Their six-year-old son came running to the parking lot and looked over my car. "Where's your flag? Where's your flag?" I asked him what he meant. "Your flag, you need to put a flag on your car so you can be safe."

The most difficult thing about living in Portland, I guess would be the winters! [Laughs] I've never thought about the difficulty, other than the winters. I have an illness that is affected by the cold weather, so I have a hard time in the winter. But as far as the community, the work and my surroundings, I love Portland. I love the sunsets. I love the natural essence of it. It kind of surprised me one day when I was driving, that I said, "Oh, I might just stay in New England."

I think my approach to my ministry, the ministry that God has called me to, may not always be understood by the clergy or some of the activists in the community. I like to be in the trenches. I don't really feel there's been a lot of obstacles because I'm in Portland, I think the obstacles are just obstacles that an activist faces. I'm a feminist. I'm a *mujerista*. I believe in women's rights. I do what I feel I'm called to do to make sure that women are able to have a voice in the community. And I'm not by any way perfect or whatever, it's just that I follow the spirit, and sometimes I mess up! And people might misunderstand that, and I've had to deal with that because I can tend to be a little bit overwhelming for some people.

Without a doubt, I have encountered discrimination toward myself. It's very interesting to me. I don't choose to wear my collar, every day. I've never been too much into that. But I notice the difference in how I'm treated. I can go into a 7-Eleven and people stare at me. You're just treated differently. Or you go into a mall area and people follow you. Police officers have stopped me a couple of times. One time I was stopped in Portland and then another time in Biddeford, and both times I was wearing my collar. And the minute they saw the collar their whole attitude changed. I notice that also happens a lot whenever I take people into the Department of Human Services. It does make a difference whether I'm wearing the collar or not wearing the collar as to how people are treated, myself included.

It's very important to me not to lose my language and my culture. I was raised in Texas, and my grandmother spoke only Spanish, so that was my first language, but once you go into the school system, they take that language away. We weren't allowed to speak Spanish. So, for many years I didn't speak it in the house, because my mother decided that we would only speak English in the house because of the law and the pressure that kids were under if they were caught speaking Spanish.

I remember being in nursing school. I was already nineteen years old, and the professor caught me speaking Spanish and put me out in the hall because I was speaking Spanish. My culture is beautiful, and I believe that it's very important to keep as much of it as I can. I do that with my daughter. I always try to talk to her half-English, half-Spanish. That's part of the culture too. We even speak some of the barrio talk that we grew up with—slang, the Spanglish.

And here in Portland you don't have a lot of opportunity to hear your music or smell your food where in the neighborhood where I grew up you just drove into the neighborhood and you can hear all your neighbors playing all the different beats of Latino music and smell the food coming through the back yard kitchens, and things like that. And so, every opportunity I get I try to listen to my music, and speak the language.

I sometimes feel a certain pressure to assimilate to the dominant culture. This is especially true for me in the fact that I'm in the Church. I remember one time we were having a conversation about diversity in the Church, and one gentleman just said, "Well, I don't see that it's an issue. People just need to assimilate. You're here. Just do it, and things will be better for everybody."

I am often saddened by the fact that I assimilated too much. I think I live in two worlds, and it sometimes makes me very sad that some people say, "You don't even have an accent." It kind of makes me sad that I don't have an accent. But I think that I have given up a lot of my culture already.

It's very interesting because I don't usually have free time. With the free time that I have, I love to wake up in the morning and say my prayers, and I'll look up at the sky. It's just time to be with God.

We were talking earlier that I really feel like it's difficult for me to be involved in a relationship—a serious relationship—because I'm in love with God! So my free time is there. It's been almost a year since I've really gone on a silent retreat, and here we are on the night of my silent retreat, and you are interviewing me. So, I don't really have a lot of free time.

I like to write poetry. I like to paint—that is something new. Living with artists moves you into that direction. I like to read a lot of books. What, how, who are we? What is it that we need to do to reach our higher consciousness?

Where are we as a universe in the knowing of ourselves? Those are the things that I do when I do have free time. And I wish I had more free time to pray, to be in that place of knowing myself, because I think that we need to do more of that in order for the world to be in a better place.

I'm part of the board for Immigrant Legal Advocacy Project and The Center for the Prevention of Hate Violence. I belong to a feminist board up in Rockland. I'm very, very active in the League of United Latin American Citizens.

There is also the most recent emerging of a nonprofit organization, Tengo Voz, which I am the founder and executive director of. This is an organization committed to Latino women and their families in the Portland area to help with finding jobs and housing, to deal with domestic violence, prevention and referral, and for cultural support and spiritual direction. We also have Latino women's focus groups, educational referrals and support, social service collaboration and referrals, and interpreting. I think that getting involved in these kinds of things is very important. So that's what I do.

What are my hopes for the future? Well, I hope that I'm an ordained deacon, and I'm hoping that I will be priested soon. I have canon privileges to do a lot of things, but I think that it's important that I be able to be in the full ministry—especially for the Latino community. I'm able to marry and baptize and all those things, but being able to model that to the community is very important. I also hope that I can make a difference in this community, where the Latino community has more voice, on how things are done to benefit them. So many poor people all over the world, especially in Latin America, survive on the money sent home from their relatives here. I'm grateful for that.

I find hope in my faith and the people I minister to. There is a fine line between the divine and human, the "is-ness." When I am confused or don't know what to do, that is where I go, to nature, the trees, the night sky, that silent place within each of us where we remember hope.

My fabulous daughter is just the heart of my life. She keeps me going. Many nights when I can't sleep, I count my blessings, like that Bing Crosby song. The blessing of Lupus has debilitated me into an unbreakable relationship with the divine. My faith is quite clear on the fact that we are family, that what happens to you, happens to me. I have survived by silence. *Nada cambió, entonces cambia.* Change takes forever and then it happens.

Because the civil war was escalating in El Salvador, Hernán and Marta both decided to flee from their rural village in the late 1980s. They arrived in Massachusetts, where they married. Since they had family connections in its small but growing Salvadoran population, in 1993 Hernán and Marta relocated to Portland where they both found work at a local food processing plant. By 1995, they had saved enough money to purchase their own home. They have a son and a daughter with whom they attend Catholic mass each Sunday. Their goal is to provide a safe environment and good education for their children. At the time of the interview (2004), Hernán and Marta were thirty-four and thirty-six years old, respectively. (Hernán and Marta are pseudonyms. As such, a photograph of Portland's Salvadoran restaurant appears in lieu of the couple.)

A view outside Tu Casa Restaurant Salvadoreño.

7

Hernán and Marta

We Left because of the War

Hernán: We've been here in Portland for eleven years now. We came here because of an uncle of mine who had moved up here. He lived at 26 High Street, a big building on High. He let us know that there was work here, and he wanted us to move up here.

First I came to see what it was like. A woman brought me, so that I could come see if I liked it. Then we decided to move from Boston. We were in Boston for two and a half years, I think. We liked Boston a bit, but then later, because of the work and the pay, it was really too little. I worked in a company called New England Casting. The work wasn't so good. At the time they were paying me almost minimum wage, $4.00 and something an hour, I think. It was difficult even if you were sharing the rent with the family, so people helped each other out a bit. But if you lived alone it wasn't enough to live on. And then to send to the family, it wasn't enough either.

There are a lot of Salvadorans here. When we came here in '93 there weren't many. Then later they came. There were only a few, only the ones who lived in that building on High Street. That was the only building. Yes, the only one. A lot of Salvadorans lived there. My uncle was one of the first. He came first with an aunt of mine and others; a cousin of hers was there too, and a cousin of theirs. And the husband of one of my aunts, but they returned to El Salvador. They liked it, but since they already had their kids there, and all, well, they decided to go back there.

The Salvadoran community is pretty united. They do things together. They have parties. They get together at times. When there's a birthday, a wedding or things like that, they always get together. Maybe there along Congress [Street] somewhere there's a discotech that they have; I think they have dances every Friday or Saturday night. Before it was on St. John [Street] but it seems that there was a bit of a problem there so they moved here to the center of Portland, to downtown. I don't know what part, but it's around there. I think they gather and have parties there, dances and all. We've never been, because apparently they drink and all.

They used to have it at a restaurant on Forest [Avenue]. They used to have the parties there, but they had problems there. They no longer wanted to rent to them there, so now they say that they're here [in downtown Portland]. They say that they come from all over, but the ones who do the music are Hispanic.

The Latino community gets along here very peacefully. Maybe there are a few who do not, but I know the majority does. At times you'll see someone and you don't know them and if they talk to you, you say, wow, they're talking to me and so then you talk to them. You can't talk to someone that way if you don't know them well, but, yes, you don't hear anyone saying there are problems. There are only problems when people are drunk at a party. That's where problems are likely to start.

The majority goes to the Bodega Latina to shop. We do too; we do all our shopping there. The only thing is that Immigration was bothering people there. Apparently they were grabbing people from there when they were leaving. Apparently they had planted themselves on the corner, and also where the Greyhound bus stop is, since the majority of Hispanics goes there to shop at that store that's on St. John [Street] in the little plaza, since food is cheaper there. Everything is cheaper there, in the supermarket. We go shopping there too. It costs less there, right, they were coming from there with their food and they made them drop the food and there they took them.

From what I hear, they grabbed something like forty [people] and then they grabbed, I don't know how many more. They were all Latinos, Salvadorans, Guatemalans, I think, and Hondurans, from all countries it seems, even Cambodians, from what they say. They never bothered us; we never saw them. They came to Barber Foods too. They say they came but that day was the day that I got sick, I think, the day that I had the accident. The next week I think they came. Someone told me that they came. There they didn't take anyone, I think. No one told me so.

Marta: I like the work at Barber, more or less.

Hernán: Yes, we like the work.

Marta: I think work is never good.

Hernán: They treat us well. We don't have any problems because of that there.

Marta: There the important thing is to do one's work and if one does it well, everything is fine.

Hernán: Other Latinos work in shellfish, in seafood companies. I think that's where Ana [Manza] was working when she got sick, the one in South Portland. Only Latinos work there in that company. I don't know what it's called. The second in charge at the Bodega Latina, he sends people there too, part-time. His name is Juan González. He knows the name of the company and he sends you. You talk to Darío or anyone there. He's Dominican. He sends people over there too, and another guy named Jim, and he's Salvadoran as well, I think. He has his office there, it seems. They say he has it at the Bodega.

Marta: Not at the Bodega, at work.

Hernán: Yes, at work. Apparently he has an office at work, in the company. I don't know if it's outside the company. He takes people to work there. At times, it's hard to find work. I've been working at Barber Foods for eleven years, almost. We've been there ten years. [We are] not experts yet. They also work with those shellfish . . . lobsters. And that egg that they get from the ocean, the spiny one.

Marta: Sea urchins. Right, they call them sea urchins; they're spiny. They look like thorns, and they get them from deep down.

Hernán: A lot of Hispanic people work at that too, and Cambodians. And in all the shops, there are a lot of Hispanics who work in shops. And at the Jordan [Meats processing] plant too. It's only for seafood I think. They bring all kinds of fish to that company. In Atlanta, Georgia, I think it's called. Yes, it's another from the Jordans that makes hot dogs.

Marta: Maybe so many Latinos work there because of Juan; where they say there's work, they go there because the important thing is to find it quickly.

Hernán: Or because of the salary too, maybe they pay better.

Marta: Because if you work in production you get paid according to how much you do.

Hernán: Because in shellfish you're working in production. If someone produces a lot, they get good money just in a day. There it depends on how fast you are. But, also, if someone's not fast, they don't earn anything there.

We've been about two times to Tu Casa [Restaurant Salvadoreño], the one that's on Washington [Avenue], that's all.

Marta: We like the food; it's Salvadoran food.

Hernán: But they don't make pupusas as good as she does. When I've gone they make them just from cheese, I think. They don't make them from pork cracklings, and . . . it seems like mostly Americans go there. Yes, that's who goes there mostly. Americans and it looks like French [Canadians] is the other.

Marta: Since Hispanic people make that food, they're not going to go there to eat the same food they make.

Hernán: The majority who go are those who work Saturdays and Sundays, they order food out because they don't have time to cook, perhaps, because they're tired. They come home tired and they call, or, if not, they come by and take out food. That's how it was in Boston also, since there are lots of restaurants everywhere now. They order out food. They don't like to cook much hardly; on Saturdays and Sundays the restaurants fill up.

Marta: We go out, but only to stores, we don't go out to parties.

Hernán: Sometimes, when we're invited to birthday parties or weddings, we go out, but when they do dances like that, then we don't. We get together with friends, like that time you came, right. For example, at Javier's, with him, like at the party, we almost always get together with them. They come over here, and that way . . .

Marta: But they're Mexican. They live in [Old] Orchard Beach.

Hernán: There are lots of Mexicans in Portland, for example, lots of Mexicans work at Barber Foods. Many work there. Many part-time, and there are many who work for the company too. Those are the majority here, Mexicans, I think, more than Salvadorans. And there are a lot of Hondurans. Well, now a lot of Salvadorans are coming. Now it's true that a lot have come here. These groups are the majority here: Mexicans, Salvadorans, Hondurans, and Guatemalans. Everyone gets along well at Barber Foods; the majority who work there are Cambodians. Vietnamese, and many Africans and Russians work there, and from Bosnia, more than Americans, many languages too.

Marta: Fourteen or fifteen languages, they said, something like that. They put little flags out for all the countries that come there. The Salvadoran flag too . . . flags from all the countries.

Hernán: When they had the meeting at the hotel, I think they told me there were more than one hundred languages there. We were both born in El Salvador.

Marta: There are different religions among Latinos. For example, the ones who are Catholic, the ones who are Adventists, the ones who are Evangelicals. There are no problems, because there's respect, see?

Hernán: The only thing is what the religion demands of the people. For example, Catholicism doesn't demand anything from anyone, but the other religion requires that they . . . but everyone respects one's religions too.

Marta: If they respect you, there are no problems.

[What] we like best about Portland [is] that there's not much traffic like in Boston.

Hernán: And there's not much danger in other things either. Because in Boston you can live with a lot of annoyance: the rent, at times you can't have your things, they want your cars, your videos. Here in this place, in this area, you live really well.

Marta: It's a very complete and full little city, in the center. It's nicely enclosed and so since it's a closed city everything is there.

Hernán: A family lives better here in this state. They can go to school. . . . They don't have a lot of danger either. The schools are good, too. From sixth grade on, they teach Spanish. They're teaching Elwin [their son] Spanish. Elwin speaks Spanish well, but he can't read or write it.

Marta: At home we only speak Spanish and he knows it all. Our daughter knows more than he does.

Hernán: Yes, she does know everything. He doesn't read or write Spanish. The girl does. She reads more. Here it's only Spanish we speak to them. So they don't lose it. At least if they don't learn to read and write, if they travel, they can at least talk to people, right? Because there are a lot of people who don't like to speak Spanish at home with their kids. They only talk to them in English, and they forget Spanish, and if they travel outside the country, they only speak English. And they lose their Spanish. Because there are a lot of people, I've seen; there are kids who maybe don't speak English well and they only speak English at home with them, and that's not okay.

Marta: It's a bit different and hard to maintain one's culture. But if one wants to, they can keep the customs from there, like food and that, just like there. We cook the same so we can maintain it.

Hernán: We don't feel a lot of pressure to lose our culture. Maybe there are some people who lose some things. But you never lose your language. . . . You have it engraved in you . . . but there are people who want to get ahead. There are a lot of people who come to this country and . . . they speak a few words of English and then they don't want to speak Spanish, so they speak English.

I have an uncle who doesn't speak Spanish to anyone, only English. And he speaks normal street English. He's always spoken to me in Spanish when we get together, but he doesn't speak to my brother, or to anyone he sees [in Spanish]. It's not the same uncle who invited me to come here. It's another. He's the youngest of all the uncles. It's really amazing; he says he's already forgotten Spanish. Since he's arrived, he can't speak Spanish. He came when he was nineteen or eighteen or around that. He's young, but he's already maybe twenty-eight, twenty-seven. He won't go back to El Salvador. He doesn't even write to his parents. And he doesn't want to see them either. He works there in a shop, in a seafood company. It's difficult. It depends on the individual, but coming here and wanting to forget the family, that's not okay either.

We went home not long ago. It's going to be a year since we went. I wanted to travel next year, but it's going to be hard because I had the accident and they tell me I can't travel. I'll wait, maybe for Holy Week another year. [We return to El Salvador] something like every year or year and a half, because to be traveling when you have a house and all, and the tickets are expensive, and with the whole family you end up spending a lot. Before we weren't allowed to travel, but now we are because we have residency. If we want to, we can vote, but we don't want to. I don't think we can vote, but lots of people say you can.

Marta: We're not citizens.

Hernán: No, just residents, that's all. I think that when you're citizens, then, yes, one's obliged to vote.

Marta: Maybe when they go off to college, we just might go back to El Salvador, when life is calmer and we no longer have to work. Besides, we have to see that they finish high school and go on to college, and then we'll see what . . .

Hernán: We're from Chalate. It's near the border with Honduras. I mean we were raised not in the city nor in the capital but in between, in the countryside. We're from the countryside [so] it's a shock to come to the city because one gets accustomed after all. We were born in that place. Even if it might be ugly, if one is raised there, they always like it. It was ugly before, now it's prettier. Now they've built more houses. Now it's like a little town. But before it was just a house scattered here and there. And there it's a *canton* [village/neighborhood] where we used to live, and there was another little valley where there were a lot of houses together. Now there are a lot of houses that they've built there.

We left because of the war.[1] The war was bad at the time [in] that place. It was fierce. There it was the most dangerous, more than anyplace [else] because that was where the war started, in Chalatenango. We lived there. Soldiers always passed by, far away perhaps. We never saw them.

We met there. We didn't marry until we were here. We didn't come here together. There was something like two months difference. There were no big challenges here in Portland, except the first days. That's how it is when you move to another state; that the first days you feel a little crazy, as they say. You don't want to go out because you don't know [the area]. That's how it was for us before I moved. We walked, took the bus, we'd go to the store and shop, and then we had to call a taxi. Later I bought my little car and we used to go to the shops and we got to know a bit. It's helped a lot to have our own car. Now it's easier to go out. I like it here better. To spend time, to support oneself, I think it's a better place here. More than anything else, there isn't much danger.

We're involved in the [Catholic] church. There are [Latinos] at other churches also.

Marta: Yes, there are many. We've never been to any.

Hernán: There are a lot. For example, here on Park Avenue they get together from the Adventist church, I think, or it may be another. And around here there's another where they get together also. There are many churches where Hispanic people go. For example, when there are wakes, a lot of Latinos get together then. For example, there was a funeral here when a girl died recently.

Marta: Reina, I think, was her name, the one that was killed in the fire. I don't know how it was, she stumbled, she got hit, I don't know. They put it in the newspaper. Some say she jumped, others say no. I don't know, but they pulled her from inside. She was from Guatemala.

Hernán: Some say she was eighteen or nineteen years old.

Marta: No, twenty-two.

Hernán: Well, they held a wake for her here in this funeral home that's here on Forest [Avenue], where the train crosses. There's a church there too. I think it's Catholic. They say there were a lot of people. We weren't able to go. The same when there was the other wake in the Catholic Church. Then the church filled up too, there were a lot of people.

Marta: It was a little girl, three years old.

Hernán: Then they get together there. Everyone gets together, all the people from the other churches. It doesn't matter what religion, any religion. Every single religion got together that day too.

Marta: For weddings they all get together too. They choose not to see . . .

Hernán: They don't check to see which religion you are. This also happens whenever there's a birthday and parties. When there are parties, it doesn't matter, they get together. There are many opportunities to get together. People say there aren't Latinos here, but there are a lot. When you notice you see that, indeed, there are a lot. Yes, there are Latinos.

Marta: One doesn't know them because one works in one place and another in another and they're not seen.

Hernán: Because a lot of them also work in restaurants; in the ones where they have Vietnamese [food], for example, at the mall. There are lots of Latinos who work there, or Cambodians.

Marta: They're not Cambodians, they're Chinese.

Hernán: Yes, the buffets are Chinese, right? But not many Latinos are in those buffets, only a few are there. They're in other restaurants. They do cleaning or cooking. A lot of Latinos work there too. You don't see them because they work seven days a week. They're there all night and during the day they sleep, that's also why you don't see them. A lot of people say that they're only a few Latino people in Portland, but I don't recall how many there are, but it's true that there are a lot now.

Marta: The hard thing is that here you have to study and go to work at the same time, go to school. When we came here from another country, [we struggled] to learn the language well.

Hernán: One has to work very hard.

Marta: We've been in ESL [English as a Second Language] classes and still are.

Hernán: She [speaks] more than I. Not much of it stuck for me, so I didn't continue. They offer classes at work too. There they have a school for the workers. I used to go. They gave two hours. They also have computing for the people. You want the work that you most want to excel in.

Marta: After the classes, most work right there, or they give you a job like secretary, or supervisor, for more money, if you make the grade . . .

Hernán: And they also pay you to go to school.

Marta: And they pay for childcare for your kids too. It's true. You have to look for a place outside, and then they pay you and you pay for it. The owners are Americans. He's from Armenia, the owner. But the children are American.

Hernán: He came here as an immigrant like the Latinos, and they say he faced a lot of discrimination from Americans for being from another country, having another language. He decided he was going to start a company and he did. I don't think they discriminate against him now. I don't think they can. Here in Portland, there are very few men richer than he is probably. Now they make millions there every day.

We haven't faced a lot of discrimination. The owner doesn't care. If he gives you a job, then he gives you a job. Whether you speak one language or another matters to others, but not to him. Instead, he gives you classes so you can learn a bit at least to be able to apply yourself, or understand each other a bit at work and all that, understand the areas, what this area is called, what that one's called, and like that. But he doesn't care if you don't know English; the important thing is to know one's work. They don't bother us if we don't speak English, just knowing thoroughly the part that you work on, that's all, or not making a mistake. And for that reason they let you know everything. If you make a mistake then it's hard afterward because in the training they've told you what it is that you have to do. When I got hurt, they were critizing a little because the doctors didn't know. But being a doctor, he has to know if someone's really injured or not. He just touched me like this, said that I was fine, that now I could go to work.

Marta: But the problem was that the doctor, if the patient doesn't give permission, he can't say what the patient has, and that's what happened.

Hernán: Also without any document from the doctor, he couldn't tell me to go to work either. He also had to wait for identification, a statement from the doctor. If they had also said, "Let's wait and see the results from the doctor, how the accident happened, how you are, if you've broken anything." But no, I just stayed like that and started to work again. They also apologized afterward. The only thing is that the nurse told me that I might lose my job if I didn't go to work. That I should go to work with one hand, and then they told me no, that I couldn't work with one hand. Then they ended up looking bad. They recouped because before they also did it to another guy. And it looks like they got rid of the nurse. But he brought a suit against the company. The other guy also suffered almost the same accident that I had, but they operated on him. They were making him go to work too. And then after that, he decided to talk to a lawyer. He sued them so they'd get rid of the nurse. I was also thinking about that as well if they told me they didn't want to pay me or if I no longer had the job, then I also had my lawyer to talk to about what the motives were. So then I could sue them as well. But not now, because everyone's been good up to now. They even told me they're paying all the medical bills and they're also paying me the same salary I was earning. I'm not going to file a suit, not for now. If later they tell me that I can already work or [they can't pay me], or some other thing [then I will reconsider]. They're treating me well for now, because they have to.

In any case, everyone there knows me too, how I work and all. The work that I did, no one else does it as well. That's what my supervisor told me.

She said, "There's no one who does the work you do."

I'm an expert, because I was the one who took care of that line. It wasn't just intelligence that you used, but then afterwards you don't need to get all worked up with thinking if you do the work quickly. Then you just know. But when they don't know and something breaks down here or there, then they start running down the line. But not me, I just let it go, to see where the problem is and then I come, and then it starts running again. They notice how I work. They can see that I work hard. I used to work at 5:00 in the morning and I'd leave and it took me almost two hours there and back and sometimes I'd leave at 3:00, 3:30, 3:45. At times I'd be very tired, because sometimes there wasn't even time. The supervisor also said that sometimes I took breaks and sometimes I didn't. I'd only take the half-hour break and nothing more. Sometimes there wasn't time. With all that, they gave me a good score. The score they gave me, there isn't anyone else who has it there. They gave me 100 points. I'm doing well there. It's a good moment.

Then afterwards we decided to look for a house. Because for us to be paying rent is money that you could say goes away and never comes back. If you have a house, at least [you are] depositing in the bank a bit of money that you're going to see again after you finish paying. Then if you want to sell, the house is yours. We bought it in '95, I think. We've had it seven years now, seven or eight. I don't remember the date.

We send money to my dad and mom in El Salvador. And Maria sends [money] to her mom too. Sometimes, we send [money] through Western Union, or if not, sometimes [with] people who travel there. I think Western Union charges less than the traveler charges. The traveler charges like 5 percent, and at Western Union I think they charge 3 or 4 percent. The traveler comes from El Salvador. A lot of people who travel come from El Salvador. There's one who comes here who comes up this far. It's like a company that he travels for. I think they take out a license, a document to travel, a visa and all that. They can't take just anything. They don't allow them to bring just anything either.

I didn't go to school in El Salvador. When I was growing up, there weren't any schools there. The schools were far away, like four hours by bus, so I didn't have the opportunity to study. I regret it a bit.

Marta: I went [to school] for, like, three months, when I was very little. [I stopped] because the war started and the people were afraid. Our professors then were also guerrillas. Our parents didn't know that they were with them. I remember that they'd put on their radio when they would say they were going to attack so that they could run away. Since we were little we didn't know. When we got bigger and the FMLN[2] radio would go on, then we played a lot and we didn't know anything. When they would talk to them and tell them that we should leave, they would run away. The people were maybe telling them that they were going to attack.

Hernán: Or maybe it was that they were communicating from there in the other canton that . . .

Marta: The parents didn't know that they were guerrillas, and we were there in the school with them. Only we knew, but since we were little we thought since they were talking we didn't pay attention to what they were saying. Because kids don't pay attention when grownups are talking. So what were we going to say to our parents? We didn't know.

Hernán: They were nearby. For example, where we used to live is a canton. On the other side was a canton that was about an hour's drive away that really was a big valley. It was a big canton and it was from there that they came. Many of them who were professors from there were the heads, like leaders, so they had the group organized with the same people that were there, I think, except that there they wanted to add a dad, or a cousin and a dad, another uncle. There were about six. [One was] a cousin of mine. What surprised us [is] we were little; I must have been about the age of Elwin [eleven years old]. What amazed us was that every Sunday he'd come to the house, and they'd cook some chickens to eat and bathe in a pool there that was really big, where there was a ravine. He would take them cookies, sweets, for everyone there. It was a lake, like a pool that rivers have, where the people bathe. And they'd eat and they'd take beer there, or liquor, tequila, something like that. And they drank there and everything. Well, two of the planners would come, the professor who was like the leader, and they also wanted to have my dad. There were like six, the ones that we had at . . .

Marta: This was really strange: At the Catholic Church there were something like the mothers and the ones who serve the priest and they were with them too, and they were undercover. They would arrive dressed that way, or maybe it was that they would dress that way so that the people would see they were with the church. Because they would be all dressed like that. And the leaders thought that they were from the church.

Hernán: So they wouldn't suspect that they were up to something.

Marta: Or maybe they weren't with the church and they dressed that way . . . that could be . . . because in the Catholic Church . . .

Hernán: No, but since they could belong to the church and be in the other group as well.

Marta: When they killed handfuls of priests or what were they from El Salvador? Six Jesuit priests and two nuns who were working with them, something like that.

Hernán: That was really awful. And some days after my dad's coming to the house since they met there, around three or four weeks from then, they were wandering outside because they wandered around attacking people and then everybody started running.

Marta: That was really nasty: to see people that were going to live in the mountains and abandon their homes. Little children sleeping in the mountains because they were going to come there.

Hernán: Since they had already given a warning that they were going to come to the houses, if they didn't go and they gave them whatever they had, if they had weapons or money or whatever.

Marta: Anyway they killed people. Not the military, the guerrillas.

Hernán: Civilians, since they all dressed like any civilian, like us.

Marta: But they were guerrillas.

Hernán: They went around like civilians. They were already armed going around like that.

Marta: And the bad thing, see, when they went around like that, they'd pick on kids just like Elwin and they'd get them and the soldiers would attack, and then the kids would die there. They killed those children because they were already mixed up with them.

Hernán: Since they already had weapons and all.

Marta: They had it in for them. They'd set them to fighting, and when the soldiers would attack, those children died there. That was really nasty. It was all really nasty.

Hernán: The people were really afraid of it, more than anything, because it started near a canton. So the people were already more afraid of it. Even though they didn't do it to kill the people that way right away, since they were civilians just like we were. They didn't confront people face to face. They didn't have the courage . . .

Marta: And the bad thing was that they'd burn busses full of people. They'd light them on fire. All the people there would be burned. Yes, that was nasty.

Hernán: Yeah, but then that was closer to the center of Chalate. Yes, that was nasty, right.

Marta: When my grandfather died . . .

Hernán: There was a place there that everyone really feared. It was called—that place, they called it the wells. There they really hurt you. Everyone, whether they were on foot or in trucks or going by bus, they got everyone down. There they simply set fire to the cars. There it was really very nasty. Around that time was when we came here, I think. We couldn't take it any more. That was in '86 or '88. It was around that date. In '87, '88, because in '88 we had already come here. I came alone.

Marta: The whole family stayed there. I also came alone.

Hernán: Already by that time from 6:00 p.m. on, no one could be seen outside; you had to stay inside your houses because planes, helicopters, and small aircraft were bombing. Since the guerrillas had already taken power somewhat through other people. They were hiding there. So, then, anyone was killed there, good people, bad, everyone alike. There everyone died. Farms, livestock, everything [was] leveled. It was really hard there then.

I came here first. I already had my brother in Boston. He was younger than us. And he came, because there was a relative of ours who helped my brother with money so that he could come. After that, with my brother here, I told him that I wanted to come. Well, I'll see how I do here, I got the money and that's how I came here. Then afterward a lot of people came. The whole family there where we grew up, they all came. There's only one sibling still there, no more, but he's disconnected. He has his family too. He's pretty different. They don't see each other; they don't visit my mother. She's pretty lonely. She has two sons there, married with grandchildren. She has my brothers there. My brother, the one who lives in front of my mom's house, he was living here with me. He went back in '94. And the other one who came here first went back in '93.

Marta: They married and made their homes there.

Hernán: All of them now have a family. But now they've been left alone. There are only two at home. My mom and dad were left alone after the whole family no longer fit in the house. There are a lot of us. We're seven males and two females.

Marta: In my family, they all got married too and live apart from one another. My mother lives alone, but she lives in the city. She moved away to the city, to Metapán, but they're coming here, all of them are coming in the summer. They always come in April to spend the whole summer here.

Hernán: I'm thirty-four. I turned thirty-four last night, yesterday. My son celebrated my birthday here last night.

Marta: He gave him toys he plays with as gifts.

Hernán: He shut himself in here, and closed the two doors. He was doing something and after awhile he called me and he had already prepared everything. They did it last year too. Last year I was sick, I think, as well, from flu or I don't remember. And that day I went to sleep, or I came home from work and went to sleep, but they were waiting for me to fall asleep. But one of them was arranging things here and the other was keeping watch there in the hallway so I wouldn't go downstairs. And after awhile when I woke up, they were watching for me to wake up. In a little bit they told me to come downstairs. They gave me something to cover my eyes and after that I opened the door and they had the light off. Then they told me they were going to turn it on and for me to uncover my eyes, and they had the whole table arranged. With candles, and it said Happy Birthday too. Wonderful. In our family they never celebrated birthdays, because [of a] lack of money, or because they weren't accustomed [to it].

Sometimes my Mom remembered, "Oh, yesterday was your birthday."

She was pretty busy. Because there were only men, there was no one to help her. She did everything for everyone. Sometimes she didn't even have time for anything. All day she would be out washing clothes. Like they did washing there. She was the one who did the wash. She would go to the stream to wash clothes. And sometimes she'd be there all day until she finished washing all the clothes that were dirty. As a young boy I was raised just with my Dad, just working. I was the first in the fields. We grew a corn and bean crop. That was customary.

Marta: [I am] Thirty-six.

Hernán: The hope we have for the future is that our children won't have to work like we've worked and suffered. We worked hard so that they can get ahead and go to school. Let them say what career they want to pursue so that we can support them in it. They have to decide so we can support and help them. For example, right now my son likes sports a lot, soccer, playing ball. That's what he likes best. The finals are on Saturday, and he plays like three games it seems, in Saco [Maine]. They're in second and the other team is in first place. And so that day they'll play against each other to see who will take first place and second.

I also played in my country, and when I came here I liked to, but not anymore. After I injured my foot, I wasn't okay anymore. But I liked it a lot. We used to play a lot there. When I was growing up there, we always had tournaments and all that. You have a great time too, just like with basketball. My kids love basketball. Before, I didn't understand it, but now I do and I like to watch it. I don't play it. With them, we play outside sometimes.

There are not many Latino soccer teams here. Sometimes they play. It seems they have one that plays indoors. What's it called, inside turf? Not long ago they opened one there on Warren Avenue. I think the Latinos have one there. In the summer they play outdoors sometimes. We used to have a team in the summer, about four years ago. I have a uniform. It was called Maranátame. And we played well. After that we lost control a bit. Some people wanted to do more than others and so it got out of control. The team had people from all over, Mexicans, Hondurans, and Guatemalans.

We used to go as far as Boston to play. We went to Boston maybe two times. Or if not, they would come. We'd issue them a challenge so they'd come. And that way they'd come here, and we had to go there for a return game. We'd bring them the deposit of $200 and then if they didn't come, they lost the deposit here, if they didn't come to a return game. Then if they came we'd give them the deposit. You ask for the deposit because if you don't ask for the deposit they don't come. That deposit is used for buying other things, like if we needed to buy more balls or other uniforms. Then with that we almost had enough. Yes, you have fun, right. More than anything, at least people enjoy it. There are a lot of people who like to play, and a lot who don't like to play but they like to watch games too. They like to have fun.

Now, it seems that my brother is in charge. They're doing tournaments there in the canton [in El Salvador]. They get people from all the cantons now, where I was raised. There we have a field on the side of the road. But everything was ugly. Now it looks like they've fixed it up. They went to ask for permission because it's by the road so it's national. When they came to hand it over, I was little so I don't remember, but the papers got lost, supposedly. I don't know how they did that, but supposedly the papers had to be in the town hall. When we went there, [the papers] didn't turn up at the town hall. They had come from San Salvador to hand over this playing field, because it was national there. No one can say that you can't use this field. My brother then went to talk to the owner to see if she'd give permission to fix it up.

And she said, "Yes, fix it up."

And they've done it and now they have tournaments there. A lot of people go there on Sundays. All the people don't fit anymore. It's pretty there. It looks like this year it's going to be there and another year it will be in another canton, and that way it will continue to happen. A lot of people get together. I don't know how many come. I think that some fifteen get together. They all have to go play there at the canton. There are cantons that have up to three teams, two, three, first and second, or they have another youth team as well. There are a lot.

Now the canton has changed a lot. It's prettier now that they built a school and a church and all. Some of the money I send there goes to this, and from the people that go there now, since lots of families send money.

Marta: Like yesterday at church when they collected money, the community takes care of that money.

Hernán: But it also comes from the community itself, the church. They've put up a clinic, too.

Marta: Or if they want to do something they tell them how much they're going to spend, and if they can help everyone gives their part.

Hernán: Or if not, they also let people here know that they need something.

Marta: Or it's just like the church here, that they say we're going to do this, and this is what we're going to spend, and then the people give money.

Hernán: When we go back, the people think we are rich for living like this, all the people. But, it doesn't bother us. Since now the people from our generation [are in the United States], there isn't anyone left there. Now it's people that were born after we came here. Now it's different. A new younger generation is there. I didn't know them, and they didn't know us. But there the majority are really poor. Sometimes they only have their house, just enough to live, no more. Since my father has work there, he has really supported the people that are working with him. He gives them work. If not, he gives them half-time work. He pays half and half for them, and that way they've gotten ahead a bit. It's very difficult there. Life is really hard. Because there the day you go to work is for no more than getting through the day. The next day you have to go to work again, too. You can't live like that.

Marta: It's not like here where there's work and you go to work. Not there, there there's no work. So the people can't [work]. If there were work just like here, the people would get ahead, but not there. Everyone works for his own good.

Hernán: Everyone works just to get by, that's all, to get by with the family.

Marta: There they don't have [programs] so people can work to be teachers or something like that, because the government has schools for that, to work with students.

Hernán: But always if there's no money, how is someone going to work to become a professor or another level? If they don't have anything, they can't in any case. There in the canton, there aren't classes beyond fifth grade.

Marta: And the other advantage here is that it's not the same. Here when they go to school, the kids don't have to go well dressed. Not there, they have to go well dressed. There they have to spend [money] on clothes. The teachers tell them what clothes they have to wear, which shoes. Well dressed. So if the parents don't have money for the kids to go to school, chances are they don't send them. It's not like here where they just go and wear any clothes.

Hernán: There the kids have special uniforms, but the teacher tells them which one it is, one for each day. They have to change their uniform every day. Every day they have to go well dressed. And if there are five days, five uniforms. But that's only in town, in the city. But when they start improving, start moving up in grades then they no longer allow them to go, they have to go that way. For example, in the canton, at four or five years old they can go just like here, they go in whatever clothes, but then if they enter the university then it's different. If it's a low grade, it's okay. As one moves up, they start requiring books, what they work on in school. The parents have to pay for it. That's why parents there don't make the kids continue with school. It's very expensive.

The other thing is that the school is far away. They have to travel or stay in town or in another canton that's far away too, so that they can stay there to study. It's not like here where big schools are nearby.

Notes

1. El Salvador's civil war lasted from 1980 to 1992.
2. The Farabundo Martí National Liberation Front (FMLN) was an insurgency group that sought to overthrow the military government of El Salvador. It signed a peace agreement with the government in 1992.

Victoria Chicón.

Victoria Chicón, originally from Peru, is a filmmaker, mother and grandmother. For the last six years in the Portland area she has immersed herself in every media venue available to her. She helped organize the Center for Cultural Exchange's Mundo Hispánico to ensure that Latinos had access to those events. Today she is the host of WMPG's radio program Cruz del Sur. She teaches children Spanish at her grandson's school. Victoria often states that she has more energy than she has time and can't imagine a time when she will stop getting up every day to explore new sources for her imagination and creativity.

8

Victoria Chicón

My Life Has Always Included Change

My name is Victoria Yolanda Chicón Yarleque. I was born in northern Peru, in Piura, in a little town called Catacaos, which is a town of artisans who are very famous for their clay and silver work. I'm sixty-two years old. I was born in 1943, on the 10th of March.

My Mom is from Piura. Her last name, Yarleque, is written in part of our history, because according to one historical theory, they say that in the north there was a Tallán group, the Tallanes, who are the product of an immigration from the north; I mean, they don't know about the Mayas or Aztecs, that settled in the north of Peru, in Piura. There aren't many traces now, as it's on the coast. It seems that the sea erased a lot of evidence of that ethnic group, except the last names, including Yarleque. A general somebody or a prince, named Mecnón, from Central America, came through there, and his deputies are Yequeces. That was the name of his deputy generals. And now there is Yarl-equec and Pan-equeck, right? So there are a lot of last names there in Peru, in Lima, I mean, in Piura. Yarleque is one of mine, that's very well-known too. And Panaque, Yarleque, Zarnaque supposedlly came from that ethnic group.

My father is a Chinese immigrant. He supposedly arrived in the thirties or forties. Leaving at the start of the revolution, the struggle between the nationalists and the troops who were starting the revolution. I think they had first gone to San Francisco because he told us stories and talked about San Francisco. He talked about Panama.

I didn't realize that my father was Chinese until I was already an adult. He was just my father, that's all. In Peru there are a lot of Chinese. There are Japanese, Chinese, Italians. So, for me it was normal. I didn't feel that my father was different. I hadn't discovered that my Dad was a foreigner. So, that's the story; my Dad was from China, and my Mom is from northern Peru.

As for me, I came to Portland. I came here because my children came in '85. I got married when I was twenty-one, in '64, maybe. But we separated just about two years later. My kids were very little when we separated.

We practically didn't know where their dad was, see? Then in the eighties, when they were grown, he appeared and said he wanted to be with them. He went with visas and everything. So, I said, "Well, their father is young. He might just be able to extend their stay," right? They came here to Florida with him in '85. My son started to study. Their dad promised to help them pay for their studies. But it seems that he didn't. So my children did the best they could for themselves.

Then my oldest, Victor Aima, got into college. He did journalism. He studied to be a reporter there in Florida. My other son also went to high school. My oldest son was already in college, in Peru, when he came. He came when he was nineteen, I think. And my other son when he was seventeen. So time passed, and they were living in Florida.

I wasn't granted a visa to come, even though they came. Once they operated on my son . . . My son Daniel is a cancer survivor. They took out his stomach, but they refused to grant me a visa to come. Finally, they gave it to me, and I came to take care of him, when he was recovering, for three months, and then I returned.

From then on, I could come every once in a while to visit them. My oldest son joined the Marines. He married Jane, whom he met at college in Florida. Then he went on his tour in the military, in the Marines in

California. First he was in North Carolina and after that in California. After that he went to Japan. And then they settled here, because my daughter-in-law is from Maine, from Portland. And my son thinks that this is a nice place, and safe for the kids.

So when they had their second one, they called me so I could help them. That coincided with a hard time in Peru as well, because I was working two jobs in the same place, in a school, like SMCC [Southern Maine Community College]. I taught film and video there. But I still needed to find a third job in order to support myself and my daughter who was at the university. Then my son said he was going to help his sister, and for me to come. So in '98 I came to take care of my grandson Gabin. I've been here six years.

My daughter is still in Peru. She's there for her law degree. She's going to present her thesis, and she doesn't want to come because she's studied to practice there. But I don't know what will happen. I never wanted to come. I never knew that I would come. I never even imagined it. Or that I would stay, and now I've already been here six years. And I like it here. It's pretty. Here I've found a lot of things that I imagined, for example, living near the sea. When I first came here there were pansies in the window boxes, my favorite flowers. A lot of things have coincided with my ideas of life. I like it. Well, the climate is hard, but here inside the house, well, you don't feel it.

In Peru, up in the sierra, only in the luxury hotels do you have heating, but not in your home. Well, I hope they have it now. I don't know, but they're making a lot of progress. But here you feel it. For example, it's winter now, it might be snowing, and here we are. I'm fine in a blouse.

I like the people here. They seem like good people. Since I came here, I've tried to find my own niche, I mean the way I lived in Peru, right? In Peru I did journalism, I worked for children's rights, for women's rights. I've taught—despite not having a degree, right? I'm a filmmaker, because I learned by working. That is, as soon as I left my job, I started working in film. Since about '62, I've been doing film. As an editor, my world is that of journalists, intellectuals, professors, teachers, cultural circles, museums.

I tried to look for something here, because my son wasn't going to leave me to work in a supermarket. Since I'm not the type of woman to just stay at home, I started to volunteer in the children's museum to see what that was about. I'm fascinated by everything. Everything's new for me. I never stop learning. So I liked it.

I've been a volunteer here. I've volunteered teaching Spanish in my granddaughter's school, and going to libraries. In the library in South

Portland I met Tom, who's a wonderful person who speaks Spanish. And he always found books in Spanish for me, so that I could read here to my grandchildren and my students. And that way, I made myself.

I went to the public television station. Here you're fortunate to have public access channels. I registered in the course, right? As if I didn't know anything about video . . . to find out how the language is different. What they use, even though I've learned to make films in English or in German, because the manuals for the first film editing machines were in German. I don't know German. But because of the job I had to start reading the manuals to understand what I was moving. And my boss was French. So there was all this combination of languages. Now I've learned a bit of English, but I'm not a polyglot, either. But I try to understand. That's how I tried to get my bearings here. That's how I got to know people and the media.

And, I like living here. Actually, since I'm a Pisces, I think that any water is good for me. My life has always included change; it's always been in a constant state of change. I've had a lot of problems in life that I've had to face. My family has helped me a great deal. So I think about what's to come. I don't know where I'm going to be. I try to see the best in the place, in the people, that I have to relate to.

I don't know how to see the bad things. That's a problem. I don't know how to be suspicious of people. Now I'm fine here. I've practically made a way of life. But you never know! I mean, my son is in Florida. My granddaughter is just seven months old. I'd like to help him too, like I've helped here. I'd have to move, change my life. If I have to do that, I want him to come here, because it's prettier here but it's different. They're from Florida, they're different, it's like coming to another country, too. He'd have to leave his job. Because of the baby they've tried to come, but it's hard to find a job. They have good jobs.

Also, my daughter's in Peru, I mean, I have a triangle. I don't know who's going to need me first. Now they need me here first, then suddenly I'll have to go there for Dani, and then to Silin. I try to make life be as good as possible. You know that in my life I've moved practically every year. Well, it seems to be one of the signs in my life: moving. I try not to think about . . . I don't create conflict around what I might have to do. I have my way of seeing the good things, the bright side.

Here it's hard to find a job. Of course, if I go to work, say, at McDonald's or at a supermarket, I'd have money, right? But I don't know if I have the energy for eight hours of work, of forty hours a week. Still, now I have my two-hour job at the school. After that, well, I teach Spanish an hour a week, or sometimes two hours a week. I also have a job with kids at the Center for Cultural Exchange because, fortunately, kids like me. And I like kids a lot. But now there aren't any funds, so I don't work there anymore, but I worked there for a year. And, so, there are the little jobs that are volunteer. I mean, I do radio and television as a volunteer, on WMPG. My show is called *Cruz del Sur* (Southern Cross), and Rosita does one for Latinos. My program is every Thursday at 1:30. Then I put on Peruvian music, because it's what I know best. I try to put on music from South America and news of the community. Now Manuel is helping me, and I think it's good because he contributes a lot of things from Guatemala. And now we're trying to get more people to come to tell their things. We have so many traditions to share in all of Latin America, right? Every country is different. There's not just one Latin America. It's really diverse. You know, there's a saying. How does it go? "As long as you have more to learn, you stay young."

I like to work with children. Back in Peru I've worked with adolescents and kids. And with adults too, but I like to work with young people and children more. Here I've found work of that sort. I teach Spanish to children [as] a volunteer in my granddaughter's school. I taught them when they were in kindergarten, first grade, second, until third grade. Then they didn't call me anymore. So I got a job here in the Language Exchange school, with Valerie. She has her school here in South Portland. She just happened to have moved to South Portland, which is good for me. There I teach Spanish to groups of children. I also work in the school on Brown [Street] helping when it's time for lunch and recess. I have a job on Sundays too, during the Unitarian service. I stay with the kids and they like me pretty well and I like them pretty well, too. I'm with the little children, up to three years old. And after that they go to Sunday school. The people are very nice at that church.

And I also did volunteer work at the children's museum a couple of years. I'd like to have a daycare in Spanish for our kids, and for the people [who] really like to speak Spanish here. That way I earn a little money. My work has always been a pleasure, because doing film is a pleasure. If you set me to editing it's as if no time passes. I can get up early and I don't get tired. I was a very good editor. I'm a very good editor according to the directors with whom I've worked. I have a lot of creative possibilities. I mean, I'm very creative in that sense. That's one of my strengths. So I try to take full advantage of it.

What's been hardest about living here in Portland is the food and the customs. For us food is really important. It occurs to me that that's why we're a little chubby. It's very important. When I arrived here, I saw that the cupboards are full of food. So I thought, what must they be spending on food? But I can't eat this pizza, packaged goods, canned soup, no. I mean, we don't have that because in Peru it's expensive to buy that. It's very expensive.

I remember when my children were little we bought food at the market, in the neighborhood. In every neighborhood there's a market with fresh food. But then, little by little they started having supermarkets. Sometimes you go to the supermarkets, which seem cheaper, but you spend more. And my kids, what they bought there was peanut butter or some packaged cereal. They loved it, but in brands from there, from Peru.

Here I started having some gastritis because I didn't know what time to eat. For us, you arrive home and you eat with the family. I needed to wait until the kids got home to eat. But the kids eat at school, and then they don't want to come home to eat until late, until the evening. When the whole family is here. So it took me a couple of years to get used to it. Until I said, no, I can't. I'm going to make my soup, my rice, and my stews.

So that's how I started cooking and so my daughter-in-law and everyone else got used to my cooking. And the kids eat. Of course, I try to make what they like, their noodles that they eat here, what they call "noodles," with their canned sauces. But I make their vegetables. I've gotten used to cooking here and to eating on my schedule. I have to eat at midday. I can't wait till the evening to eat a big meal. I mean, my main meal has to be at midday. And after that I keep going, and I can eat at night. Well, actually, to tell the truth, I eat all day.

And then, another thing that took me a long time to get used to: the clothes! In Peru, you dress in "fashion," as they say here. You dress up to go to work, long dresses. The girls wear jeans a lot, but they have their pretty blouses, their earrings. You put on makeup and perfume, and everything. But not here. Here I had to put on a big coat with a hood. Shorts! Sneakers! I'd never worn sneakers! I wore my high heel or low heels for walking, but I never wore sneakers and shorts and those polos.

The clothing is very different, and the food, and people's schedules. I mean, well, getting up early, I've always gotten up early. But the mealtimes, I mean, in the morning back in Peru—I think in all of Latin America—at 6 a.m. everyone's going out to buy their bread. That doesn't happen here! Here the bread is already packaged, right? There the bread is hot. In every neighborhood you smell the bread at 6 in the morning. The kids get dressed quickly and go to buy bread while the mother's fixing breakfast. You hear the sound of blenders making juice so the kids can drink it before going off to school. Fruit juice. Papaya, with strawberries, or milk with something. And then, well, the kids come home for lunch, because they're in school till 2:00, and they don't feed them bread or lunch at school. They have to come home to eat. The mother has to prepare the meal at home. And so they come, and now since there are so many children in South America, well, in Peru, there's another shift in the afternoon. I mean, the kids that go to school in the afternoons, that start their school day at 2:00 in the afternoon; they've already eaten their lunch before they go. So, there has to be food at home. And at night when I got home from work, for example, I'd stop by the market, which still closed at 5:00 or 6:00 in the evening, but I could still get fresh things to cook. And cheaply too. Here I spend twenty dollars, and I buy a bunch of celery, a bag of rice . . . Two or three items! But there with twenty dollars I buy for a week. With meat, chicken, and everything.

So, the food, the schedule, and clothing. I mean, I had to get used to a different way of dressing, a more comfortable style, sporty, casual. Not there—everyone dresses as if they were in Boston, everyone with their nice coats, all pretty. Jeans are pretty common, but with their blouses, everyone nicely made up, with perfume, and . . . with their little jewelry. Not real jewels, of course, because there someone will snatch them from you. Here you can wear gold every day and silver every day.

The biggest challenge I've had is achieving my own status. I mean, getting together with the kind of people that I'm used to dealing with. For example, here the newspapers just have news and not much more; they're not very cultural. There, in our newspapers, magazines, they have lots of cultural things. And because of the language, too. Just recently I'm trying out an English class for writing and reading. I read more easily than I speak or write.

And, of course, the movie scene. I tried to go to a film company a couple of years ago, when I didn't know much English, I guess. I tried to interview the director of the company who's a filmmaker from here. And the secretary asked me if I was looking for work. I said no, that I was a filmmaker and I wanted to meet the director. Then she said, "He's very busy." So she gave me a card so I could call him. In Peru that can happen, too.

But then I tried another angle. I was really happy that Tim moved here, Tim Rice, who's from *Moviemagic*, the magazine! He moved here. At first I thought he was a little farther away, but still in Maine. I was pretty happy because I was hoping there would be a filmmaking triangle between Florida, California, and this side of the East Coast, but no! I tried to approach them and I sent my screenplay, but I think they didn't read it. But I filmed the whole contest, the first film festival that the magazine here in Portland had a couple of years ago, I think, two or three years ago. And I sent it to Tim. His son goes to school where my granddaughter went. That's as far as I've gotten. I haven't tried to go farther because there isn't that interaction yet.

I have to pay to join the association, [but] sometimes there isn't money. It doesn't cost much, fifty dollars, but not yet. I don't have it. I've tried to go to a couple of events. I joined a group of screen writers. I also joined an association of screenwriters from here [in] Maine. Their business was in Brunswick, I think. But my problem is getting there. I still don't have a driver's license. And there's no time to practice, because someone has to be with me to practice. And that's hard to manage. My son is very busy. My daughter-in-law, too. Everyone has so much to do. So, I still haven't gotten a license, and that limits my mobility.

I get around by bus, though. I mean, since I've been here I've gotten to know all the busses in South Portland. But it really took me time to learn all the schedules! In Peru, you go out to the corner and there are five of them. The whole street is full of buses to wherever you want to go—but not here. You have to wait an hour, or half an hour, or a quarter of an hour, and sometimes they're late, so I'd think they'd already gone. I'd start walking when the bus was just coming. It was something to learn. It took me awhile, at least two years, to learn how to manage with what to wear, the food, the weather, and the busses.

I've faced some discrimination here. You know what? I ran into a woman who treated me very badly—just because she felt like it—here in the supermarket. And she treated my grandchildren very poorly, too. I spoke to my daughter-in-law about it, and she talked to a woman we know who works at the grocery store, and it seems that the woman spoke to the manager. Maybe he said something to the woman, because every time she sees me she gets all red in the face. She's an older woman. I was with my grandson with the cart that has a car attached in front that they have at the grocery store. My grandson was lying down. Then she told me that I had to take the boy out of the cart. I was at the checkout.

I said, "But why? I can go out with the cart with the boy in it."

My grandson bought some candies, and she threw them down on the counter. I said, this isn't a normal attitude. That attitude is because I'm not . . . because I'm a little different. I hadn't done anything! I was in line and there weren't a lot of people. She was the one running the checkout, taking care of the customers who were buying groceries. And she told me I had to take the child out of the car.

I said, "But why? I can take the boy out in the car. We don't have much to buy." My granddaughter bought some little candies, things like that. And the woman threw them, after scanning them through the checkout.

And another time at the bus. Several times I had to wait for my grandson. It was winter, too. I hailed the bus, but he said, no, that he took a different route; twice, a couple of times. I also went with my daughter-in-law to the bus company, and we told them. Supposedly the driver had some problems. I don't know. Those are the two instances of discrimination. Here you don't see discrimination, because the people are very friendly. But sometimes it happens, right? For example, the other day I was selling some of my crafts. A friend, a man, said to me, "Very nice. Very nice! As long as they're not Sendero pieces!" From the Sendero Luminoso (Shining Path), from the terrorists in Peru. And I thought, what?! I mean, how does he know about that? He's well informed. Why does he have to connect my things, my experiences, with the Sendero Luminoso? I mean, they know about the bad things, that's all. And so there isn't discrimination, but fear. So, you have to be careful.

And I've often seen social faux pas. That they want to do something, but since they're not really aware, you know, in Latin America, in general we're aware of things. I mean, on a corner you see some old people or some kids at the bus stop and they're talking about what's happening in the world. But not here. I mean, here, you know the news from here, but not the culture of the whole world. American culture, I mean, they're completely absorbed in that, but their historical past doesn't interest them. But we have so much of that, the whole historical question, our heritage. We have the advantage of seeing things more broadly.

With language it's very complicated. I mean, I try, for example, to speak Spanish here with my grandson. It's easiest with my youngest grandson, but the little girl, who's older, has a harder time because she's already at an age where she doesn't want to make mistakes. And my son didn't speak Spanish to her from when she was little. My son in Florida was trying to speak Spanish to the baby. I hope he can manage. But I think because communication is very important, the one who's talking, like my father, when he speaks Chinese he might think that I'd miss what he was saying. So sometimes that happens to me with my grandson too. So I talk to them in English. And they correct me too. They help me. They correct me.

But the language is very important, right? But so are traditions! I mean, for example, I'm not very religious, but how you celebrate Christmas, right? On my father's birthday I put out his picture. I tell them that he was from

China, that he sang, what he was like. They have a little different background, where their family came from. My son has made a very nice web page with everyone in the family, so I hope that they'll have more and more access.

Now with my grandsons, the language might get lost if we don't keep insisting very strongly. My granddaughter, for example, is taking French instead of Spanish at school. I tell her, good, that's an advantage, because she's going to know French, Spanish, and English! So, we try to treat it that way. I think that if they listen and listen, it doesn't matter if they don't talk, because someday they're going to try to understand. And, besides, you don't learn anything if you don't need it. You can't learn a language out of luxury. Here you've studied another language since you were little, at school. But they don't practice it, so they forget it. I hope that they can go to Peru for vacation and then as they play with their cousins there they'll find a motive, a need to communicate; that way they'll come to enjoy the language.

I don't have a lot of free time, but I enjoy the time I do have. Fortunately, I don't sleep much. Lately I've been more tired than before. But I used to sleep just two or three hours, and I was happy because I could get all my things done in the morning. Now I get more tired, but I try to keep very busy. And suddenly I'm deficient; a person who's very diverse. I do a lot of things. And then I lose focus on what I should be doing. So I'm trying to work on that, on keeping focused. I don't like to get frustrated. Since I have such big dreams, for example, of making movies. It's complicated, of course. I'm moving forward, but I do other things that are fulfilling for me, that make my day, that keep me going.

When I was in Peru, I'd start sewing. Then you see something completed. There, I did something! Because you can start something and finish it. That's one of my defects, the diversity of interests. Since I know how to do a lot of things, at school they taught me to do many things. I can do anything. Then I try to put it into practice. I don't lack the opportunity to leap from branch to branch, like a little monkey.

With Latinos, we tried to create the Centro Latino. But before that, I tried to get involved with the people who went to the Center for Cultural Exchange, where there were performances of Latino artists here, and by going to church where all the Latinos are. There are a lot of churches that I've never been [to in Peru] because I was raised as a Catholic, see? But here, because of the community, I've gone to visit them.

There are a lot of Peruvians here, too, in the Catholic church and the Adventist [church]. There's even a priest from there. An Adventist pastor that

I met there. Incredible! I've met more than sixteen Peruvians here. But they say in Connecticut there are sixteen hundred included in the census! And there are more than thirteen organizations of Peruvians. So, there are Peruvians all over the place.

I wasn't here in 1974 when César Chávez came to Portland. I just learned about him here, because of the prize. . . . I'd only heard a little bit before, not much. But now with the prize you got, I learned about César Chávez. I think it's very important that they've given him recognition. There's even a César Chávez prize established here in Portland.

You know, I'd like to work in the community. In Peru, the schools and the university are the centers where there's real movement around cultural issues. And after schools and universities, it's in magazines, newspapers and magazines. I'd like the schools here [to] have involvement with cultural activities. Donna from the Center for Cultural Exchange does that work, I think. Because at the Center for Cultural Exchange they have passport programs. So she goes to the schools and takes local artists. But they talk and teach about Brazil. She does a beautiful job for the center.

What was good in my school, for example, [was that] every classroom had the name of some country in Latin America. In that classroom you worked on that country. You studied its history, or you did something, the flag, the national anthem, you sang, and all of that. And on the anniversary of its independence you invited the ambassador, and the ambassador came. So then you would celebrate the anniversary of Brazilian independence, and so we wouldn't just learn about it in books, but in person, and directly, about what Brazil was, about every country in Latin America. So we can do that here. That's my dream. I hope some day it can happen.

Now, with the creation of this association of Latino students in USM, I think it's very good. I felt a different atmosphere at the university. It's not like there. A Latino association is formed, or some association for X is formed at the university, and the whole university is there. But there weren't many here. There weren't many people. There was us Latinos, but there was no one from the university, very few from the university were there. Not in Peru, all the students go to see what kind of thing it is, what the group is doing. To oppose it or to support it, but they're there. That makes a society dynamic. I don't know if it's possible here, but [the Latino-Hispanic Student Association at USM is] on the right path. I think it's important in the university and where Luisa works as well, in the Multicultural Center.

And I think the Adult Education program should be given an award. I love the Adult Ed school. I don't know, it seems like an excellent program to me. The teachers are excellent, and you can see the variety of the world there.

My goal is to make films. I hope that before my time is up I can make a couple of films. But I know that it's very hard, but it's not impossible, either. There are others who have done it. You have to be dedicated to it. That's why I have to fight with my distraction. My son is helping me a lot. He bought me a digital camera and an Avid editing system, which is an extremely expensive thing that I never dreamed I'd own. I'm trying, but the bad thing is that I don't know about business. You can put me to work like a slave, but not when it's dealing with business. That's my misfortune: I haven't found the partner who can be the manager for me.

In Peru the majority of filmmakers make film, because women are the producers. In my case, I'm the filmmaker, but I haven't found a man who can be my producer. I haven't found the manager. I'm limping along without my other half. It didn't work out. Even though I had my second daughter, I got together with a filmmaker, but we were both artists, not businessmen. But he can do more things than I can on his own. That's my dream and, of course, having my own little house. That's all I want. Sometimes I've had my cards read and I have the star of triumph, or the sun of triumph, or something. So, I keep on moving forward. They say that one's life is already written. Maybe, I don't know. But every day you make everything change. People's will is such a spiral that you can twist it all or head it all in a certain way.

What I'd like to add is that everything I've done, I owe to the support of my family. I mean, my father, my mother taught us to support each other. There are four of us sisters, and I'm here, alone. My sisters who are there go around together with a whole clan of more than thirty following behind, including my cousins. In my family my aunt thought she was my older sister. She lived with my mother and father's family. I have my three brothers and my two cousins. That's the family that gets around together like little ants. They support one another. My sisters Elsa, Blanca, and Lili work together for the whole family. They worry about the toys, they worry about the family's problems, about the little ones that are growing up. I have several nieces, nephews, and grandsons. I'm very proud also of my children who have made lives for themselves practically alone.

My Victor Aima, who's now a programmer, is a photographer and he was a painter and musician. My Dani was also doing computer work, but after having worked for the company fifteen years, at night, that was really a bad thing, he was a supervisor, but they didn't give him the chance. I think that's a bit of discrimination, too. He's a hard worker and he's very responsible. He asked them to change his schedule, but they refused to do it for him because he's Latino. So he had to leave a job after fifteen years! Start all over again! Because he has to be with his family, right, his little girl and his wife.

Well, I'm very proud of them. They've made their way practically all on their own. My daughter is going to be a lawyer soon, too. And she knows English, she knows Italian, she's learning French. They're so nice, the kids are. I mean, I hope they have good luck. My grandchildren are really lovely too. I'm very fortunate in the family I have here. She's [my daughter-in-law] very nice, too. I mean, I've met her friends and her family. I've found a good place. I mean, I'm really fortunate.

Juan González.

Born in the Dominican Republic, Juan González enlisted in the U.S. Army as a young man. He has the heart of a family man whose traditions are deeply rooted in the Catholic Church and love of his community. He has the mind of an entrepreneur who saw a need for a store that would provide traditional food and nourishment for the soul. Thus was born La Bodega Latina. Regular customers include people from Latin America, the United States, and Africa. In recognition of what he has done to advance the promise of equality for all, Juan was awarded Portland's 2004 César Chávez Leadership Award. Since the interview took place in La Bodega Latina, the recording also captures people talking, bachata music, sounds from a kitchen, and the creaking of a door opening and closing.

9

Juan González

Roots Are Important

My name is Juan Gonzáles, and I'm thirty-five years old. I'm from the Dominican Republic, and I arrived in Portland because of service in the United States military. During my last six months in the service, I was transferred to the Brunswick Naval Air Station, and that's how I came here to Portland, Maine, around 1997. I've been in this area for seven years now, thank God. My family is here, too: my wife, Rosa González, and my two children John and Johana, and my sisters Beni González and Jazmín Durán, and my mother, Marta. I have a lot of family here. We're a big group.

We have a spiritual family, too. We always go to church on Sundays. Whenever we can, we go [to] the church that's on Mellen [Street], Sacred Heart. We're Catholic, so we're active at church. We're a close-knit family. This is fundamental in any business, and the family is like a business. We have to be close to get ahead.

When I moved here, there was a cousin of mine named Becky Ross, who was the first to come to Maine, and she lived in Portland. When, by chance, they transferred me to Brunswick, and she was already here, I stayed with her the first two weeks while I hunted for an apartment here. I would commute to Brunswick. It wasn't really out of choice, but more by chance.

But I love Maine. That is, I love Portland. It's a beautiful city, and the people here are wonderful. They treat you with a lot of respect. It's good. I like it.

When I left the service, I had some little temporary jobs. I worked for Taco Bell for a few days. I worked for a cleaning company for a bit, too, while I waited for a call. I'm a telecommunications engineer so I had my resumé posted on the Internet hoping that someone would call. I really didn't know New England very well. I did whatever job came up to support the family. After being here a month and a half, I got a job with a company in Boston called John Hancock. They're brokers. I would do telecommunications for them. Then I commuted from Portland to Boston every day. I kept it up for eight months more or less, until the first snow. And I said to myself, "I can't support myself this way." Then I had the good fortune to get a job here in the hospital, in Maine Medical Center, doing the same thing, telecommunications. That's how I supported myself until we started the business, and I became independent. Now I have my own telecommunications company, and we serve . . . the Bank of America account, which was Fleet Bank. And I still maintain their telephone exchanges.

But La Bodega Latina was something we needed. We like to eat plantains a lot, and when we arrived here in Maine, there weren't many plantains. We had to hunt for them and bring them to Portland. When I had to go to Boston, I'd bring them from there every day, and it was sort of uncertain. And so I said, "There's a need here. Why don't we try to do something?" First I started to sell them from my house. I'd bring five or six boxes of plantains, and they would all get sold.

People started ordering from me: "You, papa, you go tomorrow, bring me this, bring me that."

And so we started that way, and I said, "Well, this business might work."

That was it. We decided to put [it] in a small place; that's how we started, with something small, and, thanks to God, we've gotten to where we are now. Now La Bodega is no longer just for the Hispanic community, as we started it. Its nickname is "The People's Market." Everybody comes here. Africans come here, Somalians, Hispanics, I mean people from everywhere, everyone comes here to shop, thank God.

And with the restaurant it happened the same way. The people themselves started asking about food that we didn't have. That's how we started a prepared-food service. I mean, it took me some time, because the restaurant business is sort of delicate. I have to say it's tricky. They say that about 85 percent of restaurants fail here. I didn't want to run that risk. Up to now, all of the businesses that I've started, with thanks to God, have been successful. I took my time with the restaurant. We gave them . . . we got it started, and up to this point the people are giving us their support. It's working. It's still in diapers, but we're paying the bills. People eat here no matter what. We have some good cooks in the family.

I was educated in the Dominican Republic, but I finished my studies in telecommunications in the Navy, in San Diego. When they gave me the Small Business Award of the Year in '99, we were competing with a lot of businesses on the state level. We were well received by the Small Business Administration. They chose us as the first. That was a memorable experience. Then at the beginning of this year they gave us the César Chávez award. It was also a really great experience. And the rally that we had against the INS [Immigration and Naturalization Services], that was an unforgettable experience that I'd repeat. I'd repeat it over and over again, every time this happens. That was also an experience that had a positive impact for me even though it was something negative in my life as well.

The most difficult things about living in Portland are the taxes. We pay a lot of taxes here, but it's part of the business. They say that doing business in Maine is tough, and it is tough. It's hard, but you can do it. The problem of having to pay a lot of taxes is difficult, but it's manageable.

Whether luckily or unluckily, I've never directly had problems with discrimination here for being Latino. I don't doubt that they can see in my face that if something happens to me I'm not going to keep quiet about it. I've experienced it through other people who are close to me, friends, family, and they really have suffered discrimination for one reason or another. For example, people who have gone to get [an] ID at the DMV [Department of Motor Vehicles] get questioned more than an Anglo who goes to get an ID.

Just because someone's white, they can get a hearing and they don't get questioned as much as they question Hispanics. Because of their color, they make it much harder for a Nicaraguan immigrant, a Salvadoran, a Mexican, a Dominican. That's where discrimination comes in. The same as when you go to request a loan from a bank or something like that. You sign, "González," and they say, "Fine, wait a minute." Let's see what happens. You sign "White" or "Smith," and they don't question you so much. I've had people who've brought that kind of complaint to me. They have had a hard time getting loans at the bank for their home, for whatever, because of that situation. And it's definitely because of discrimination. I know people who have a perfect record. I mean, they don't owe anything, they haven't been delinquent in anything, and still, they make it much more difficult for them. But those are uncommon. It's not something that happens all the time. They're not extreme. It's not that they tell you that because you're Hispanic, we're not going to serve you, no. They draw it. They use tactics when they do something like that. They take their time, subtly. You know because [when] you analyze it, you realize in the end that's the reality. It was because of discrimination that something didn't happen.

Of course, it's important for me not to lose my language or culture. In my house we speak both languages. I speak English to my kids, and my wife talks to them in Spanish. Automatically, when they talk to me they speak in English, and when they talk to my wife they speak in Spanish. And if the four of us are together talking, they switch back and forth. They talk to me in English, and then with their mother in Spanish. I don't want that to get lost. Roots are important.

Sometimes you feel pressure to assimilate. At first I did. The advantage I had when I arrived to this country for the first time [was] I immediately entered the military. That was the best experience that could have happened to me in the United States, because there I learned everything I needed to see about United States culture. There I learned politics; I learned economics and sociology. I learned everything. I learned to manage within the system. So when I came from there out to the street, when I came to civilian life, it was a little bit easier for me. It affects the reality of life because the training in the Navy helped me adapt. It helped me adapt to the new system. I was coming from a third-world country; entering into a military power like that of the United States was a big step for me. Then staying in it for four years without any problem was an even bigger step.

For the kids it was a little harder, especially for the boy, the oldest, because when he came here he was already four years old, three or four, and he already spoke Spanish. He didn't speak any English. When I enrolled him in school, luckily we found a program in Reiche school where they helped people with disabilities with the language. But it was hard. It took him a little to get adapted to the system, but after the first year in that program, he assimilated. Now he behaves more like an American. I mean, now my son is twelve years old; he's in sixth grade and his grades are good. He's always one of the ones with high grades at the school. At first it was hard for him. For the other one, Johana, she was born here, and my other two sisters are American, too; they were born here. That was the easiest way to adapt, because they were born in this culture.

The only thing is we keep our roots from our country. I mean, in my house, one culture rules, the one I brought here, as my parents taught me in Santo Domingo. I'm not saying that I follow the culture of teenagers here. No, I don't buy that. My daughter isn't going to be on the street, no, my daughter's not going to be seeing it and not knowing what someone's consuming. She's going to be at home with the rules. And it's because we've been growing up in that system, and thank God, everything up to this point has been that way. Despite the fact that we're in a different culture, I still impose the culture that made me, where I come from. And they've been assimilating it perfectly inside the home, that's the culture that rules. None of them talk back. That doesn't happen in my house. Of course, they interact with friends and that's fine, but in the end we always gather together and share and set an example.

"Look, do you think this is possible? Tell me if you think that this is okay?"

They keep quiet; they say, "No, that's not okay."

They realize that what we're doing is for their good. Maybe now they see it as being a little hard. They see it as a lot of restriction, but in the long run, they're going to be the ones who benefit.

I say it to my twelve-year-old, "If you don't have a career, you're not worth anything. If you take and you enjoy life now and forget to study, in time you're not going to be worth anything. The only thing I think I can leave for you is an education, and that's what you're going to have from me, an education."

And, so far, they're assimilating well.

I love Portland. I love the state of Maine. The people, the climate, even though sometimes it's hard when it's snowing. But that's pretty, too. What do I know? I feel fine. I feel good here. I participate in a lot of events. I belong to . . . what's it called? ILAP [Immigrant Legal Advocacy Project], the association of lawyers that helps with immigration issues, the ones who help Hispanics who don't have the resources. I'm part of their board of directors. And a group that's called the Rotary Club, I'm a member of Rotary. There we always have the opportunity to deal with a topic that affects the community, not just Latinos, but in general. . . . I also participate in that.

Every time that something happens here, that has to do with my people, I have to stick my neck out. I'm totally involved with my people. I wasn't here yet when César Chávez came to Portland. But I was here when Portland celebrated his birthday in 2000. . . . I saw it. It was a good. It was very nice because it recognized a patriot of ours, a hero of Hispanics. Yes, that was very pretty.

As far as hopes for the future . . . I want to see Hispanics in the legislature here in Maine. I want to see Hispanic power involved both at the local level of government and at the legislative level in Congress. And I know that they will be. If it's not us who do it now, our children will do it. And that's why I strive so hard for my children to have a good education, because I'd like to see someone come out of the González family who says: "Look, I come from an immigrant who came here, doing this, and, look, now I'm the mayor of Portland, Maine, or governor of Maine," or something like that. We can do it. Our children are the ones who can do it.

Sitting in the waiting room at Lourdes' International Beauty Salon is a testament to the diversity of Portland. On any given day you will find Asian, African, African Americans, and Latin Americans of every persuasion (Caribbeans, Mexicans, Brazilians) waiting for a style and cut that only she can deliver. Lourdes opened up a shop that is very much like a Latin version of the film "Barbershop." Hers is a gathering place for connection, coffee, laughter, and Spanish-language TV. Though Lourdes had to fight long and hard to obtain her beautician's license in the United States, with the help of a friend, she completed the process successfully. Despite being the only non–English speaking person taking the exam, she passed two-thirds of her test requirements on the first try.

Lourdes Carpenter.

10

Lourdes Carpenter

Trying to Move Forward

My name is Lourdes Maria Carpenter. But everyone knows me as Lourdes. I'm from the Dominican Republic. We're from a town which is called Santiago. Santiago de los Caballeros. I arrived in the United States first in New York because my mother has been living there since 1984. She did the petition for us, and I arrived in New York in 1996.

I was in New York for a month but I didn't like New York's atmosphere, especially for my son, who was really little. My brother lived here, and he said to me, "Come here," and we came to live here. I arrived in Portland on October 30th, in the beginning of the fall of '96. I have been here a long time. I've had to sacrifice a lot. Now I feel better. But in the beginning it was very hard for me.

I mean hard in the sense that I didn't speak any English. I didn't understand. There weren't many people who spoke Spanish here. I would just go with my brother to the supermarket and then there weren't as many Hispanics as there are today. I would hear a Hispanic person speaking and I would get excited and look around to say, "Ah! You speak Spanish! Oh, how great!" Yes, I would have to say that that's something that makes you feel excited, to meet another person who speaks Spanish. There were very few people. But with time they have come. The Latino community here has grown a lot.

What can I tell you? Many hard times where perhaps you find someone who wants to extend a hand to you, can translate for you, but you can't always find people to help you, and yes, you suffer, you cry, in many moments I felt hopeless. You miss your country, and you get depressed for whatever little reason, you feel useless, you feel disabled, and that's why now if I see someone who needs help, I try to give them a hand.

I had to work a lot. Many times I left some places crying because people didn't understand me. And this made me feel really, really bad. But, you know, one struggles and all that. But they're things that give you strength to struggle ahead. You say, "Never. I'm not going to surrender. I have to manage to move forward."

For example, when I [was in] my first job. It was cleaning. I cried. I felt so bad because I've been a hairdresser in my country since 1984. I had my business ever since I graduated. We didn't have any illusions. Things went very well for us. We weren't rich. Yes we lived poorly, but I was happy there. Because I took good care of my son. We had food, we lived poorly but we lived well. But you sometimes don't believe, it's like your mind is saying, "Ah, there everything is better. There there's lots of money."

There are many people that believe that here you find money walking along the street, like the leaves. Everyone's dream is to come here. I had someone to take care of my son there. I had someone who would cook for me, who would lay out my clothes, because that's not expensive. If you work hard you can pay for a servant in your home. So, for me to come from there, to arrive here and scrub bathrooms, that was very hard. I began in Macy's vacuuming, when my supervisor in the store came to talk to me, I understood him through hand signs.

Sometimes I felt bad, and I was so depressed that sometimes I would cry for any silly thing. For example, when one day he told me to put a plastic bag on the vacuum and to hang it on the vacuum so as to go along and throw in it the papers that were around the store so that they wouldn't get sucked into the vacuum, and then he said to me—I didn't understand! And he said, "Forget it," as if he had gotten frustrated with me. I thought that he had said a bad word, and so I told my brother, and he said to me, "No, he meant that you should forget about that."

Then after that the head boss of the company came to visit Macy's, and I think he's Portuguese, and he speaks a little Spanish. So he talked to me and I guess I made a good impression. He said to me, "Ah, I'm going to tell your supervisor that he give you a job that's more comfortable for you so that the work will be better for you."

It was hard for me to begin working in that job. I was depressed, I cried, I didn't sleep. But I had no option. I went to various salons and they told me that they couldn't give me a job because I didn't speak English and I didn't have a license. They told me what I had to do in the meantime to get my license, and after that I had to learn English as well. It's not easy. So while I was working in Macy's, I began school.

So, when the boss came it seems that he said to the supervisor there that he should put me on cleaning the bathrooms. I didn't know at that time that the bathroom job was, for the women, the lightest job. But when he told me, "Okay, the boss just said to me that I should put you on cleaning the bathrooms," this was like a humiliation. I began to cry in front of everyone there.

I said to him, "Look, I'm sorry." I told my brother, "Tell him that I only clean bathrooms in my home, and not even in my own home in Santo Domingo did I clean bathrooms." I began to cry, and cry there.

Then I told him that I was leaving. My brother had given me a ride there, and he had dropped me off, and I said to him, "Don't go, because I'm going to leave, I'm not going to scrub bathrooms." I felt at that moment that scrubbing bathrooms was the biggest thing that had happened to me in my life.

So my brother said to him, "No. She's quitting. She's leaving."

The manager, as if he had a little bit of soft spot for me, said to me, "Don't go."

So I said to my brother, "Tell him that if he lets me keep pushing the vacuum, I'll stay in the job. But not the bathrooms, no."

We were already leaving, but he waved to me like this, "No, no, come here. Keep pushing the vacuum." And I turned around.

That is funny because there were some people from the Philippines who were friendly with me, and we would eat lunch together. In Philippine [Tagalog], some of the words are similar to Spanish. There was one Filipino who cleaned the bathrooms when I was pushing the vacuum. Sometimes I would sneak away, I would go to the bathroom to talk with him, and would help him with the mirror, and that's when I realized the truth: That the easiest job was the bathrooms! So I said, "But it's true!" After that I wanted to clean the bathrooms.

I adjusted. I went to school. And my son went to school, too. I lived alone with my son. After time went by, I got my license. My brother,

Anthony, helped me a lot with a car; it wasn't very expensive, and I began to drive. I went to work, and I began to learn a little English. I began the paperwork for my cosmetology license.

To me, that was very, very frustrating. They didn't allow me to have a translator. They didn't let me use Spanish in the exam. There were many requirements. After I filled out the application, since I had my license in my country, I brought my diploma, I brought everything, I had to return to the Dominican Republic to get letters from where I had my business, how many years I had it, signed by the mayor of the city, from the school, with the director, with how many hours, everything, all the requirements; and it's a lot of things that they demand of you. Just my diploma wasn't enough.

So when the application was all ready, and I thought that we were going to have a little bit of good luck, they said no, they don't give the exam in Spanish. They wouldn't let me use a computer that would translate it for me. They wouldn't allow me to have someone with me.

So, I said, "What am I going to do?" Because I didn't know any English, very little, "Good morning" you know, "How are you?" But not enough for an exam of that level. Well, I began to study and study, and I had already learned a little, and I decided to take my exam.

"Well," I said to myself, "I am going to try to do what I can." I went and I didn't know any English. They sent me a pamphlet with all the things that would show up. Let me tell you that I didn't know much English, and for those cosmetology terms, in Spanish, I would have passed it in a split second.

I didn't know even "row" . . . I didn't know what that meant! And I said, "God, what am I going to do?"

Since I gave the $89 for the application fee, they sent me a pamphlet with the statement below that you need another exam, a whole day from 8 in the morning to 5 in the evening. In the morning they give the practical exam, and in the afternoon they give the written exam. Well, I go, and I bring everything. They sent me a list of what I was going to need, and all that.

I told the lady who was going to give the exam, because I heard her say at first, quickly, "You have ten minutes to do this and this." Since she said it really quickly, I said to her, "Look," with the little bit of English that I knew, "I don't speak English. *Yo hablo* (I speak) a little bit." I said to her, "But if you explain me what I'm gonna do, slowly, you know, I can understand better."

Then, as if she understood me, she said to me, "Oh, you don't speak English? You are so brave that you are here."

And so, she treated me as if she respected me a little for that. I didn't understand what she had said to me. So when I would motion to her, she would repeat it. "Part the hair in four sections. On this side, do a complete relax, on the other side a retouch relaxing, on this side do a new color, and on the other side a retouch color." In other words, let me tell you, I passed my exam, the practical, and I was really nervous. I don't know how I passed it. I knew how to do my cuts, I had my model, which was the doll, a mannequin, and I just concerned myself with my work and that all my hairs were even. After that, since we had completed the whole exam, they don't give it to you all at once: the facial, the makeup, and with that you're done, so they don't tell you if you pass or not, they just go along making notes. They take you to another place and there they give you the written exam, about the Maine laws. I had read a lot, because they had sent me the pamphlet. I did it, with a lot of effort, yes. I dwelled on some questions, checking them, looking them over. I did it!

After that came the big one, the written cosmetology exam. It's some three hundred questions. It was unbelievable. It was just guesswork. I knew that I wasn't going to pass that exam, because I said, I don't know any of this. If they were to give it to me in Spanish—but, you know, the language. When I went home and they sent me a notice: I passed the State of Maine exam! They themselves told me that almost all the Americans go up in flames on that one. They were surprised that I had passed the exam. I passed the practical!—all of it!

But I crashed and burned the other part with just sixty-one points, since it was seventy-five that you needed. I got frustrated, and I said to myself, "Get to it," you know, "Study." I kept on. Sometimes my friends came to my house and helped me.

I walked the floors of the cosmetology schools finding out what I could do to pass my exam. I found a school in which the director told me, "Look, I want you to tell me something: How is it that you passed the State of Maine exam? Almost no one passes that exam, hardly anyone."

Then he said to me that if I gave him $2,500 he would prepare me for the exam. But I didn't have that much money and it was a lot of money, and so I said to him no, that was impossible.

So I asked him, "What should I do?"

"Ah, well, we have a little book, that has questions that you can read."

"Ah," I said, "How much does it cost?"

"It's ten dollars." That book was my salvation. It had all the questions—there are quite a few of them, so I set myself to studying and studying—but let me tell you that I took my exam four times because what I was missing was the written. What happened? I took the exam one September. You have until the next September to pass it. If you get to September again and you fail again, the other two that you passed expire. That's why I was going crazy and was so stressed, because after one year if you haven't completed the three sections, then the other two expire, too. Then you have to start all over again. Then, that's not all. Each time that you take the exam you have to send a money order for $89.

So I was due in September, and it was already July. July was the last exam that I took. And then if I didn't pass that one, I had a chance in August, one that they were going to give in Bangor, another that they were going to give in Augusta. But you had to be quick, because if you lose time in registering yourself, you also had problems. So that was when I got the little book, around June, then in July I was going to take the exam. I worked at it night and day, day and night. Everyone was helping me; my friends would come to the house and they would ask me the exam questions. By that time, I knew a little more.

And so, I took the exam. The lady who came from Florida to give it, I'm not sure of her name, she knew that I had problems ever since the first time, that I didn't know much English—I won't forget her because she thought so much of me that she gave me an extra half hour because she knew. I sometimes had to spend a few minutes on one question. Of course, the questions come with four answers and sometimes, you know, I would be there looking for the meaning, because it's a big deal when you know what the answer is, but you don't understand. You know what it's about but you don't know the meaning in English for the cosmetology terms. The words that they use are very hard.

When I went, God knew that I had worked hard, and that time—I knew that I had done well, but you never know. They take two weeks to give you the results. But what happened? You have another date by which you have to write your money order if you don't pass, to take the last one. So I was worried. I said, "I can't go back and pick up the other two," which were the two that I had passed. So I called the lady in Florida and I said to her, "Look, I'm really worried. I haven't received my letter which informs me whether or not I passed my exam."

And she said to me, "Oh, don't you worry. It will come in a few days."

And I said, "Look, I'm worried about this because the registration for the last exam, if I don't pass it I'm going to lose everything." It was the end of August and if it got to be September I couldn't take another one. "So I have to register."

Then she said to me, "Don't worry about that. I can't tell you anything because it's confidential," but she said, "Don't worry about it."

So then I felt, *Ah!* I began to jump and say, "Oh! I know what it is! I passed! I passed!" And when it arrived, it was huge for me. I felt a release, where you say, "Oh, my God! Oh, thank God!" I felt very happy. I had my license now.

Thanks to God, today things are different. I've struggled a lot but I've managed to obtain quite a bit. And the last thing is that here in Portland I met my husband, and he turned out to be a very, very, very good man. I am very grateful to him. He has helped me. He has supported me in everything. I have my family. I have two more children.

I feel that I have achieved a lot. The only thing that was missing was my citizenship, and now I've got that. Last week they swore me in, and thanks to God, I have my business, I have my family, I have all my siblings here in Portland. I feel that, because I have a lot of faith, whatever happens I turn to God.

As the people say, "Oh, I've never seen him." But I do know that he exists. He has helped me. He has always been by my side. Perhaps he gave me a star when I was born. Because I have had to work, but he has compensated me, and I have arrived, you understand? I have gotten a lot in life. That is to say, that you get what you aim for, what you set your goals to be, what you propose, and all that.

If they need help, I like to help people because not many people like to help others. If someone needs help and it comes to them, well then that feels good to the person. One is thankful. I feel thankful that other people have helped me. I am very, very thankful to Victoria Hershey.[1] I met her just after I arrived here. She helped me a lot.

Another woman that I have never seen again and I have tried to locate is Lynne Rowe.[2] She helped me to translate all my paperwork. She did so much to help with my license that I owe a large part of it to Lynne. Wherever I am I think of her. Wherever she is I hope that God is with her and that he gives her everything that she wants because she really helped me without any thought to herself. She found things for me, she translated for me, she told me what I needed, and she made the calls. They're things that one always carries with them there in your heart and they are never forgotten.

Not everyone is willing to help others. There are many selfish people who are only out for themselves. I feel so good when I help someone or when someone says to me, "Oh, thank you!" "Thanks to Lourdes I did this." "Thanks to her I have this." Not because people thank you, but because you feel something in your heart that is just for you. God blesses you for the good deeds that you do. My mama says, "I always do many good deeds so that one day if my children need something God will provide it to them for me." You understand?

I tell you, I have closed my business here to go translate for someone who has a problem or to take them to someplace, and all that. I have done it many times. I feel good. Sometimes they say to me, "Oh, I missed you one day when I was going to stop by." But you are also getting something in another direction. You are helping those people. Mamí always says, "You never do your favors so that they thank you. God will thank you." It goes on building up with God, and those are blessings that God will throw your way. When you have a good heart toward others, God blesses you and things go well for you.

You can't just stay on a corner there. I am one of those people, you know, that has their moments of despair. One gets depressed. But the next day I bounce back up, I throw myself back into it, and I continue up and out, because you can't stay on a corner depressed because you're going to die. One always has to be trying to move forward, and to make progress and try to do better.

I feel comfortable because Portland is calm. Look, now I almost never go to New York. You go to New York and it's a huge difference. If you put on a blindfold and you go to New York, you say, "I'm in New York," because you feel where you are. I don't like that, perhaps because I've gotten used to being here. But my kids are calm, and my son goes to school. I try to always lead him along the straight and narrow. I teach him the good. If he does something wrong, he knows what the consequences are. I always try to make him understand me, so that one day he's not going to have the chance to say, well, they didn't tell me how it was. You always try to guide your children along a good path. I have three children. I have a fifteen-year-old—he's going to be sixteen—that's José. And I have one that's four—he's going to be five this month—Michael. And Mariah, who's going to be three now. I feel at peace. I feel comfortable and ready to keep moving forward.

How do I say it? I, myself, haven't felt so much that I've been discriminated against like that, as a person. But yes, discrimination, I don't know what you can call it, in a city where they don't let you take an exam, a person who speaks Spanish and doesn't speak English. My thought is that there are many legal immigrants who need their driver's license ID but don't speak English. There are many cities that have it in Spanish. I understood when I went through the incredibly long process of getting my license that I'm the only Hispanic woman in Maine that took the cosmetology exam here. There was a woman before me from Peru who couldn't do it. She had to go to Boston and do it there and work there because you can't work here with a license from another state, either. You need the one from here.

It's very hard for many people who are indeed professionals and who don't have the opportunity to do the exam in their language. I got frustrated. I suffered a lot. I cried a lot, and I despaired because at the age that I arrived here you know that you're a professional. I think that I began in '97 the paperwork and it was in '99 that I came to get my license. It was a really, really long and hard time.

It is difficult. There should be more people who speak Spanish. Because, let me tell you, the Latino community has grown a lot. I haven't seen Hispanic police officers here. It's hard for people to be understood, it's really difficult.

I have not felt rejection based on my color—no, the opposite. I have been in the hospital various times, I had my two children here, and I have felt very well treated.

There are many people that don't do it. Sometimes there are Hispanics that are ashamed to challenge it. Not me. I learned. Because of all that I have gone through, it has taught me many lessons that one should defend yourself and your rights.

But, thanks to God, I don't speak perfect English, but I know enough to get myself out of problems, to defend myself. I can defend someone else, too. I wasn't able to finish school, I was in the seventh level, and I was taking conversation classes, and Adult Education. It has helped me a lot. That's what I mean, that sometimes people say that there is discrimination. Well, I say something: Maine, the State, really helps people in the sense that there are schools, and if you don't have a good income to pay for the classes, they give the classes to you for free. That helps a lot.

Notes

1. Victoria Hershey is a Portland community activist and journalist. See page 228n25.
2. Lynne Rowe was a Spanish teacher in a nearby high school and a volunteer at the Center for Cultural Exchange.

Iván Cantor's mentor Armando Vives at his Gold Boot Two Shoe Shine & Shoe Repair shop.

Born to entrepreneurial parents in Colombia, Iván Cantor regrets not having heeded their counsel. The consequences of living in the moment have had a sobering effect. His time in Maine was marked by isolation and discrimination, particularly as he struggled to get a job with his limited English. During his eight years in Portland, he felt as if bad luck and bad timing were his constant companions. Despite these setbacks, Iván continued to marvel at natural beauty, especially Maine's fall colors. The Preble Street Resource Center was a safe and welcoming place for him, where he could get some rest, connect with friends, and even help someone else out. Shortly after this interview in 2004, he left Portland. Armando Vives, pictured above, was a mentor to Iván while he lived in Portland.

11

Iván Cantor

Everything Has Its Good Sides and Its Bad

My name is Iván Cantor. I am forty-one years old. Not so young, but a little, perhaps. I was born in Venezuela, but since I was born on the border, I lived half of my childhood in Venezuela, and the other part I lived in Colombia.

I arrived in Portland, Maine, well, first because I had the luck to travel here, to Miami, with a tourist visa. There I met some Peruvian fellows, and we became good friends. Since I didn't know anything about the United States, nor the world of New York and Chicago and all the cities, my friends said to me, "Would you like to go to Nashville, Tennessee?"

And I said, "Why? That doesn't interest me!" And I said to them, "Well, Okay. Let's go to Nashville." So we went to Nashville, why not? And I liked it a lot. It was really nice, a big city but not that complex. We also went to Memphis, and from there we went to Alabama. We didn't like Alabama very much; it was very lonely. So we went to Nashville again. From Nashville we traveled to Washington, from Washington to New York, and from New York to Boston.

But after that there was a period of time where I got lost. I didn't know where my friend was, since we always wandered a lot. So a friend said to me, "No, he went to Portland."

"And where is Portland?" I said to him.

"It's in another state, the State of Maine. There's work in the fishing industry."

So I decided to come here. But when I came the first time, I didn't like it much because I came from a large city, and you can see how it's very small. I didn't feel comfortable. But I went back there, because everything has its good sides and its bad. I really liked the tranquility here. It's not a city that's super-safe, but it is quite calm, and somewhat safe. I liked that.

When I went to Boston again, I was in that large city, you know the complications that are there, so I began to think. I said, "No, this isn't any good." So I came back here again, and now I've been here seven or eight years. Yes, a long time.

I don't have family here. I arrived alone. It's different, of course, because you have to rely on yourself completely. Even if you stay with close friends when you arrive, you always have the help of a shelter, right? One has some food, well, sharing whatever food there might be. And there's also help adapting to the city. They know a lot, or some things, with the relationships that they have. For ideas you have more options, right? But when one arrives and one doesn't have any friends that might have connections, you arrive without anywhere to live, without much money. Well, that's more than a little hard.

During that time there were far fewer Hispanics. Now there are more Hispanics. But eight years ago, there were far fewer. Therefore, it was, how can I say, harder to find people who spoke Spanish.

The question of church for me has always been very important, no? Because I believe that man is not just flesh, that man has a spirit, a soul that has helped a lot. You don't have to go once to put on the halo. There's always a support for you. What will never be, will never be. It is more about your esteem. Even though you can't see God, in worshiping him, one feels something strange, as if you are supported, yes? Well, there I met Don

Armando Vives. He is a Cuban gentleman who has lived in Portland more than forty years. The stories about him, he definitely could do an interview like this [chuckles] because he sure has a long history. He's a person that helps people a lot. He doesn't pay attention to nationalities, or if you're Mexican, Central American, or wherever you're from. He helps everyone. He always goes to church, the Adventist church, which is one of the Hispanic churches, and it is one of the churches that has more people. So, he took me there. I like to go, because first of all I'd say that I need the support for spiritual reasons, for God. Secondly, the pastor is Puerto Rican, too. He speaks good Spanish and good English. There are a few people from each country; there are Peruvians, there are people from Brazil, Central America, Guatemalans, Mexicans, all of them. One feels that you're with family, more or less, because everyone speaks the same language. I like to go for that reason, too.

I've lived in Portland nearly eight years, and instead of life getting better for me, it's the opposite. The best years were at the beginning. Now, after September 11th for me it's been not a disaster, but I've had lots of work problems, you know? That is one of the most important things to me and the most difficult because it's all money, right? It has made it very hard for me to get work, and there are many companies that require too much, for jobs that don't merit that sort of thing. I don't know if there's a connection. But since September 11th until now I have seen that even the very same newspapers that before on one page of the paper you would see four, five lines of jobs, now sometimes there are two or three, tops. This has been one of the more difficult things for me, because, well, I rely on myself. That's a really big barrier, not being able to find work, because I always have worked. I live to work. I like to work, because that's the way it should be, right?

I've always lived a little better, you know? Sometimes in your family there are some nephews and nieces that one wants to help with some things. That's why one always hopes to be able to help out with something. But if you can't, like me—I have a nephew who is studying business management at a university; well, right now, I can't send him anything any more.

So, like I told him, "Son, the will is there," you know? But this is the thing, many times people don't have the will. I would say that it's not that the will is weak, but that I haven't been able to give.

"No, Uncle, it's cool. Don't worry about it," he would say. But then that bothers you a little, too. They hope you can because in any part of the world it's the dollar that has the value, right?

Education is very, very important. It always depends where one is born, and the situation in each country, with what they offer to help people. We are three siblings. We always studied in good schools because we were never rich but we've been quite comfortable. Overall, that's why we've studied in good schools. Ever since you're a kid, your parents always say to you, "Study because that's all you'll have. Take advantage of it."

But when you're really young, kids don't think about that. The other thing is that the assistance from the government isn't as much as it is here in the United States. You can study this, or you can study that, and you can get that degree. So, in turn, my sister, being the youngest, instead of being the opposite as it should have been, she's the professional, the doctor. Those of us that are older than her, we didn't end up having any profession.

My parents have always had a wholesale business and a store. Of course, I'm not going to say that it was like Shop 'n Save or Hannaford [supermarket] or anything like that. But they were good businesses. My brother learned to drive a trailer. They bought a truck for him, and he began to look for work with his truck. I always worked with them. Therefore, I didn't have any reason to be looking for work elsewhere. It was the easy life. We had restaurants, too. We worked in the restaurants.

Then later my brother traveled to here. Then I decided to come here too, but the issue of studying language has always been a barrier. There are, like, three English classes, a basic, a medium, and an advanced. There are people who are very advanced, but it's always worthwhile and one goes to speak. One can't be asking the teacher, "Teacher, is that . . ." First of all, it's that I'm behind in the classes, second that it's . . . shameful. It's very expensive. So for these reasons, well, I haven't been able to study here.

My best memories here are that I see that this is a very quiet state. I've lived in many states. When I tell people the states that I have lived in, they say, "Oh, you've seen more than the North Americans themselves." I have seen lots of cities. I like it here because it's calm. Although it's not that it's super-safe. But comparing it with other states, it does have more security and calm. One of the nicest things that I've liked about here is the woods, because I've had the luck to see a lot in the northern part, like Bar Harbor and other places.

One of the nicest memories that I have is that, with the church, we traveled to a summer camp, and there is a beautiful river and there are many trees that you see. It's gorgeous. It's really, really nice. But one of the memories that I had, there are roads that you travel on and there are little towns that look like they're out of a movie. There are some stores that seem old, they even have the same signs as in old-times. And the bell rings, "jingle-jingle," and all that. But then behind the store there were some tables, and what I liked most of all was that I always found many people there, and that below there is a huge river and across the river there are some little houses. The people who live on that side take a little boat and cross the river to get to the store. They come into the store, and they make their purchases. I was sitting that day with Don Armando, and they come in this boat to cross the river. And I said, "How kind are these people!" That is just so nice, and I like that very much.

Also, just to add onto that, around that time we went to buy a plane ticket for a friend. And there were the magazines from all over the world, and there was a magazine that said, "See Maine in eight days." They were going to come when the leaves change colors. In one day they visited Lewiston, Auburn, and so on. And another day they visited Caribou, Bangor, and on the last day here in Portland. They have some photos, and they saw some parts, but one can't see it all, right? But it's beautiful. That's one of the things that I like very much about Maine.

One of the things that has been hard about living in Portland, aside from the importance of work, because if you don't work you don't have anything, is that rent here is too expensive. There's no control over the rents. The houses that were worth seven hundred are now worth nine hundred dollars, and up to a thousand dollars. Now there aren't apartments. I have seen many apartments these days at a thousand dollars. In order to pay a thousand dollars, the father, the mother, and the son have to work, all to pay one thousand dollars.

Then there's also the charge for the phone, there's the electricity, and all of these things add up to a thousand dollars. There are many people who have told me that it's like that. There are many jobs, but they don't raise the wages much within those jobs. But the rent they do. So I see that as really hard, because in Miami or in other places like in Nashville, the rent isn't so very expensive as it is here. There are places like the YMCA, but the rooms are too small. I tell you that to charge one hundred fifteen dollars weekly for those rooms, that's too much money. The rooms are very small. They don't have anything, not even a kitchen, just a small little room. So that is one of the things that is really hard, because the rent is too expensive. You have to work a lot. Sometimes you have to work two jobs to pay the rent and the utilities, and to have something to save.

There is some discrimination. Everything is different, you know? There are some that have that. I've had those experiences, but not a lot. One day I went to apply for a dishwashing job, and I arrived first before all the rest. At that moment when I arrived, another person arrived, but that person was from here. So it turns out that they gave the job to him and they didn't give me the job. Lots of times there are people who don't say it to you directly. But they tell you, "I'm going to call you." They do this so that they don't have to do it in the moment, you know? So they don't say no to you, but with that you realize that it's something like discrimination. It's not just in jobs, sometimes you go shopping with your own money to some places, and one sees the—not so much disdain, but it's not the ordinary style, so despotic. On the other hand, some people are very different, much more friendly. They treat you as they should, normal.

I think it's very nice and it is very important that people hopefully speak three, four languages. But there are people that don't value that. In Miami, when I lived there, in the store there was a Vietnamese woman, and what I noticed was that if a person came in that spoke English, she spoke English. And if someone came in that was Vietnamese, even better because that was her language. If another person came who spoke Spanish, she spoke that, too. Not because we were the best, but there were many Vietnamese saying, "Cómo está usted, amigo? ¡Gracias, amigo¡ ¡Gracias!" They don't speak a lot, but they keep talking to you, so I realize that it's good.

At least I wasn't born here, but while I don't speak English, I would like to speak English. I can't see the solution, because there are people that say to you, "Why don't you speak English?" Some people say to you, "This is North America! Speak English to me!" But, I was born elsewhere.

I have some Japanese friends and I'm not going get upset because they're speaking Japanese because they were born there. They also speak English. But there are people who think that someone who's speaking their language is talking bad about them. With no more reason than that, they say to you, "Speak English!"

For me, I like to speak my language, and I would like to speak English as well. We're all humans, and while everything is in order it's not important, but when something is out of order, for whatever reason, that's different. If the person is in line, you have no reason to show them a bad face like that. So you prefer to speak your language. It's because since you were born there you speak it better. It's like I said to someone, "If you were born in Italy, you would prefer to speak Italian." We're not saying no to English because, as I said, I met this Vietnamese woman who spoke Vietnamese, and she also spoke English. It seems to me that probably it's good that people learn other languages.

With my free time, although I like to read a lot, there aren't many books for Hispanics here, you know? Nor do I read a very advanced level of English, so sometimes I grab a book and I understand and I don't understand, but I like to read a lot. There isn't a place to buy them. Not because I don't want to read in English. I read it, too. But I don't get the point from the story or the history that the book means to explain.

I also like to rest and relax, as well. Sometimes there's time and sometimes it seems that there isn't a lot of free time. Well, there's time but there's none that's free. You have to run here, and over there, and back again, and so on. One is going to take advantage of it if it's summer, to be able to go to the beach or to go out and walk in the park or go out to eat somewhere.

There isn't much here for social things. Here there are two Hispanic churches, but they're small. I have been to them as well. There isn't really a center, in and of itself, where people get together, you know? But really people get together if just in the dances that they do with our music. Sometimes I go there, too. It's just on Saturdays that they do them. Every once in a while I go. There isn't a club space or something like that. I like to go sometimes, because I feel good to be with people from countries that speak Spanish. I believe that it's already been figured out that one-fourth of the United States is Spanish speakers, too.

In Miami almost half of the people speak both languages. The same in Texas, almost half the people speak both. It's totally the same in New York, and in Chicago it's the same too. This makes me feel good, that people speak both languages. I know a lawyer whose name is Tom, and he speaks Spanish. He learned to speak Spanish over in Mexico. The nicest part about it is when he says, "I'm going to the Caribbean with my girlfriend, and I have no problem because I can speak Spanish." And he likes the food, and the fish. So when we see each other, he says to me, "How are you?"

And I said to him, "Good, greetings to your mother."

He says, "Of course! It's okay." So that's really great.

Although I never had the opportunity to travel to California, nor learn much about César Chávez, it seems to me that the work he did was very important because it was work to help Latinos move forward economically. He valued the work that Latinos did. Not because we're better workers, no. The Latinos and Hispanics are the people who do the hardest jobs here. Like for example, if you go to the majority of the fields, you don't find Vietnamese there, you don't find African-Americans there, or Africans, you don't find them there. What you find more than anything are Hispanics from Guatemala, from El Salvador, from Mexico. But very few Americans are there. If you go to construction sites, there are many Hispanics working there. If you go to the fish factories, 70 percent of them are Hispanics, because there are many who would like to work there. Absolutely, César Chávez valued the fact that those people work very hard. It's not for really low wages, but it's not tons of money. What he did is exactly to value the work and the effort that the Latino here does, because there are many areas here in the rural areas where in the majority of these places it is all Hispanics working.

My hopes are very high. For what? My hopes are to learn more English and to have a good job, but a job that isn't too special either. A good job, I couldn't ask for more than that. God give me health, nothing more. Those are my hopes. Now, if I could ask for something more, well obviously I would like, but I don't demand, that much wealth. But if wealth comes, I'll take it, you know?

I would be interested in knowing more English. I wish that, speaking of Spanish, which is the language in which I express myself better, because I met people who sometimes have told me to seek work where they speak Spanish in Miami, they've told me, "Ivan, you speak better Spanish."

Despite that, I know that I can express myself in Spanish, but in English I can't express myself. But anyway, I would prefer to learn more English, to be able to express myself better still. But, how do you say, I can't find the word how to say it, but it seems neat to me that a person would speak like

I'm speaking to you but in two or three languages. That is wonderful, interesting. Yes, I would like that, and a good job, and a little better health, yes. That is what I would wish for the future. As I always say, if I can have more through my own efforts, well I would like that even more, obviously. I would like also, hopefully, to go to school, take a welding or carpentry course. We'll see what the future brings, right? Thank you.

Olga Alicea.

Born in Puerto Rico and raised in California, Olga Alicea grew up speaking Spanish, eating traditional foods, and attending Catholic Mass. Though her brother is dark-skinned, Olga is light-skinned. As a result, people do not always know that she is a Latina or a native Spanish speaker. At times having to prove her "Latinohood" has been frustrating, but it has also led to some soul searching about what it means to be Puerto Rican. Through her work at Portland area social service agencies, she has been an advocate for the homeless and other marginalized populations.

12

Olga Alicea

You've Got to Practice It

My name is Olga Maritza Teresa Alicea. I am thirty-two years old. I was born in Puerto Rico, outside of San Juan and lived in Carolina. When I was three years old my family moved to Los Angeles. We lived there for a while, and then we moved to Stockton, California, so I grew up in Stockton, went to San Francisco State University, and lived two years outside the United States in a country called Kyrgyzstan. When I returned after those two years, after living a month in California, I moved to Alaska and was there for a year and a half, and finally I decided to get in my car and come to Portland. Here I am in Portland.

I did not have family here in Portland. The only thing that I tried was to go back to school, and I left when I lived in Anchorage. What I was doing in Anchorage was over, and it was time to either move or travel or have a new experience. So by chance a close friend of mine came to visit and spend a few months with me and she helped me make the decision to end what I was doing in Alaska and pile myself into my car and travel a little. She suggested that we go to Portland, but she didn't know anyone. She had come to Maine when she was eighteen years old. It was like a really ideal place, really different from where I had grown up, good like a postcard and I decided that it would be a good place to go.

I've been on my own here. Since I moved, I've noticed that it has been more difficult for me. Normally I'm the type of person that makes friends easily, or perhaps it has taken me a while because I'm a little more reserved in how I relate to people. It has taken me time to make friendships that mean a lot to me. But I have them, and over time I have made them, but I don't have family. Sometimes that is hard for me.

I was raised Catholic, and it was always assumed that, as you say in English, I lived and breathed being Catholic, but when I was a teenager many things happened and I questioned many things. Ever since I was a child I questioned many things, and one thing that I questioned was not being able to understand exactly what I felt about being Catholic. Also it was part of questioning my parents, and so, to rebel against them meant to have power as a young person. Sometimes one looks for things that mean the most to your parents. For my father, being Catholic [was] a big part of who he was. Sometimes to make him mad, I didn't go to church.

Finally, for a few years, not that I didn't identify as Catholic, because for some reason I have felt Catholic, I rejected the church, that type of spirituality. But I always have had a connection with something larger, you know. I went through many things, and in my early twenties I came to be aware of my relationship with God. Because I am Latina, I don't know, but I always have identified as Catholic, but Catholic in my own way, because I know that there are things that I believe that cannot be, [that are] contrary to the Church or contrary to father's ideas or my grandmother's ideas. But I also believe that the God in which I believe is much larger than ideas, philosophy, or the beliefs of religion, of any religion. But yes, I am Catholic, but I define it differently than another person.

I went through times where I didn't go to the church for a while. But I don't go to church, I feel empty sometimes because I haven't gone, not because I feel that God is going to punish me, but I feel that there is something special in going to church, to go to a Catholic church, because I feel something when I receive the Eucharist. That's why I feel as though something is missing when I don't go to church. There are other things that I feel that I have to constantly keep doing in my private life that I don't do. It's more than going to church. Having a relationship with God is every day.

I arrived here in November 2000. When I came to Portland I didn't have a lot of expectations. I didn't have anything definite in mind about how I was going to make my life. At the same time, I knew that it was going to be a calmer life, because I imagined that I was going to live in a rural place, very country, with a dog, and a pickup and without many neighbors. But I arrived in Portland, which is what you would call a city, but for me, it lacked many things, like the culture that you could find in a place like San Francisco or New York. But one of the things that I realized is that it lacked people of color. You didn't see many Latinos, much less Puerto Ricans. You get used to having a certain thing around, and you don't even know that you miss it, until you notice that it's not there. Sometimes Portland is one of those places where the people are really nice and are good, and everyone welcomes you, but at the same time when you begin to move to a new place and make friendships with people from work, wherever you meet people, one begins to have intense conversations, and one begins to notice that the people begin to make statements that are not necessarily racist but statements that show their ignorance. I'm a person that to look at me I could look like any other person in Portland; I have light skin, and I can express myself perfectly well in English.

I like cultures that I can "absorb." I can act like the people around me and then one begins to notice that one says something that has to do with being Puerto Rican, about missing something, and sometimes a little joke—something that reveals you. It doesn't get you far, being the Puerto Rican. It's making me feel a little uncomfortable. Yeah, don't get too cultural.

This I discovered with a particular friend, and it made me sad especially because of the people I know around me. I was missing a lot of things, I didn't have family, I didn't have anyone with whom to identify culturally, necessarily spiritually. Maine is full of people who are not so progressive as the people in California, because everything I compare with California. It's one thing to move to Portland from California and notice that many things can't be done and you accept the thoughts, you tolerate them. It's another thing to go to a place where everything is possible, where things are nice but remember that things can be different. That's how I feel. I missed it.

When I traveled to Maine, I hoped that things would be a certain way. I thought that things would be good. And they were, but I didn't feel like, "Oh God, this is the place." And I'm always looking for that place. The place where everything will fall just as it should fall, and I'm going to feel, "Aí, this is my home! This is where I belong!" It wasn't like that.

People always ask me, "How do you like Portland? Are you thinking of staying in Maine?" And I always feel that I couldn't say for sure without jumping to a conclusion. I definitely couldn't say, because I didn't feel like this was the ideal. Something was missing. But interestingly, I began school, and I know that I have to stay at least until I finish school. But I was always thinking of another place. Sometimes you begin to see the things that were in front of you, you begin to find friendships when you weren't expecting to find them, and you decide, "If this makes me happy, then I should try to seek those situations out."

I like the nature because, let me tell you when I'm driving, I feel that I'm in a beautiful place. In many ways, it doesn't compare to where I was raised, in Stockton. It is more beautiful, a quieter life. It seems like the people here in Portland have that same fervor for the nature. They want to preserve the sea, that beauty. There are other things that are lacking where I was raised. I began to notice particularly when I returned to California that it was all very hurried, even within my family, within my friendships, it was like another type of life, it was different, how they dressed. Not that all people in Maine think like I do, but sometimes in solitude one begins to turn within yourself more and find that you develop more as a person. And in doing so, it seems that I began to develop a relationship with my environment, in my own surroundings. I also feel a little bit committed, and I can't say, "Oh, yes, I'm going," right now until it gets a little harder for me. But that's something good, you know. I feel a little more sure. I come home, and I feel that this is my home, although some things are missing. But I think that maybe I am going to find that this is the place.

When I think of New England, I think of the trees when they change colors, I think of the lakes, I think of the loons, I think of many things, and when I realize that I am living that moment in time, that is when I have the best memories. When I think about the autumn, I think about Halloween. One sees movies, one thinks about New England, one thinks about New Hampshire and things like that. My experiences with nature may not sound that specific, but, for example, when I had been living here about year, I went on a haunted hayride, and it was absolutely traditional, it scared me, but it was more about being with good friends, that type of experience.

I always look for work that is related to social work, social services, because they pay me well—not necessarily, but they don't pay badly. I am a person who feels very, very grateful, because as soon as I arrived in Portland, I spent one or two weeks, but I decided to make a call and in almost an instant I felt that it was that easy to find work. Once I was determined to find work,

I had found it. It is not necessarily due to talent, I feel that someone was looking out for me, you know?

I always find work. Although I may complain, I always feel that there are opportunities, however limited, because I find that like teaching and the social services don't pay like they should pay, my experience with the field has always been good. But I look around and I feel that the pay here in general is not as good as in other places. But I'm content. I feel that work has gone well for me, depending on who you ask.

I worked with boys that were disabled, and for one it was hard for him to study, others had problems with their behavior with adults, and others were a challenge. But one has to develop relationships with them to be able to make a change, they have to trust you. That's why my good experiences in Portland are my friendships. I have a personality such that I can be serious and all the rest, but more or less I like to laugh a lot, I like to play, I like to be candid, I like to be a little crude in how I say things, I like to be able to be who I really am with the people around me and I have been able to find people who accept me. The students accepted me, my coworkers accepted me, and the friends that I have made. That is what has made these experiences unique.

I decided to go to Boston College, by my own choice. I had a dream of the type of university that I wanted to attend the second time around. The first time was a very good university, especially for what I wanted to study, which was English and Creative Writing. Many of the professors were writers, and for this reason it was a very good experience, very vivid, but I didn't milk the opportunity as well as I could have. That's why I decided that I was going to work incredibly hard. I also wanted a Catholic school. This was part of the nostalgia of being young and the experience that I rejected while I was still young. It was like reliving my youth, to have that experience at thirty-something years old.

I can't talk about other peoples, but for many Latinas I think that they maybe feel rejection due to how different they look. I am not saying that that's how it has been for me, but they don't reject me completely. Because of parts of my personality and of my way of being, for many people, the majority of the people, not Latinos, but mainstream persons it's easy for them to spend time with me because it seems like we're the same. But when I try to show that I have more than one dimension, that it's not a dimension which is part time, it is who I am as a whole, then there are people who are a little ignorant and thus, they assume. People assume who I am.

In the big picture it's a matter of perspective. Still I am very thankful for what I have not had to go through. Sometimes I know that there are people who struggle much more than I. In telling about the things that I have noticed in moving here is not to say that I have been mistreated. No, no. It's that life has been different from what I remember from California. But I am not a person who's suffering or anything like that. And the bad experiences have been few and they are personal. They aren't anything that would have happened specifically in Portland or in Maine. They are things that happen in life.

Maybe the other thing that makes it hard for me to live here is that I feel I have a need to live close to my family. And that is what is hard for me. Yes, that is what is very hard. That is true for many Latinos, and it's worse than what I feel because I made the decision to come here. There are a lot of reasons why I feel like I had to do it. If you ask my family, they say "You know that you have to do it."

But I know that there are people who have no other choice. They come to the United States, they come to Maine, to suffer discrimination, and live in fear, or they live hidden, or they don't get paid well and know that they shouldn't say anything because they are so grateful that they have a job, you know. That isn't my experience. The experience I live is only because I want to be a really compassionate person. I keep that in mind so that I am always grateful of the fact that it isn't my experience.

I can't say if I've faced discrimination, as I think you might be defining it. I am going to say no. But I want to take discrimination to another level and try to break it apart. I think that discrimination exists in not being able to see any representation of who you are in your environment, to feel like the person that you are is completely unaccepted. That it is easier to make fun of yourself than to present this person to the people that you think are your friends, that sort of thing. That's discrimination.

Sometimes I've found more discrimination among Latinos themselves directed toward me and not necessarily from the majority of Anglo people. Many of the people with whom I share my time that are Anglos, are more progressive people and good people who accept you as you are, so that's why I haven't seen a lot of that. They are more open people.

I prefer not to walk around with a Puerto Rican flag so that the whole world knows, "Hey, I'm Puerto Rican." But it's really interesting that sometimes the same people that suffer discrimination are the ones who reject you without knowing who you are. It's happened to me many times. Interestingly, it's when I speak Spanish or say that I am from Puerto Rico. I have to make some sort of Latino gesture so that they say, "Okay, you're all right. You're one of us. Hey sister, you're one of us."

This happened to me recently. There was a woman who I saw in a meeting once and I liked how she spoke in public and so I introduced myself to her. I knew that in the future we were going to work together on something, so I introduced myself, not because I was Puerto Rican and she was African-American. It wasn't a "minority bonding moment." It wasn't like that. What I wanted was to introduce myself to her. I said to her, "Hi, I'm going to be working there . . . You're going to be working there . . ."

And she looked at me like . . . I understand that look because I can say that sometimes I'm guilty of it too, not necessarily outwardly, but I'm guilty of thinking it in my head, that sometimes I judge people, too. She looked at me like, "Yeah, whatever, white girl." Kinda like that. I can't say that was what she was thinking, or what she meant to say with that gesture and that way of holding herself, but that was how I felt because she didn't look me in the eyes. It was like she rejected me.

Some days later there was a situation where again I was with this person and we were in a situation where there was a person talking to us who spoke Spanish and she tried to speak Spanish to them but that person was already talking to me, and I began to talk to her very naturally. You know, it's my language! It's my way of movin'! I could feel her on the periphery watching me, and she said, "Oh! You speak Spanish!" But she was another person altogether. She struck me as a completely different person.

I said, "Yeah, sí, I'm a Puerto Rican. I speak Spanish." Perhaps I didn't even tell her that I was Puerto Rican, but I told her in a way like I'm not asking to be accepted by you. I do speak Spanish, that's right. You just assumed that I didn't. Or you assumed whatever it is that you assumed about me. And that's your own loss, that kind of thing. And then I moved on. How she relates to me now is completely different.

But that happens to me a lot. It's as though I have to prove my Latinohood. Not with everyone, but so that people take me seriously. Sometimes there are people that assume that my experience hasn't been as hard as theirs, and that could be true, but the experiences that I have had in trying to be two things at once are my experiences, and they are worth no less than anyone else's experience.

It's incredibly important to me not to lose my language and culture. I thank God that my father always spoke Spanish to us at home. They never spoke English at home. They speak English, and they speak it well, with their pretty accent, right? But they never spoke to me in English. They always spoke to me in Spanish. I learned English in school.

What makes me sad now is seeing the people that come from other countries, the immigrants that live here, the refugees that live here, what they feel. I'm not judging their situation, but society puts a tremendous pressure to conform, or become part of society, in order to be part of this community. Sometimes they feel like they have to encourage their children to learn the language. It's a trade-off. It's better that they learn the language and lose their language in the process, than that they suffer discrimination, or hardships, or not be able to go to college. It makes me sad that one has to decide between one or the other, that it can't be both.

I didn't have that experience. I always was completely proud of being Puerto Rican. I always knew that I was Puerto Rican, I knew that I was completely different. But at the same time I knew that I was something that was different, I didn't fear anything. I was proud because my parents had that pride.

When I think about how I was raised, my experience was really quite Mexican. The Latino experiences that I had when I was being raised were Mexican and Puerto Rican. Because my best friends were Mexicans, the friends of my parents were Mexicans, the food that I loved—that is, other than my mom's and my grandmother's Puerto Rican food—was Mexican. If I'm talking about Stockton [California], there was the Vietnamese culture as well, but more than anything it was Mexican culture, Mexican, Vietnamese, and Puerto Rican cultures. But there are very few Puerto Ricans in California. We always spent Christmases with family. I had my uncles and aunts and cousins and all that, and the music!

But it's really interesting, because I spent much more time with my mom's family that lived in California. My cousins, they all talk to me in English. My dad's family lives in Florida and in Puerto Rico, and those cousins have maintained their accent, like is typical in Puerto Rico. That's why I was raised as I was with the language, because I didn't have it around me all the time, because even though I had lots of Mexican people around me, many of them spoke a few words of Spanish but they never spoke it like we spoke it because we spoke it at home. Even with so many Latinos in California, the culture is still oppressively white.

Oh, I have the flag in my car! I have the flag in my living room. I have who knows how many pictures of Puerto Rico at home. I think that to stay the person that you want to be, whoever that may be, if it's a strong person, if it's a confident person, if it's a person with integrity, if it's a person who's Catholic or Latino, whoever it is with whom you identify, you've got to practice it. You have to learn about your history. You got to constantly read your Puerto Rican writers. You got to constantly listen to Puerto Rican music—not all the time—but you need culture, and cultures are always moving and changing. Sometimes you have to be careful that the culture you think is Puerto Rican isn't nostalgia. And that's okay too. But, you know, culture isn't a thing. That's why in saying that I'm Puerto Rican, I also have to say that that yes, I'm Puerto Rican, but I'm a Puerto Rican from California, influenced by Mexican culture.

So, basically, one has to be conscious. If I stop speaking Spanish, my Spanish is going to disappear. If you are conscious that it's a decision, a conscious decision, fine. But one has to be careful because the main culture is so dominant that things happen to your culture as a minority that you don't even realize until you're thirty-two.

One could have an entire conversation about what it means to "be Puerto Rican." What it means to be Puerto Rican to you, could be completely different, or it could be the same. But culture is fluid, culture is how one wants to see it, it's your perspective. Just speaking Spanish doesn't make me the same as a Guatemalan, as a Mexican. I've totally learned that with as few Puerto Ricans as there are I've had to join a group of people where at least they speak Spanish and at least some things are similar. The religion could be something that makes the cultures seem similar but one could have a meeting with a ton of Latinos and that's where one realizes, "Holy Mother of God! We are not the same!" And that's okay.

I remember that when I was being raised, the way my mother raised me is Puerto Rican child-raising. We can have a debate about it, but that's just my experience. She was a really strict person, for whom everything had to be just so, and if you misbehaved, well . . . I would go to school and talk to my girlfriends, and I realized that my mother was the only one who raised children this way. I didn't know that when I was rejecting my mother's way of being, it was Puerto Rican. I just knew that I was a twelve-year-old girl and how she did things weren't like everyone else. I know that there are things that as a young person it takes many years to realize what you have lost. You don't know what's happening at the time. You don't know what you're losing. But I know what was missing in my youth. I know for sure, it was something to say to my parents, "Oh—what a magnificent culture you have!" Or that there were some other Puerto Ricans around, or that there was some way to be able to share what it is to be Puerto Rican with the community, and for them to celebrate it. Or that I could have seen someone on television that is

Puerto Rican, something that would have been visible, that had a more omnipotent presence. To have had that experience of sharing my culture and the community would say to you, "Yeah, being Puerto Rican is nice! This is really cool . . ." You know, acknowledging it. To also know that I'm not just Puerto Rican, I'm a girl that speaks English, and now I live in the United States, and that's good, too. But that's not what happened. My parents did the best that they could, but they too had to change and do what they had to do to adapt.

I've never felt pressure to assimilate without knowing what's going on. Until one reaches a certain age and compares the family members who stayed in Puerto Rico or who are surrounded by many more Puerto Ricans, there are things that you miss. In assimilating, I probably learned the history of the United States. I probably became very proud of the United States, and, in the process, I never learned the history of being Puerto Rican.

This is a really poor example, but I was raised always with people calling me "Olga." That's my name. Since I was little, people called me "Olga." And it took me going to Kyrgyzstan and being around Russians calling me Olga to be able to say, "Holy God . . ." You know, I've never liked the way it sounded, but that's the way they did it. And I didn't necessarily correct them. And I always said "Olga Alicia," or "Olga" . . . I always said "Alicea" but sometimes I would say "a-lee-SEE-ah" so that they could pronounce it, and it took being an adult to say, "Why?" "Why is it that I have to learn to do all this?" My name is: Olga Maritza Teresa Alicea. If you can figure it out, good! You know, you realize you're giving in to make it easier on the majority, because it's so much easier sometimes. It seems like you have to question yourself, but sometimes it's just easier to do it in a way that they'll be able to handle it.

I like Portland. It has nothing to do with Portland, it has to do with me. I can decide to find things here that make me happy, or I can constantly be thinking about another place. That is an illness of mine. It's not necessarily that it's Portland. Yes, I like Portland.

I've spent more than a year with Centro Latino. What has happened is that this organization of people is dedicated to uniting based on being Latinos and to better the quality of life for Latinos. How this is defined for each individual within the organization has been interesting. It has been an interesting experience to know that to be Latino doesn't necessarily mean that we are all the same. We are all individuals. But it has been interesting in that I think that organization is constantly evolving.

What I've noticed is that we are all, while different, some of us are very similar, but we are all people who want to be there and we still stay together as a group. Someone from the outside might say, "And what exactly is it that Centro Latino does?" There is a dedication among us to unite. We feel that, "Hey, you know what? We have a right. We can build a community. There is a community here." There's definitely a Latino community. I don't feel connected just to the Latino community. I feel connected with immigrant communities in general, because I feel that many of the challenges and many of the experiences are similar. I think there's a lot of potential in Portland.

In my free time—this is going to sound like the classified ads—I like to go hiking. I love to go hiking. If you ask me how many times I have done it, there aren't as many times as I would like there to be. I would like to do more with my time where I make an effort to walk outside. I like to write. When I am more disciplined, I write every day. I like to read a lot. When I shower, I like to sing. When I'm relaxed, I like to sing. I like to spend time with my *amigas* and with my *amigos*. I like to do lots of things.

I like to think about my future. Or should I say: I like to obsess about the future. I like at least contributing to organizations, I like to look for ways to help people. Some days I do it better than others. I like to get in my car and drive and get lost and try to find my way home. But that's the story of my life.

For my future, well, in general, I want . . . I don't know. It's funny. I'm someone who's always thinking about the future. But if someone asks me what I'm going to do when I graduate, what I'm going to do a week from now, and can we make a date a week from now? I just freak out. So you're getting a roundabout answer: A little house, a dog, to have kids; it might be that I stay in Maine. I would like to do something with my master's in Social Work. I envision myself living in another country, trying to live in a place where life is a little simpler, to be useful in some way. That is always my constant mental anguish, I think, to feel that I'm not contributing, or that I'm not sure what my purpose is, or that I'm not trying hard enough. So, anything that has to do with making sure that all of my drive is being put to use, or that I'm being honest with myself.

My idea of happiness is being cozy, safe, and comfortable enough to do whatever, wherever my whim takes me. And that doesn't always happen because I don't always feel comfortable, I don't always feel safe. And I don't always feel supported. I have to say that's one of the things that I feel fortunate to have. I feel support from so many different directions. That's my deep thought for the day. This has been very nice.

Conclusion

Toward a Fluid Latino Identity

Robert Atkinson

> We owe it to each other to respect our stories and learn from them.
>
> —Robert Coles, *The Call of Stories*

> There's so many new energies coming in, and there's so much for us to learn about each other.
>
> —John Connors

The narratives presented here reveal much about how a person constructs, reconstructs, and represents a subjective understanding of their own identity. From these very personal and revealing stories, two implicit principles of the narrative approach are clearly elucidated. The first is: The world will tell you who you are until you tell the world. The second is: The story we tell about ourselves is who we are.

The approach used here is not only designed to facilitate and bring forth an expression of this in narrative form, it is also built upon a respect for individual storytellers, an appreciation of the way in which people make sense of and communicate meaning, and a recognition of the sanctity of the relationship forged in the telling of and the listening to the story.[1] We have tried to allow the reader to step inside the personal world of the storyteller and, by identifying common themes and motifs across lives, discover larger worlds consisting of both differences and similarities.

Our goal with these narratives, though each of our interview styles is somewhat different, has been to be as consistent as possible in the questions used and the content covered. In this conclusion, I do not interpret the narratives, but only let the words of the storytellers be heard again to identify some common themes, concerns, struggles, hopes and dreams, and to address the question of a possible "next phase of Latino identity," as mentioned in the Introduction. After all, each person is speaking only for him or herself, from individual experience, as an individual, and no one individual speaks for others in any of the Latino groups or communities represented here.

We can now begin to put together how people of diverse backgrounds, even within the deceptively broad and general category of Latinos, find community beyond their common language. We have here a wide range of backgrounds, experiences, and identities (including age, gender, class, religion, nationality, and ethnicity) of the people of Latin America, community leaders and everyday people, who are engaged in the ongoing process of adapting to their new lives here, and who have made connections across their geo/socio/political/national—and, to some degree, even cultural—differences.

Even the many differences between the Latinos in Portland can not keep them apart. As Olga Alicea found out, "one could have a meeting with a ton of Latinos and that's where one realizes, 'Holy Mother of God! We are not the same!' and that's okay." Centro Latino, an organization that is "constantly evolving," was formed for this very purpose, not only to "better the quality of life for Latinos" but to build a group of "people who are dedicated to uniting based on being Latinos."

As John Connors aptly puts it, "There's twenty-something odd countries and cultures and different backgrounds and histories and food and music. When it comes together, there's an energy that's exciting to all of us. . . . There's so many new energies coming in, and there's so much for us to learn about each other." It also includes a "reaching out" to learn more about others and build relationships that go beyond the Latino groups themselves to include other ethnic communities in Maine and other states.

Perhaps what might be considered our most intriguing finding from these powerful and intimate narratives is that while the Latinos who have settled in Portland, Maine, for various reasons are a very diverse group themselves, and because they have come to a predominantly Anglo area, with a recent influx of other immigrants—and refugees—from all parts of the world adding to a growing diversity here, their own process of forming, reforming, and adjusting their own identity has caused them to become remarkably fluid in how they see themselves.

These narratives illustrate that a new Latino identity as fluid and evolving over a lifetime of change may be most characteristic of their experiences described here. Each individual whom we have come to know through reading their own voice has told us in one way or another that they view both their community and their personal identity as fluid. Their collective identity as a Latino community in a predominantly Anglo area is changing and dynamic. At the same time, their strong sense of place is also fluid; they eloquently express feeling comfortable in their new home.

The identity development literature (which informs at least the fields of psychology, human development, counseling, sociology, and anthropology) is helpful here as it includes many identity models that share both similarities and differences covering historical, structural, sociocultural, psychosocial, biological, and narrative concerns and contexts.[2] Allowing for the centrality of culture and ethnicity, many of the ethnic and "racial" identity models that exist are helpful, as well; they account for experiences of oppression along with efforts to maintain cultural characteristics and deal with the process of acculturation. These, however, are stage or phase-based, usually implying a linear progression from one stage to the next with little, if any, allowance for a dynamic process underlying the way one negotiates the stages. They are also primarily built upon quantitative responses from Likert-type scales (responses from most to least likely). Some reviewers of these measures have called for, among other things, the use of "alternate (e.g., qualitative) methods of assessing identity" as well as moving beyond "thinking about ethnic identity as necessarily stable."[3]

In the Latino identity development literature, the nonlinear dimension-based identity model that includes the six dimensions of Latino integrated, Latino identified, subgroup identified, Latino as "other," undifferentiated, and White identified is also helpful, at least in pointing out the wide range of differences across acculturation level, skin color, national origin, and other distinctions that there can be among Latinos.[4]

Another very helpful approach is the Personal Identity Model, built upon multiple identity constructs and the A, B, and C dimensions, which move from the least changeable identities to the less visible but potentially changing identities to the identities built upon historical contexts and other external factors. These three dimensions provide a holistic view of the person while allowing individuals to define and determine which dimensions have the greatest salience for them at a given point in time.[5] This is a model that indicates considerable within- and between-Latino ethnic group differences as well as a greater fluidity to identity than most of the other models.

Currently, the increasing recognition of bicultural identity and multicultural identity makes it clear that everyone carries multiple identities at the same time, that each of the identities we carry are part of who we all are as whole persons, and that these multiple identities also converge and interact with each other continuously, in different ways depending on the circumstances.[6]

This leads to what may be most relevant in understanding the formed identities of the storytellers here; it leads to what we might think of as a fluid identity model. The central question of all identity models, indeed many spiritual traditions and practices, is: Who am I? This is the question that often sets us off on a search for our essence. This is also the framing question that led Wayne Muller, a minister and therapist, to explore the beauty and meaning of our lives from cultural, psychological, and narrative perspectives, and to conclude that our acknowledgment of who we are is no less precious or necessary than it was for Buddha, Moses, or Jesus. The "naming of who we are" sets the course of our life, determines how we live, and "what gifts we will bring to the family of the earth." On the other hand, "if we are unsure of who we are, we will live tentatively," not knowing what we should do. A strong sense of our own nature guides us toward what is necessary for ourselves. It is in this context, and from having listened to the powerful stories of many of his clients, that Muller asks, "Can it then be that what we call the 'self' is fluid and elastic? It evolves, strikes a different balance with every new breath." It "expands and contracts: the heart opens and closes, the lungs and abdomen rise and fall, the earth itself as it moves through space expands and contracts through the seasons—winter, spring, summer, fall, winter. When we cease to move in this way, we die."[7]

A fluid model of identity development would emphasize elasticity, evolution, balance, and wholeness in one's life, because we have to learn to navigate the changes and transitions we encounter throughout life. It would take into account that, despite being in the midst of continuous change, there is a "hidden wholeness" within us that expresses who we are at the core of our being. In our twenty-first-century global village environment, this may be seen as both necessary and healthy in response to the circumstances around us, a resilient way of adapting to the ongoing change we experience in the world today.

When we are afforded the perspective of "life as a whole," as we are from the personal narratives here, we can gain a clearer picture of not only how personal identity is formed but the subjectively important themes and issues of one's life that have shaped this identity. The narrative approach allows us to see more clearly the outlines of the dynamic process that is always involved in negotiating the changing circumstances of life. It also helps us to find the balance between putting too much emphasis on what may be considered generalizations—or stereotypes—and throwing them out completely. The strength of the narrative inquiry approach is that it focuses entirely upon listening to the individual voice that is telling the story.[8]

As such, the themes from these narratives are kept in the words of the storytellers themselves, to illustrate that there are similarities, differences, and uniquenesses among them. In some cases, traditional Latino values are reflected in the narratives of their experiences, and in other cases some may have learned to go beyond these culturally common values to adapt and fit in as a minority in a newly adopted dominant culture.

Many have spoken about how important, even necessary, it is for them to hold onto, and pass onto their children, the values and traditions they had inherited from their parents or elders, while also being flexible enough to adjust to new circumstances in their lives. This may be why the key to their lifelong identity is fluidity, added to the traditional values that have defined and identified them and their ancestors for many generations.

Today being fluid, adaptable, and resilient is as much a key to maintaining a strong and healthy identity across the lifespan and throughout all of life's changes as is holding firmly to their ancestors' traditions. Highlighting the following themes, struggles, concerns, and hopes from their life stories will further illustrate the dynamic, evolving, holistic nature of their identities, and how each one has negotiated tradition and change in their own way.

Connections across Differences

Discrimination

Because mainstream society perceives Latinos as different, discrimination is one of the shared experiences that should not be overlooked as a force that brings them together. It is well established that minorities in the United States, in general, routinely face negative stereotypes, prejudice, and discrimination. Some scholars refer to these adverse experiences as "exclusion."[9]

Those whose life stories are told here have all expressed quite clearly and movingly some direct or indirect knowledge of discrimination, be it subtle, overt, or otherwise. Laura Ochoa, one of more than eighty Latino students at the University of Southern Maine, may be the exception here. She says she honestly hasn't noticed discrimination while living in Sanford or in Portland.

Then she adds, with her infectious laugh, "Probably because I'm a nice person and everybody loves me!" But she does find that, as the president of the Latino-Hispanic Student Association at USM, it is sometimes hard being a minority in a leadership position. Lourdes Carpenter, too, hasn't "felt so much that I've been discriminated against," in fact, she noted that when having trouble taking her licensing exam because of her lack of understanding English, the person helping out understood what she meant "and she said to me, "Oh, you don't speak English? You are very brave that you are here." She took that as a sign of respect. However, she knows that there are many legal immigrants who don't find the sympathy she found in similar processes dealing with their documentation.

Olga Alicea has somewhat of a mixed reaction, as well, in this area. While many of the people that she shares her time with are "Anglos," who are "more progressive people and good people who accept you as you are," she adds that she "could look like any other person in Portland." And while she is "always grateful of the fact that [discrimination] isn't my experience," she has felt that "being the Puerto Rican" is "a little uncomfortable." It made her sad when it felt like she was getting the unspoken message from a friend, "don't get too cultural." Another experience was very revealing to her in a different way. When she introduced herself to another minority woman after a meeting, she was taken aback by a response that indicated the woman perceived her as white. But when the woman later found out that she spoke Spanish, she related to her completely differently, and she felt "it's as though I have to prove my Latino-hood, not with everyone, but so that people take me seriously." She notes very wisely that discrimination can have many levels, explaining that "discrimination exists in not being able to see any representation of who you are in your environment, to feel like the person you are is completely unaccepted." Other Latinos, she also noted, do "come to the United States, to Maine, to suffer discrimination, and live in fear, or they live hidden, or they don't get paid well and know that they shouldn't say anything," while others "feel rejection due to how different they look."

Juan González "never directly had problems with discrimination" in Portland either, but his friends and family have suffered different treatment, such as "being questioned more" than Anglos, or experiencing a normal process as "much harder." Iván Cantor, too, has "had those experiences, but not a lot." One example he gave was of being the first one to walk in to apply for a job but at that moment another person arrived who "was from here. So it turns out that they gave the job to him." Blanca Santiago has "definitely felt singled out for discrimination and racist attacks," and she has witnessed other people being discriminated against, as well, even in public service settings where she has had to step in and say something. This is partly why some people "don't want to be seen," which contributes to the "idea of 'invisibility'" of Latinos.

John Connors, later in his life, experienced a similar singling out, what he calls "racial profiling," when he was "surrounded" by "about ten customs agents with their dogs" in an airport luggage claim area. Victoria Chicón says she has "faced some discrimination here," too, noting especially supermarket and bus settings, as well as assumptions or stereotypes linking her to terrorists, which may be based as much on fear. And the Reverend Rincón states, "Without a doubt, I have encountered discrimination." Stopped by police officers, "the minute they saw the collar their whole attitude changed."

These kinds of experiences of discrimination can have the impact of going much deeper than the moment; they can change the way people choose to interact socially, and even whether they choose to struggle any further to preserve their own cultural traditions or values. Sometimes the discrimination faced in being who they are makes them stronger. This is even a belief that is expressed in a number of Spanish proverbs: *Cuando una puerta se cierra, otre abre;* (When one door shuts, another opens); *A más riesgo, más provecho* (The greater the risk, the greater the gain); *No hay mal que por bien no venga* (There is no evil from which some good cannot be derived).[10]

Beyond, and partly in response to, the experience of discrimination, a number of common strengths emerge from within the Latino community; many other inherent, culturally rooted, clearly strength-based factors connect Latinos. Preserving any aspect of one's culture is a constant struggle in today's world. This is a classic example of the conflict of opposing forces (traditionalism-modernism; or, continuity-change) playing out every day in the lives of those who arrive in this country carrying a strong tradition. The very desire, and commitment, to maintain one's culture, because of the ongoing struggle it involves, adds considerable strength to the individual, the family, and the community.

Language

A common language goes a long way to bring people together, and connect them in deep ways that perhaps nothing else can. But not everyone here had the same experience with their native language. Though Spanish is the second-most-often spoken language in this country, and most prefer speaking Spanish in the home while increasing proficiency in English,[11] many here found themselves struggling in this country with a native language that is not encouraged, and either unconsciously losing their language or, worse yet, not even learning it at all at home because of external pressures or expectations. This was the case for Blanca, who now not only speaks Spanish but has worked as an interpreter, too. When she first had the opportunity to use Spanish every day she was "totally engaged and alive," and found "this whole part of me that's not being used." It was the reverse for Ivan, who, born in Venezuela, has found that "language has always been a barrier." Having come here in his thirties, it was difficult for him to learn English, even in classes, and it was expensive. This barrier has also been a factor in his not being able to get the training or jobs he has wanted. He adds, "I like to speak my language and I would like to speak English as well."

Laura and Lourdes had similar language problems when they first came here. Even though Laura did learn English in Mexico, it was still "hard." She says, "You think that you know it, six years studying English, and then I came here and tried to speak and people didn't understand. I didn't understand them." Now she is bilingual, and speaks Spanish at home with her daughter, who is bicultural and bilingual. Lourdes didn't speak any English when she came here from the Dominican Republic, and would "feel excited" when she met "another person who speaks Spanish." Not speaking English was her greatest difficulty in getting her cosmetology license.

Even though she was born in Puerto Rico and raised in California, Olga noted that her parents "feel much more comfortable speaking Spanish, and that's why I was raised as I was with the language." She added, "It's incredibly important to me not to lose my language and culture. I thank God that my father always spoke Spanish to us at home. They never spoke English at home." Ana and Eliseo found it "a bit difficult to maintain the language for the family" but they "always speak to them in their language." Hernan and Marta, also, "only speak Spanish" at home with their children "so they don't lose it." Juan and the Reverend Rincon also spoke strongly about how important their native language is to them.

The Latinos in Portland are part of a broader movement toward bilingualism. Their strong preference for maintaining their native language makes for a significant and growing bilingual community, within which there are varying degrees of language proficiency in both Spanish and English.[12] There are many reasons for this increase in bilingualism, including reducing the discrimination against them because they don't speak English, while maintaining their native language.

Religion

Perhaps the one factor that most brings people with other differences closer together is religion. Not all of those interviewed were raised or still are Catholic, however. There is, in fact, diversity among Latino groups in religious and spiritual affiliations, beliefs, and practices, partly a result of the unique and fascinating blending of indigenous influences, Catholicism, and, in some cases, African elements. One of the contributions of this collection of Latino stories may be to help us better recognize the distinctions between Latino value orientations and beliefs systems. Only by understanding the individual and unique aspects that make up each story are we able to move beyond a monolithic group image, and thereby identify both the differences and the commonalities that do exist among the members of a larger, disparate group.

It is such differences that can actually create a close interrelationship between spirituality, religion, cultural practices, and a way of making meaning.[13] As is evident in Olga's experience, even though she was raised Catholic, she "questioned many things" as a teenager but always "had a connection with something larger." In her early twenties, she became more aware of her "relationship with God," always identifying "in my own way" as Catholic. The Reverend Rincón, too, was raised Catholic and felt her call at quite a young age but at age thirty left the Catholic Church because as a woman she could not become ordained. She switched to the Episcopal Church, is now answering her call by ministering to the community in Portland, and loves "to be able to help somebody."

The link between religion, family, and community is sometimes almost indistinguishable. Juan has a lot of family members here, and they are a "spiritual family too." "We have to be close to get ahead," he added. John says "religion has always been important to me in my life. I think it is to most Latinos," and concurs that "it's also an important social piece." For Ivan, too, church "has always been very important," since "man is not just flesh." The social aspect of the church is a big factor to him, as well; as he says, "one feels that you're with family."

Hernán notes "everyone respects one's religion," and that "everyone gets together, all the people from the other churches. It doesn't matter what religion." The Spanish-language Mass has served a social as well as religious function for the community. As Blanca sees it, "The Catholic Church here is a big unifying force. There's also a big Seventh-day Adventist population, and then there are the Episcopalians, and each one of these has its own spiritual leader." Each of these spiritual communities came together, not as religious communities per se but as core groups forming Centro Latino Maine, a secular organization serving the social needs of Latin Americans in Portland.

Laura was one who found her spiritual community here. After years of personal struggle, and not having attended church in Mexico, she "had this necessity of a spiritual something . . . I really wanted more like spiritual relief." She found her spiritual home at the local Unitarian Church after the pastor welcomed her and prayed for her. She became a member of the church and also its treasurer, and her daughter has sung in the choir. "I think that this is important for her," she said.

Culture and Tradition

Cultural traditions vary from one nationality or ethnicity to another, but those that are consciously carried on, especially in a new land, become a real strength. The traditions still living in hearts and lives of the Latinos we interviewed give them great pride. In some cases, these are often their highest priority; in other cases, their value is realized later in life, and then become a priority. John's grandmother gave him some very important cultural understandings as a child that years later made even more sense to him. It was after he was married and had children, when he visited Puerto Rico for the first time and saw the celebration on Three Kings Day in the square in old San Juan, that he was able to say, "Yeah, that was what Gram was talking about." This experience, he said, "really convinced me that I needed to become more involved and more active in the Latino community overall." After becoming a leader in the community, and getting the word out that "there's a lot of history [about Latinos] to learn here in Maine," he reminds us that "those roots go back a long way and run very, very deep."

Laura strongly identifies with her indigenous roots, even though that is only part of her heritage and was not emphasized in her family when she was growing up. "I feel more indigenous in my heart than Spaniard," she said, adding that she feels "really connected with the Aztecs, which are my ancestors, and their rituals." She is personally drawn to the Day of the Dead ceremony, as it is celebrated in Oaxaca, which is rich in history, food, music, and art, with the ancestors being honored because death "is another stage of humanity."

Olga was "always completely proud of being Puerto Rican . . . because my parents had that pride." Her parents' best friends were Mexican so she grew up with almost as much Mexican culture as Puerto Rican, and she especially incorporated a love for the food and music of the culture into her life. To stay the person you were brought up to be, and to keep your culture, she says, "You've got to practice it. You have to learn about your history." Ana and Eliseo spoke about the Dominican tradition of the whole family getting together on the one-year anniversary of the death of a family member. Even with strong cultural and family values, the acculturation process threatens the survival of those deep-rooted traditions.

Juan said, "It's important for me not to lose my language or culture," and, in an even stronger tone, added, "We keep our roots from our country. . . . Despite the fact that we're in a different culture, I still impose the culture that made me, the one where I come from." The Reverend Rincón said the same thing about not wanting to lose her language and culture, and added, "My culture is beautiful, and I believe that it's very important to keep as much of it as I can. I do that with my daughter." Victoria also says that traditions are very important. One of the ways Blanca says she maintains her traditions is living by and passing on the cultural values she has inherited, particularly those of humility, respect, and pride.

Family

The importance of family is very evident throughout the interviews although the way, or specific form, it manifests itself varies drastically. Scholars concur that *la familia* plays a central role in the identity and well-being of all Latinos, regardless of place of birth.[14] Olga noted how it has sometimes been hard for her not having family members in Portland, and being on her own here. Victoria, on the other hand, moved to Portland to be with her son and grandchildren. Juan has his "close-knit" extended family, including his sisters, his mother, and a cousin. Lourdes originally came to New York because her mother was there, then to Portland because her brother is here. Though the Reverend Rincón's daughter lives in Los Angeles, she says she feels "like I have family here"; the "incredible people" she has met here "are like my family."

Family functioning is at the core of social and psychological well-being. But Latino families are in transition. The long-standing centrality of the strong nuclear-extended family unit is today being challenged. The many recent modifications in family structure have not only added to the many struggles faced by Latinos but have created new and distinct family realities for Latinos, most not encountered by past generations. There is the intact *familia,* the single-parent *familia,* the bicultural *familia,* and the immigrant *familia.*[15]

Most of those interviewed for this collection have experienced many of these family structures at one time or another in their lives. Immigrant families coming to a new country together face a disruption in the family cycle as well as greater stress put on their functioning as a unit. The intact family, with both parents living together with their children, is more traditional and may tend to have clearer roles for each family member, but in this country, with both parents likely working to keep them above the poverty threshold, even intact families experience significant stressors and challenges, such as different pressures or expectations for different generations, resulting in more intergenerational conflict. The single-parent Latino family is growing in numbers, and, though contrary to some popular opinion, does not necessarily imply negative consequences for the family or children. The bicultural family is becoming more and more common. Latinos currently have the highest rate of intermarriage in the United States. This rate will continue to increase, and Latino families will continue to experience greater and faster changes, which will have a greater impact on Latino ethnic identity.[16]

Community

A strong sense of community extends the family and constitutes another strength that Latinos share. For John, all of his involvement and being more active in the Latino community is about "community building." Hernan says, "The Latino community gets along here very peacefully. Everyone gets along well." Ana notes, "There are a lot of connections here with Latinos helping one another. When Latinos arrive, right away they come to Sacred Heart, the Catholic Church, and immediately they ask for someone, and that person is ready to help them. We're all very united."

Both Lourdes and Laura are grateful for the help they have found in the community. Lourdes says, "I feel thankful that other people have helped me." Laura, after her intense personal struggle, says, "I am trying to give more to people because I got so much." Blanca has found "a sense of a united community amongst Latin Americans, particularly at the church" emerging, as well as around other new grassroots community organizations, schools, centers ("where people can actually congregate and tell stories about what's happening in their lives"), human service agencies, and both community celebrations and tragedies. Victoria has experienced a sense of extended community as well, especially through her work with the Center for Cultural Exchange. All these settings beyond the family serve to unite the diverse Latino community. Community resources, such as clergy, folk or religious healers, cultural centers, grocery stores, personal care services, and social and personal empowerment agencies, are all the kinds of sources of help that strengthen individuals, families, and the entire community.[17]

Nature and the Environment

Another common strength emerges from a strong connection to the environment. Olga has had an affinity for nature, and almost without trying she "began to develop a relationship with my 'environment'" in Portland. Juan says he loves "the climate, even though sometimes it's hard when it's snowing." Ivan, who has so little, is so grateful for the beauty Maine offers, especially the woods during peak foliage. He says, "It's gorgeous, it's really, really nice . . . there are little towns that look like they're out of a movie." Victoria also, feels "it's pretty here," and likes "living near the sea." And the Reverend Rincón, too, likes "the water around" her. She says, "I love Portland. I *love* the sunsets. I *love* the natural essence of it." Eliseo, too, notes that he likes the "peace and quiet" here, that that was "why we decided to come up here."

A Sense of Home

Not only being able to adjust to a new and different setting, but to think of Portland as home is one more strength shared by everyone here. Victoria captures it best with her attitude of understanding and acceptance. She is used to moving "practically every year." She says, "Life has always included change." So she has adapted well. "I never even imagined" coming here "or that I would stay. Now I've already been here six years. And I like it here." Olga, similarly, never imagined coming here, until she acted on the suggestion of a friend while in Alaska to pile everything into a car and take off for Portland. She didn't have a lot of expectations, but Portland ended up being "one of those places where the people are really nice and are good," and, even though she "was missing a lot of things," she began to "feel a little bit committed," and eventually "a little more sure." She said, "I come home and I feel that this is my home. . . . I like Portland."

One of the factors that points out differences not only in the Latino storytellers here but in the people they interact with as well is that people are often cited as a reason for why a place feels like home. Even though they have been targets of discrimination, many have also found allies or other people around them who are just good people to be around. Juan reports, "I love Portland. It's a beautiful city, and the people here are wonderful. They treat you with a lot of respect. It's good. I like it." Ana and Eliseo "like it quite well here in Portland. . . . We feel at home here. The people are really nice, the neighbors and the landlord are very nice." The Reverend Rincón agrees, "I like Portland a lot. . . . I like the people." Blanca said it was her work as a Spanish language interpreter and service provider for the Latino migrant laborers that helped her "feel more a part of my community." Ivan said, "I like it here because it's calm," and because the people are "kind." Lourdes, who met her husband in Portland, echoed this sentiment when she said, "I feel comfortable because, you know, Portland is calm . . . I feel at peace." Laura, who came here first on vacation, says, "I just *loved* New England. I still love it. . . . It's my new home." Even though her "heart is still in Mexico," she says, "It's kind of close here. . . . It's my family, because I have my friends here. . . . I can go out to the supermarket and meet a lot of people who know me." John gets to the heart of the matter: "The question I get a lot is: Why do Latinos come to Maine? It's a beautiful state. Why does anybody come here?"

Common Values

While we are presenting the individual voices here as individuals with singular experiences and perspectives, and not as a voice for their entire group, clearly both differences and similarities can be found here. What we have heard from the Latinos in Portland about what connects them across differences corresponds quite well to what is identified in the literature as the common cultural values among Latinos as a whole. While differences are clear, cultural heritage commonalities are strong. When Latinos come from a traditional background, when traditional cultural values, beliefs, and ways of life are important in their lives and are maintained, they very often share the following commonalities and strengths: a worldview that emphasizes harmony, unity, and cooperation rather than competition; an extended family and friendship network that is held in high esteem; resiliency derived from religion and family, and in the face of adversity and barriers; a sense of debt and responsibility to one's cultural heritage; and a sense of celebration through dance and music.[18]

These strengths and commonalities might also be seen in the following values: *cariño* (affection); *confianza* (trust and intimacy within a relationship) *dignidad* (dignity, pride); *familismo* (family loyalty, cooperation, unity, interdependence) *fatalismo* (things are meant to happen); *machismo* (expressing masculine characteristics); *marianismo* (feminine moral and spiritual superiority), *personalismo* (an orientation in which people are more important than the tasks at hand, dignity of self and others); *respeto* (respect); and *simpatia* (harmonious and pleasant interpersonal relationships).[19] Even though all of these common values may not have been mentioned specifically in the interviews, they are either alluded to or are underlying, even if unstated, themes in them. As Blanca Santiago noted, these common values are embedded "in everything we talk about with each other; they are *in* everything we do."[20]

Concerns and Struggles

The successes the interviewees have had are tied to their struggles, and in particular how they have overcome discrimination and racism. As part of the significant struggle of facing discrimination in its various forms and levels already addressed, a common concern among those interviewed, as noted in the Introduction, was the recent border patrol sweeps by federal immigration agents because "it affected all of us," as well as, for some, ongoing immigration concerns. Laura not only has dealt with immigration issues for a very long time but her whole life since coming here revolved around them. "The immigration issue was the longest, longest, tedious, painful thing. It lasted five years to get my permanent residency."

Coming to a new country and establishing a new home in a new community has further contributed to a number of common concerns. One of the first is not finding many others like oneself. She didn't have a lot of expectations, but as Olga said, "You didn't see many Latinos, much less Puerto Ricans" in Portland. Another struggle for her was realizing "you're giving in to make it easier on the majority."

The lack of a familiar community and culture can force a significant adjustment. Victoria, who came here to be with family, faced a different kind of struggle, that of finding a job in an area she was qualified for and interested in but where there were no openings. She was forced to take a variety of temporary and part-time positions. While also struggling "to get used to" the food, clothing styles, and transportation challenges, her "biggest challenge" has been "achieving my own status" professionally and creatively.

This was Ivan's struggle, as well. He arrived alone in Portland "without much money," no family, and nowhere to live. He not only had to rely on himself completely, he "didn't feel comfortable" in this situation, because "that's more than a little hard." But he also knew that "everything has its good sides and its bad." He has continued to struggle, to keep a home, to find work, especially after September 11, 2001, to advance his education, and to learn English. He has noticed a decrease in the number of jobs available, and this ongoing struggle has bothered him because he has not been able to send money to his nephew who is a student in a university; and on top of this, he is finding that "rent here is too expensive . . . there are many jobs but they don't raise the wages much within those jobs. But the rent they do."

Concerns of other Portland Latinos range from personal issues to social justice issues, and many have a combination of concerns. Laura's greatest struggle was clearly her experience of domestic abuse. As someone who came here as a tourist with no means, she struggled with the language and not having basic economic needs, but managed to find on her own a shelter and eventually a community where she could start over with her young daughter.

Lourdes, also, struggled and "sacrificed a lot" in the beginning. She suffered, cried, and at moments felt hopeless, having to take jobs that did not fit her experience or interests, which was "a humiliation."

For Juan, "the most difficult things about living in Portland are the taxes" but that is "part of the business." "It is tough . . . but it's manageable." He has also been concerned about his son's adjustment, since he didn't speak English when he came here at four years old, but after the first year "he assimilated" and "now behaves more like an American," "always one of the ones with high grades at school." Blanca, having experienced poverty herself, is most concerned with assisting others, helping them move out their "invisibility." She feels that the greatest needs of the Latin American community are services addressing their spiritual and psychological needs. As Hernán notes, "everyone works just to get by"; both work and school are a necessity at the same time. Although "we don't feel a lot of pressure to lose our culture," this also "makes it hard to maintain one's culture . . . but if one wants to, they can keep the customs" from home.

Ana and Eliseo also speak about this struggle to maintain traditions, noting, almost jokingly, the significant difference between gender roles in this country and theirs. Eliseo said, "In our countries, we're always very *machista,* but when you get here to the United States you have to forget about that, because here the first one to arrive is the one that has to cook or wash or always help the spouse." Ana added, "In our countries the wife almost never works, she always devotes herself to her house and her children. . . . When the husband arrives home everything is already done, all the food is prepared, but not here. Here the couples always work, both of them." But they have additional struggles, too. She finds it "very hard" dealing with her health problems, worsened by the cold climate. Eliseo described becoming a citizen as "a difficult process," saying "it's hard for someone who doesn't know English." The Reverend Rincón also has "an illness that is affected by the cold weather," but it is her activism that involves her in what she most wants to be doing. "I like to be in the trenches," she said. "I don't really feel there's been a lot of obstacles because I'm in Portland; I think the obstacles are just obstacles that an activist faces." She mentions being "saddened by the fact that I assimilated too much." John says he is most concerned with the social issues that still need to be addressed: the border policy, unsafe vans still being used in the Maine woods by migrant laborers, whites not valuing the life of an Indian or Latino, too little access to higher educational opportunities, and the need for a higher profile of Latinos in professional and civic settings.

Hopes and Dreams

Because of experiences of poverty and deteriorating standards of living in Latin America, migration to the United States provides a sense of hope and opportunity.[21] One of the primary reasons immigrants come to this country is to improve their lives for themselves and for their children. As Blanca clearly and succinctly put it, "It's about dream building." She explained, "Sometimes we just don't think about people and their dreams. . . . We know that people want a better life. Everybody wants a better life. And we know that people want a better life for their children. . . . But are we really looking at what this means?"

Lourdes pretty much expresses it for some immigrants who make the conscious choice to leave their homeland: "Everyone's dream is to come here." Now, after much difficulty and help from others, she says she feels fulfilled "when I help someone or when someone says to me, 'Oh, thank you!'" Victoria, though she may have initially sacrificed some of her own aspirations, while coming here for her family and to help to raise her grandchildren, is pursuing her own creative goal, too, that of making films. Ivan's hopes include "to learn more English, and to have a good job. But a job that isn't too special either. I couldn't ask for more than that God give me health, that He give me that and nothing more." Ana and Eliseo had a dream, "Our hope when we started to work was to buy a house." Then they thought "that couldn't be done" when she got sick, but they ultimately "accomplished what we wanted and that was a triumph over my illness and pain."

Laura's struggle with domestic abuse brought about a personal transformation, leading to new opportunities for advancing her education through scholarships. "I was very trapped and now I'm just like a butterfly." She wants to apply the lessons she's learned to finish her education, be a nurse, work in a hospital, raise her daughter and "do something else for the community." She says she wants to help "change other lives, and I will."

Olga said she would "like to do something with my master's in Social Work . . . to be useful in some way . . . anything that has to do with making sure that all of my drive is being put to use, or that I'm being honest with myself." The Reverend Rincón's ministry is her work and her dream. She most loves helping people. She says, "When I can help people get a bag of groceries or fill out applications to get food stamps or to get a job, or to enroll in university, to better their lives, to give voice to their oppression, or to give voice to what they see about themselves, it just helps me feel like I'm answering the call." Her hope is that she "can make a difference in this community." One very important step toward this is her founding the grassroots community organization Tengo Voz.

In addition to providing a community gathering place with his store, Juan is very civic-minded with membership in the Rotary Club and being on the board of directors of the Immigrants Legal Advocacy Project. While working hard in the present, he looks into the future for his hopes and dreams. He sees a time when Latinos will be serving in the state legislature. "If it's not us who do it now, our children will do it." Hernán and Marta have a similar motivation. "The hope we have for the future is that our children won't have to work like we've worked and suffered. We worked hard so that later they can get ahead and go to school and afterwards have a career."

For John, there's community building to look forward to. "There's a lot of potential . . . a lot of hope out there, but there's a lot of things we need to put in line and develop. . . . If you come here in this point in history you can help shape what the community's going to look like five, ten, fifteen, twenty years from now. To me, that's exciting, that I can be part of what happens. . . . I think that in the next ten years you're going to see some of the things that I'm concerned about change pretty quickly."

Beyond Marginalization

Where are these shared experiences, common values, concerns and struggles, and hopes and dreams leading the Latinos of Portland? Many of those interviewed here have had experiences that have forced them to live on the peripheral of both worlds they inhabit, the diverse Latino community and the largely exclusive world beyond. Blanca, who spoke only English until she was an adult; Olga, who doesn't look Latino; John, whose last name is not Spanish; Juan and Lourdes, whose places of business serve mostly members of the minority communities; Victoria, whose considerable technical skills have not carried over from one culture to another; Laura and Ivan, whose lack of English-language skills resulted in social and economic difficulties; and Adrian, whose undocumented immigration brought him experiences of exploitation and detention. Each of these individuals have felt marginalized in their own way, and often within both worlds in which they live simultaneously. Children, even in intact families, may straddle both worlds even more than adults do.

This experience of marginalization has created a "crisis of identity" in which the question is asked: "Who are we, really?" In terms of language, is it Spanish or English, or is it bilingual? In terms of culture, is it one or the other, or is it some combination of both? One of the obvious effects of this is revealed in comments such as: "We always end up sacrificing. . . . Our kids are going to learn to drink Coca-Cola and defy authority. "[22] Those who straddle two cultures often wonder if it is worth it. How do you keep the values of your country and culture alive and still assimilate? Blanca replies to this quandary: "You wanted to change, didn't you? You looked at the pros and cons, you made a choice to change, *and* to grow."

This is what the Latinos of Portland are doing; they are not coming to this country and assimilating passively. They are in the process of turning this "crisis" of who they really are into an opportunity for growth and advancement. Through their struggles, their experiences of feeling—and being—on the margins of their worlds, they are not only asking themselves the hard, essential questions of their experience, they are learning from and doing something with their own answers.

The next phase of Latino identity, alluded to in the Introduction, and given voice within each of these fascinating and powerful narratives, is evolving within the Portland Latino community. A Latino identity is emerging that is both similar to and different from every other Latino identity. Each individual is struggling to move beyond marginalization to a place where they can begin to stand firmly upon their often-tested and hard-earned inner strengths forged from the tension between deep cultural roots and the dream of a better life.

Their answers to the hard questions forced by their life experiences point to a clear blending of dual worlds, dual cultures. Their experiences indicate the emergence of a new Latino identity, unique convergences of deeply rooted traditional values; equally deep-seated desires to build new and better lives in a new culture and come as close to fulfilling their potential for themselves and their families as possible; a commitment to actively achieving their rightful place in a new society; and, the newfound ability to feel at home in a place they have come to make their own.

In order to form this new identity, they recognize the need to not only tell their stories, and have others learn from them, but, as Adrian put it, to become activists in their own struggle "for a better life." As each person of Latino heritage recognizes and holds on to their individual cultural and ethnic strengths, while becoming more comfortable with American ways, they actively create an identity that is more their own. Latinos are not only transforming the country and its cities, they are transforming their own identities in the process (as alluded to in the Introduction).

The Latino community has come to Portland through a variety of paths. A few Latinos have been recognized as refugees because of conditions in their countries and arrived through that channel. Far more have fled countries torn by civil war or other unrest but have entered with temporary visas or with no visas at all, since with the exception of Cubans, the U.S. Government rarely grants refugee status to persons from Latin America. Some have temporary worker visas and reenter as temporary workers in repeated years. Others entered with temporary visas and never left. Many are permanent residents after waiting years to immigrate, and still others have come over the border without papers, eager to make a new life and contribute to American society, yet without the same rights as others. Many of those who arrived without visas later go on to qualify for temporary or permanent legal status here.[23] And of course, some were born U.S. citizens.

The Latinos are mostly a young community, with more young adults resettling here than children or elders. They are not only the largest and fastest growing minority nationally but in Maine, as well. Over the next twenty years, it is projected that the Latino community will have the largest percentage of increase in its population of any other group in Maine, realizing a 193 percent increase by 2025.[24]

Victoria Mares-Hershey pointed out in a 2005 column in the *Portland Press Herald* that, in reference to the local Latino community's culturally rich celebration of La Posada organized by the LHSA at USM, "The process of making America is alive and well, despite our current anti-immigration climate." Political debates about immigration tend to arouse anxiety, rather than acknowledge that most Americans enjoy the gifts of our cultural mix, or that cultural celebrations such as La Posada bring out and add to the strength of our country that immigration has made possible.[25] The narrated life experiences in this collection, as well as the many regular community events and celebrations, are ways of getting to know our Latino neighbors better, in order for us all to more clearly recognize that "it's about community building," and "it's about dream building."

Notes

1. See Robert Atkinson, *The Gift of Stories* (Westport, CT: Bergin & Garvey, 1995); *The Life Story Interview* (Thousand Oaks, CA: Sage, 1998); and, Susan E. Chase, "Learning to Listen: Narrative Principles in a Qualitative Research Methods Course," in *Up Close and Personal: The Teaching and Learning of Narrative Research,* ed. Ruthellen Josselson, Amia Lieblich, and Dan McAdams (Washington, DC: American Psychological Association, 2003), 79–91.
2. See Jane Kroger, *Identity Development: Adolescence Through Adulthood* (Thousand Oaks, CA: Sage, 2007), 29–30.
3. See, for example, Ann R. Fisher and Bonnie Moradi, "Racial and Ethnic Identity: Recent Developments and Needed Directions," in *Handbook of Multicultural Counseling,* ed. Joseph G. Ponterotto, et al. (Thousand Oaks, CA: Sage, 2001), 341–70.
4. B.M. Ferdman and P.I. Gallegos, "Racial Identity Development and Latinos in the United States," *New Perspectives on Racial Identity Development: A Theoretical and Practical Anthology,* ed. C. Wijeyesinghe and B. Jackson III (New York: New York University Press, 2001), 32–66.
5. P. Arredondo and T. Glauner, *Personal Dimensions of Identity Model* (Boston: Empowerment Workshops, 1992).
6. Tracy L. Robinson, *The Convergence of Race, Ethnicity, and Gender: Multiple Identities in Counseling* (Upper Saddle River, NJ: Pearson Merrill Prentice Hall, 2005).

7. Wayne Muller, *How, Then, Shall We Live?* (New York: Bantam, 1996), 3–8.
8. See Robert Atkinson, "The Life Story Interview as a Bridge in Narrative Inquiry," in *Handbook of Narrative Inquiry*, ed. Jean Clandinin (Thousand Oaks, CA: Sage, 2006).
9. C.T. Garcia Coll and M. Garrido, "Minorities in the United States: Sociocultural Context for Mental Health and Developmental Psychopathology," in *Handbook of Developmental Psychopathology*, ed. A.J Sameroff, M. Lewis, and S.M. Miller (New York: Kluwer-Plenum, 2000), 177–95.
10. L.I. Rovira, *Spanish Proverbs: A Survey of Spanish Culture and Civilization* (Lanham, MD: University Press of America, 1984).
11. Azara L. Santiago-Rivera, Patricia Arredondo, and Maritza Gallardo-Cooper, *Counseling Latinos and la familia: A Practical Guide* (Thousand Oaks, CA: Sage, 2002), 48–49.
12. Santiago-Rivera, et al., 59.
13. Santiago-Rivera, et al., 44–46.
14. Santiago-Rivera, et al., 149.
15. Santiago-Rivera, et al., 69–101.
16. Santiago-Rivera, et al., 87–91.
17. Santiago-Rivera, et al., 151.
18. Santiago-Rivera, et al., 182. Alberta M. Gloria and Theresa A. Segura-Herrera, "Somos! Latinas and Latinos in the United States," in *Counseling American Minorities*, ed. Donald R. Atkinson (New York: McGraw Hill, 2004), 291–94.
19. Santiago-Rivera, et al., 191–93. Gloria and Segura-Herrera, 291–93.
20. Blanca Santiago, personal communication, April 2006.
21. J. Gonzalez, *Harvest of an Empire: A History of Latinos in America* (New York: Penguin Press, 2000).
22. Blanca Santiago, personal communication, April 2006.
23. Beth Stickney, Executive Director, Immigrant Legal Advocacy Project, personal communication, April 2006.
24. *Portland Press Herald*, Special Report, "The Changing Face of Maine," June 20–23, 1999, p. 2.
25. Victoria Meres-Hershey, "Latino celebration shows strength of immigration," *Portland Press Herald*, December 27, 2005, A7.

Appendix

English and Spanish Interview Questions

What is your name?
How old are you?
Where were you born?
Were you able to go to school in your country?
How did you get here from your country?
How long have you lived here?
Do you have children or family here?
I would like to know about your experience living in Portland.
How has it been for you to live here?
I would like to know about your experiences with the school system.
Have you been to school here?
What are your best memories of your time in Portland?
What have been the biggest disappointments?
Have you ever been faced with discrimination because you were Latino or for any other reason?
Is it important for you not to lose your language and culture? How do you keep it?
At times do you feel pressure to assimilate to the culture here? What do you think about that?
Are you a member of a particular religion?
What do you do with your free time?
Do you belong or are you involved with any Latino organizations or do you participate in Latino community events?
Do you like Portland as a place to live?

Were you living in Portland when César Chávez came to visit in 1974?
Was it an important moment for you when Portland celebrated his birthday in 2000?
What are your hopes and dreams for the future?

Preguntas de historia oral

¿Cómo se llama usted?
¿Cuántos años tiene?
¿Donde nació usted?
Deseo saber más sobre su experiencia de vivir en Portland.
¿Cómo ha llegado a Portland de su país?
¿Cuánto tiempo lleva viviendo en Portland?
¿Tiene niños o familia aquí?
¿Pertenece a alguna religión?
¿Cómo le ha ido con su trabajo aquí?
Quisiera saber más acerca de su experiencia con el sistema educativo.
¿Logró estudiar en su país? ¿Ha ido a la escuela en Portland?
¿Cuáles han sido sus mejores memorias de su tiempo en Portland?
¿Cuál ha sido la parte más difícil de vivir en Portland?
¿Cuáles han sido los desafíos más grandes en Portland?
¿Ha enfrentado discriminación por ser latinoamericano o por cualquier otra razon?
¿Es importante para usted no perder su idioma y cultura? ¿Cómo los mantiene?
¿Siente alguna presión para asimilarse a la cultura de aquí? ¿Qué piensa acerca de esto?
¿Le gusta Portland como sitio para hacer su vida?
¿Qué le gusta hacer con su tiempo libre?
¿Está usted involcrado en alguna organización de latinos o participa en eventos de latinos?
¿Vivía Ud. en Portland en 1974 cuando vino César Chávez a visitar?
¿Fue importante para usted cuando Portland celebró su día de cumpleaños en 2000?
¿Cuáles han sido los momentos más memorables para usted de su experencia en Portland?
¿Cuáles son sus esperanzas para el futuro?

Index

Note: Page numbers with an f indicate figures.

Abercrombie, Thomas, 40n27
Acuña, Rodolfo, 46n69
Adventists. *See* Seventh-day Adventists
AFL/CIO, 110
African Americans, x, 201
AIDS awareness programs, 64, 124, 125
Aima, Victor, 156, 166–167
Algonquians, 39n12
Alicea, Olga, 2, 22, 27, 30, 194–205, 194f, 208, 212, 214, 215, 217, 219, 221, 224, 225
Almonte, Pedro, 91
Anderson, Benedict, 30, 47n78
Andrade, Manny, 64
Anzaldúa, Gloria, 1, 22–23, 27
Aparicio, Ana, 37n3
Armony, Ariel C., 42n39
Arredondo, P., 227n5
Arreola, Daniel, 4, 38n11
assimilation, 25–29
  Lourdes Carpenter on, 176–178
  Victoria Chicón on, 30–31, 158, 163–164
  Juan González on, 172–173
  Hernán and Marta on, 141–143
  The Reverend Virginia Marie Rincón on, 27, 34–35
  Blanca Santiago on, 57
Atkinson, Donald R., 228n18
Atkinson, Robert, x, 10, 40n26, 207–228
Aztecs, 96–98, 155–156, 216

Baldecci, John, 17
Baptists, 16, 33f
Barber Foods Co., 3f, 44n50, 76, 77, 139, 140
Baron, Marty, ix
Basch, Linda, 46n66
baseball, 91–92
Baver, Sherrie L., 37n3
Bernard, H. Russel, 40n24
Bhabha, Homi, 45n55
biculturalism. *See* multiculturalism
Biddeford Blanket Co., 60
bilingualism, 2, 213–214
  Adrian Bravo on, 79
  Iván Cantor on, 190–191
  Lourdes Carpenter on, 176, 178–179, 183
  Victoria Chicón on, 158, 164
  John Connors on, 111
  discrimination and, 89–90, 144–145
  driver's manual and, 124
  Juan González on, 26, 172
  Hernán and Marta on, 141–142, 144

bilingualism (*continued*)
 Ana Manza and Eliseo Brea on, 86–87, 89
 Laura Ochoa on, 107, 108
 The Reverend Virginia Marie Rincón on, 130–131, 134, 158
 Blanca Santiago on, 26–27, 54–55, 57, 62
Blanc-Szanton, Cristina, 46n66
Bodega Latina, 3f, 21–23, 31, 64, 84, 92, 127, 133, 139, 170–171
Booth, John A., 42n39
Boyer, Jean-Pierre, 95n2
Braceros program, 13
Brandeis University, 56
Bravo Chavez, Adrian, 9, 10, 14, 19f, 34, 66–81, 66f, 225, 226
Brea, Eliseo, 6, 10, 19, 20, 82–95, 82f, 214, 217, 222–223, 224
Brown, Timothy C., 42n39
Bush, George W., 122

Cambodians, 75, 139, 140, 144
Cantor, Iván, 15, 19, 30, 184–193, 212, 215, 221, 223, 225
Carey, David, Jr., x, 1–36, 40n25
Caring Unlimited, 105, 108
Carpenter, Lourdes, 15, 22, 64, 174–183, 174f, 212, 214, 217, 218, 222, 223, 225
Carter, Jimmy, 16
Castro, Fidel, 16
Catholics, 63, 86–87, 125, 131–132, 141, 147–148, 196–197, 215–216
Catholic Charities Maine, 58
Center for Cultural Exchange, 18f, 64, 154, 159, 165, 219
Central American Free Trade Agreement, 33
Centro Latino Maine, 6, 10, 63–64, 90, 204–205
César Chávez Leadership Award, 50, 125, 165, 168, 171
CETA program, 57
Chase, Susan E., 227n1
Chávez, César, 29, 94, 114, 125, 165, 192
 holiday for, 30, 120–121, 173
Chicano movement, 29
Chicón, Victoria, 20, 22, 64, 78, 154–167, 154f, 217, 218, 221, 223, 225
 on discrimination, 162–163, 166–167, 213
 on migrants, 34
 on multiculturalism, 7, 30–31, 158, 163–164
child labor, 68
Chinese, 92, 93, 144, 156
Chomsky, Aviva, 38n10
citizenship. *See* naturalization
Clark University, 57
Coatsworth, John H., 42n39
Coca-Cola Corporation, 123
Coles, Robert, 207
Colombia, 6, 19, 75, 184–185
Columbus, Christopher, 62, 94
Community Counseling Center, 65
community pride, 20–24, 61–62, 205, 218–219, 226
Conforti, Joseph A., 38n10, 39n12
Connors, John, 10, 22, 30, 34, 110–127, 110f, 207, 208, 213, 215, 216, 218, 223, 224, 225
 Latino Health Center and, 64
 on multiculturalism, 113–118, 207
coyotes (migrant smugglers), 69–71
Craig, Richard B., 41n30
Cuba, ix, 5–6, 12–13, 16–17, 28, 91, 187, 226
cuisine, ethnic, 54, 86, 93, 98, 134, 140, 144, 159–161

Damian, Victor, 22
Danta, Ruby, 37n3, 47n71
Darder, Antonia, 41n31
Darwin, Peter, 104
Day of Action for Immigrant Justice, 8
Day of the Dead, 97–98, 216
De Genova, Nicolas, 47n74

detention centers, 78–79
discrimination, 6, 96, 98, 211–213
  after 9/11 attacks, 92
  Olga Alıcea on, 2–4, 197, 200–201, 212
  Adrian Bravo on, 72–73, 80
  Iván Cantor on, 190, 212
  Lourdes Carpenter on, 212
  Victoria Chicón on, 162–163, 166–167, 213
  John Connors on, 115, 213
  Juan González on, 171–172, 212
  Hernán and Marta on, 145–146
  housing, 63, 72–74
  Laura Ochoa on, 105, 211
  The Reverend Virginia Marie Rincón on, 133, 213
  Blanca Santiago on, 62–63, 212
  See also racism
domestic abuse
  Laura Ochoa on, 32–33, 96, 99–105, 109, 224
  Virginia Rincón on, 135
  Blanca Santiago on, 53, 56
Dominican Republic, 4, 14–15, 19, 27, 32, 82–83, 88, 94, 169, 171, 175, 214
dreams (and hopes, for a better future), 4, 55, 61, 67, 74, 77, 80, 106, 108, 126, 135, 164, 173, 192, 223–224
driver's manual, bilingual, 125
Duarte, Juan Pablo, 94, 95n2

education
  Adrian Bravo on, 76–78
  John Connors on, 114, 118, 119, 123
  Juan González on, 173
  Herán and Marta on, 146–147, 152–153
  Laura Ochoa on, 104–106
El Salvador, 6, 14–15, 25, 136, 138, 141–142, 146–148, 153n1
environment
  feeling safe in, 12, 17, 35, 136
  natural surroundings, 4, 27, 86, 87, 198, 200, 212, 219
Episcopalians, 132
ethnicity, 26–29, 111–113, 201–204
  cuisine and, 54, 86, 93, 98, 134, 140, 144, 159–161
  gender and, 32
  See also identity

farm workers, 43n42, 53, 59
  advocacy for, 125
  Adrian Bravo on, 69–73
  John Connors on, 118–119
feminism, 32–33, 133,
  See also machismo
Ferdman, B.M., 227n4
Fernández-Armesto, Felipe, 36n2
Fernández-Kelly, María Patricial, 49n83
Fink, Leon, 37n4
Fisher, Ann R., 227n3
Foner, Nancy, 48n80
food stamps, 60, 128
  See also social assistance
Foss, Leticia, 26
French-Canadians, 108, 140

Gadsden Purchase, 38n9
Galarza, Erneesto, 41n30
gangs, 55, 130
Garcia Coll, C.T., 228n9
García y Griega, Manuel, 41n30
Gardiner, Ramon, 5
GED (general equivalency diploma), 57
Genova, Nicholas de, 36n3
Glaessel-Brown, Eleanor E., 38n10
Glasser, Ruth, 38n10
Glick Schiller, Nina, 27–28, 46n66
Gloria, Alberta M., 228n18
Gold, Steven, 48n80
González, Elián, ix
González, Juan (scholar), 37n7, 228n21
González, Juan (shop owner), 21f, 22, 26–27, 36, 64, 84, 139, 168–173, 168f, 212, 214, 215, 217, 222, 224, 225
Grandin, Greg, 42n39

Grasmuck, Sherri, 48n80
Guadalupe, Virgin of, 86–87, 125, 131
Guatemala, 5, 6, 15–16, 22, 58, 119
Gugelberger, George M., 40n27
Gurrola, Blanca, 65
Gutierez, Juan, 5
Gutiérrez, David, 41n30
Gutiérrez, José, 122

Haitians, 14, 95n2
Haney López, Ian F., 37n7
Haslip-Viera, Gabriel, 37n3
healers (*curanderas*), 130
Hernán and Marta (pseudonyms), 16, 20, 25, 136–153,214, 215, 218, 222, 224
Hernández, Ramona, 41n33
Hershey, Victoria, 181, 227, 228n25
HIV disease. *See* AIDS awareness programs
Hollinger, David A., 46n68
homelessness, 72, 74–75
Hondagneu-Sotelo, Pierrette, 47n72, 48n80, 48n81
hopes. *See* dreams
housing
  discrimination in, 63, 72–74
  Ana Manza and Eliseo Brea on, 85–86
  substandard, 69, 72
Huntington, Samuel P., 25, 26, 45n61

identity, 26–36, 37n7, 208, 209–211, 225–227
  See also ethnicity
Immanuel Baptist Church, 33
Immigrant Legal Advocacy Project (ILAP), 3f, 35f, 135, 173, 224
immigration policies, x, 8, 33–35, 109, 142
  George Bush on, 122
  Victoria Chicón on, 34
  John Connors on, 122
  detention centers and, 78–79
  naturalization and, 87, 103–104, 181
  Virginia Rincón on, 132–133, 135
  See also undocumented workers
interpreters, 63
interview questionnaire, 229–230
invisibility, social, 61, 213
Iraq War, 122, 123

James, Daniel, 40n25
job-related injuries, 145–146
Jordan Meats Co., 139
Josselson, Ruthellen, 227n1

Kibria, Nazli, 37n7
King, Martin Luther, Jr., 121
Kroger, Jane, 227n2
Kryzanek, Michael J., 41n33
Kurzman, Dan, 41n33

La Bodega Latina, 3f, 31, 64, 84, 92, 127, 133, 139, 170–171
Labor Council for Latin American Advancement, 110
Lancaster, Roger, 15, 42n37
language. *See* bilingualism
Language Exchange school, 159
Latino-Hispanic Student Association (LHSA), 10, 22, 25, 32, 105, 106, 165, 212, 227
League of United Latin American Citizens (LULAC), 90, 110, 124, 135
Le Espiritu, Yen, 37n7
Levitt, Peggy, 35, 48n80
Lipsitz, George, 36n1, 37n7
literacy, 51, 55
Lloyd, David, 47n69
Lourdes' International Beauty Salon, 3f, 22, 23, 24f, 64, 174
Lowe, Lisa, 30, 37n7, 47n69
Lowenthal, Abraham F., 41n33

machismo, 93, 100
  See also feminism
Maine Center for Economic Policy, 37n5, 43n42
Maine Migrant Workers Advocacy Group, 125
Maine, University of, 123

Manuel, Peter, 41n31
Manza, Ana, 10, 14, 19, 20, 32, 82–95, 82f, 139, 214, 217, 218, 222–223, 224
maquiladoras (factories), 34
Mares-Hershey, Victoria, 227
marginalization, 28–36, 225–227
Mariel Boatlift, 16
Marta and Hernán (pseudonyms), 16, 20, 25, 136–153
Martinez Auto Service, 5f
Martínez, Gus, 8
Martinez, Pedro, 91
Mayagüez Campus, University of Puerto Rico, 119
Mayans, 5, 6, 119, 155–156
medical care, 25, 35
Meléndez, Edwin, 38n10
Menjívar, Cecilia, 48n81
mestizaje (racial mixing), 29
methodology, 9–12, 207–208, 229–230
Mexico, 7, 8, 22, 27, 66–70, 76–80, 94, 96–102, 106–108, 114,122, 214, 216, 220
Milroy, Lesley, 40n24
Morales, Rachel, 126
Morrison, Dane Anthony, 38n10
mujeristas. See feminism
Muller, Wayne, 210, 228n7
multiculturalism, 6–8, 25–29, 140–141, 208, 216–217, 218
  Olga Alicea on, 197, 200–201
  Victoria Chicón on, 7, 30–31, 158, 163–164
  John Connors on, 113–118, 207
  Blanca Santiago on, 58–59
  See also bilingualism
Multilingual and Multicultural Program, 64
Mundo Hispánico program, 64, 154
Muslims, 113

narrative approach, 207–208, 210
Nash, June, 48n80, 49n83
naturalization, 87, 103–104, 181
  See also immigration policies
Network in Solidarity with the People of Guatemala (NISGUA), 42n39
Ngai, Mae M., 37n7
9/11. *See* September 11th attacks
North Carolina, 5, 6, 69–71
Nuñez, Elsa, ix–xi

Oboler, Suzanne, 46n68
Ochoa, Diana, 96f, 99–103, 105
Ochoa, Laura, 7, 10, 15, 22, 27, 30–33, 96–109, 96f, 211, 216, 218, 221, 222, 224, 225
Operation Bootstrap, 13, 52, 65n1
O'Reilly, Alejandro, 112
Oropeza, Lorena, 46n69
Ortiz, Wilma, 47n72

Padilla, Felix, 46n69
Palumbo-Liu, David, 45n54
Penobscot people, 118
People's Market. *See* Bodega Latina
Pérez, Gina, 24, 36n3
Peru, 9, 20, 22, 154–166, 185
Pessar, Patricia, 41n33, 48n80
Philippines, 177
police
  racial profiling by, 115–116, 133, 213
  recruitment of, 35
Ponterotto, Joseph G., 227n3
Portelli, Allesandro, 40n25
Portland Refugee Resettlement Program, 16
Preble Street Resource Center, 3f, 64, 74, 76
Programa Roberto Clemente, 56–57
public assistance. *See* social assistance
Puerto Rico, 27, 50, 52–53, 59, 110–114, 123–124, 194–195, 200, 202–204, 214, 216

questionnaire, interview, 229–230
Quinsigamond Community College, 57

racism, 16, 26, 35–36
  Olga Alicea on, 2–4, 197, 200–201
  institutionalized, 63

racism (*continued*)
Ana Manza and Eliseo Brea on, 89
police profiling as, 115–116, 133, 213
Blanca Santiago on, 61–63
See also discrimination
Ramos-Zayas, Ana Yolanda, 47n74
Rappaport, Joanne, 40n25
Reagan, Ronald, 121
Reed, Frank, 58
Reimers, David M., 43n42
religion, ix, 28, 85, 125, 141, 144, 196, 215–216, 220
Rice, Tim, 161
Ricourt, Milagros, 37n3, 47n71
Rincón, The Reverend Virignia Marie, 63, 128–135, 128f, 213, 214, 215, 217, 223, 224
on assimilation, 27, 34–35
bilingualism and, 130–131, 134, 158
Tengo Voz and, 33
Robinson, Tracy L., 227n5
Rodriguez, Alex, 91–92
Rodríguez, Clara, 46n69
Roediger, David R., 37n7
Rolde, Neil, 45n57
Romero, Mary, 47n72
Rosselló, Pedro, 112
Rovira, L.I., 228n10
Rowe, Lynne, 181
Rumbaut, Rubén G., 48n80

Sacred Heart Catholic Church (Portland), 3f, 11f, 85
Safa, Helen I., 48n80
Santiago, Blanca, 8, 10, 22, 26–27, 32, 50–65, 50f, 131, 212, 215, 217, 218, 221, 222, 223
Santiago-Rivera, Azara L., 228n11
Sassen, Saskia, 14
School Age Mothers program, 55
Schultz, Nancy Lusignan, 38n10
Scontras, Charles A., 41n30
Seaver, Lia, 55
Sensenbrenne, F. James, Jr., 8
September 11th attacks, 92, 104, 133, 187, 222
Seventh-day Adventists, 3f, 31f, 63, 75, 143, 164–165, 187, 215
shamanism, 130
Shining Path (Sendero Luminoso), 163
Shipler, David K., 45n58
Shorris, Earl, 30, 43n42
Silver Company, 85
Slim, Hugo, 40n25
Smith, R. C., 47n79
soccer, 150–151
social assistance, 25, 56, 60, 62–63, 128
softball, 90–91
Somalians, 65, 170
Sosa, Sammy, 92
Spanish. *See* bilingualism
Spanish-American War, 38n9
Stephen, Lynn, 40n27
Stickney, Beth, 228n23
St. Patrick's battalion, 114
struggles, personal (due to cultural differences), 25–28, 176, 221–223
Suárez-Orozco, Carola, 39n20

Tallán people, 155–156
Tedlock, Dennis, 40n24
Tenenbaum, Barbara A., 43n41
Tengo Voz, 3f, 32–33, 128, 135
Thomas, Piri, 37n7
Thompson, Paul, 40n25
Three Kings Day, 112, 216
Tobar, Héctor, 39n11
Torres, Andrés, 38n10
Torres, Rodolfo D., 41n31
Torres-Saillant, Silvio, 41n33
traditions, cultural and ethnic, x, 25, 29, 97, 110, 112, 128, 163, 168, 194, 211, 213, 216–217, 222
Tu Casa Restaurant Salvadoreño, 3f, 23, 31, 93, 127, 136f, 140

undocumented workers, 59
Adrian Bravo on, 67, 69–75, 79
cheating of, 70, 72, 73
coyotes and, 69
incarceration of, 78–80

raids on, 90
See also immigration policies
unions, 110, 125
Unitarians, 216
Uriarte, Miren, 38n10
U.S.-Mexican War, 38n9, 114
U.S.-Spanish War, 38n9

Valdés, Gina, 1
Valencia, Javier, 84–85
values, cultural ix, 29, 105, 211, 213, 217, 220–221, 225, 226
Vansina, Jan, 40n25
Venezuela, 9, 19, 185, 214
violence. *See* domestic abuse
Virgin of Guadalupe, 86–87, 126, 131
Vives, Armando, 7f, 184f, 187

Wabanakis, 5, 17, 39n12
Walker, Thomas W., 42n39
Warren, Kay, 9–10, 40n22
Waters, Mary C., 47n76
Weible, Robert, 38n10
welfare programs. *See* social assistance
White Memorial Seventh-day Adventist Church, 3f, 31f
Wiarda, Howard J., 41n33
Wiggin, Frances Turgeon, 41n30
Wijeyesinghe, C., 227n4
Worcester State College, 57
workers' compensation, 62–63

YMCA (Portland), 19

Zimmerman, Matilde, 42n39